D0880812

THE ELVIS FILES

WAS HIS DEATH FAKED?

THE ELVIS FILES
WAS HIS DEATH FAKED?

Gail Brewer-Giorgio

Foreword by
Raymond A. Moody, Jr., M.D.

&

Detective Monte W. Nicholson,
Los Angeles Sheriff's Department

SHAPOLSKY PUBLISHERS, INC.
NEW YORK

McGRAW-HILL RYERSON
TORONTO, CANADA

IMPALA BOOKS
LANCASTER, ENGLAND

A Shapolsky Book

For any additional information, contact:
Shapolsky Publishers, Inc.
136 West 22nd Street, New York, NY 10011
(212) 633-2022

Published in association with Stan Corwin Productions

10 9 8 7 6 5 4 3 2 1

First published in the United Kingdom and Continental Europe by
Impala Books, a division of Gazelle Book Services Ltd.,
Falcon House, Queen Square, Lancaster LA1 1RN, England
UK ISBN 1-85586-100-3
First published in Canada by McGraw-Hill Ryerson
330 Progress Avenue, Scarborough, Ontario M1P 2Z5

Library of Congress Cataloging-in-Publication Data:

Brewer-Giorgio, Gail, 1939–
   The Elvis files: was his death faked? / Gail Brewer-Giorgio.
      p.   cm.
   Includes bibliographical references.
   ISBN 1-56171-000-8
   1. Presley, Elvis, 1935–1977 – Death and burial. I. Title.
ML420.P96B73   1990
782.42166'092 – dc20
[B]   90-41533

Design and Typography by Smith, Inc., New York

Printed and bound by Graficromo s.a., Cordoba, Spain

The book The Elvis Files *could not have come about without the help of Mel Bergman, William Speckin, Carole Halupke, Ian Shapolsky, Mitch Slayton, Gene Smith, Dr. Raymond Moody, Larry and Sue McBride, Monte Nicholson, Wayne Elliott, Storm N' Norman, Bob DiMaggio, Laurette Healy, Sandra Chandler, Brian Feinblum, and Jeffrey Ingber.*

Also, the "Gathering-ites" deserve so much thanks! And a giant hug is due Stan Corwin, Maria Columbus, and a super-special editor, Donn Teal. Thank you, thank you, thank you!

To Carm, Jim, Chris, and Maria (who helped so much), and their families . . . love!

To those in the media who took the time to evaluate all of the letters, to listen, without judging, I am grateful.

And thanks go, of course, to you, ELVIS, wherever you may be . . .

Contents

Foreword

As a people and as a culture we can't let go of Elvis. He lives on and on in the thoughts and memories and dreams of his fans. He lives on, also, as the ostensible central figure of fascinating and occasionally baffling psychic experiences – reported paranormal events and mental states – which tantalize us, and which reveal, again and again, the depth of the affection which his fans hold for him.

As a doctor of medicine and a psychiatrist, I am intrigued by these accounts. They interest me for what they reveal about the human mind and spirit. They tell us a lot, I believe, about the psychological aspects of what it means to be a devoted fan, about the nature of our relationship with celebrities, and about some of the less well understood manifestations of the human process of mourning.

> *Raymond A. Moody, Jr., M.D.,*
> *author of* Life After Life
> *and* Elvis After Life*

Having been in law enforcement for almost eighteen years, I recognize outstanding investigative work as that of an investigator who leaves no stone of information unturned. It is this type of investigation that conscientious detectives conduct. For the past two years I have been privy to much of the information compiled by Gail Brewer-Giorgio, concerning the controversy surrounding the "disappearance" of Elvis Presley. If Gail left a stone unturned, I have yet to find it.

There are many people involved with this phenomenal mystery, but to date no one has put forth the effort to verify their facts to the extent that Gail has. She is, in my estimation, the most credible person to analyze and compile all of the existing information on the subject. I am convinced that if Elvis is to be found, she will find him.

---

*A more extensive reading of Dr. Moody's intriguing studies can be found in his book *Life After Life,* Peachtree Publishers, 494 Armour Circle, N.E., Atlanta, Georgia 30324.

   Such a wealth of information exists, today, on the subject of Elvis' alleged death that I have decided to collaborate with another author – another law enforcement officer – Paul Bishop on it. Bishop and I met one day in my office in downtown Los Angeles. He came armed with a copy of my earlier Elvis book, *The Presley Arrangement.* From that day forward, Bishop – the author of several novels – has, like me, become increasingly involved in untangling the Presley conundrum.

   For all those with opposing views – who strive to discredit her – take warning: If you do your homework, you will find yourself caught up in the search for Elvis, too!

Detective Monte W. Nicholson,
Los Angeles Sheriff's Department,
author of The Presley Arrangement
Los Angeles, California
August 1990

A Letter to the Elvis Fans

There is an old saying that one should never discuss politics or religion because those topics inevitably lead to heated discussions. Nowadays you can add another subject to those: Elvis' death. The topic of Elvis Presley's death will bring forth varying reactions from people of all walks of life, not just the Elvis fans. Almost everyone remembers where he/she was when he/she heard the news that Elvis had died. There are very few deaths that commanded that kind of media and public attention. President John F. Kennedy is the only other public figure who comes to mind.

I have been an Elvis fan for thirty years and a fan club president for twenty of those years. In 1977 my club was eight years old and "established" in the Elvis world. Once the shock and trauma of Elvis' unexpected death passed, I began to question the events that surrounded that fateful week of August 16, 1977. Too many questions that I asked were answered with "I don't know." Even today, more than thirteen years later, those questions are still unanswered. I am thankful that Gail Brewer-Giorgio has brought those questions into the public eye. Perhaps now, with the eyes of the world and media watching, we can find out what *really* happened on August 16, 1977.

Thank you, Gail. And to Elvis, wherever you are, we love you!

Maria Columbus, President
THE ELVIS SPECIAL
P.O. Box 1457
Pacifica, CA 94044

Introduction: Why *Is Elvis Alive?* Was Written

We know nothing about motivation. All we can do is write books about it.
— PETER DRUCKER

Since Elvis Presley "died" on August 16, 1977, the question "Is Elvis alive?" has often been asked — a question posed long before my book *Is Elvis Alive?* became a bestseller, a book that prompted thousands of responses, many beginning with: "I have actually *seen* and *talked* with Elvis Presley. I did not know who to tell; people would think me either a liar or crazy or both."

The Elvis Files gives some of those who have written in response to the earlier book the space in which to tell of their experiences. For the most part, I have only identified them by their first name and last initial, and in most instances have reprinted their letters as presented. If anyone doubts that such letters exist, my office and files are open for inspection.

The evidence keeps unraveling on the most intriguing story of this century, offered in this follow-up to *Is Elvis Alive?* The information and analysis run the gamut from intense to light-hearted, from what is perhaps important to what is trivial. Still, what may be junk to one man's mind may be food to another's.

This writer does not claim that her analyses are 100-percent correct or that there may not be logical explanations for many of the enigmas related. If the complete answers were known, they would be presented. The question remains: "Is Elvis alive?"

- What about the sightings, many of them by very, very credible people?
- What about the mass of contradictions surrounding events at Graceland on August 16, 1977, and in the days and years following?

- What about the mystery records and mystery voices heard since 1977?
- What about the amazing parallels with his "death" that surround Elvis' spiritual leanings and readings?
- What about Elvis' intense governmental connections?

There are so many puzzles that even as this book goes to press there is no bottom to them.

It is true that I have been under fire often for posing the proposition that he may indeed be among us. Yet "Is Elvis alive?" has passed one test of time: the question regenerating of itself.

I AM OFTEN ASKED WHY I WROTE *IS ELVIS ALIVE?* WHEN I WROTE THE book it was an attempt to make sense of what happened to my novel, *Orion*, as well as to parallel events that (1) had raised questions and (2) at times had seemed senseless regarding the death of Elvis Presley. Questions had been raised by many of the fan clubs, as well as by the press and the general public, from Day One – that being August 16, 1977.

I was not the originator of such questions, nor was I responsible for the many contradictions in the official documents such as the Medical Examiner's Report (or death certificate), which states that the body was found in the bathroom in a rigor-mortised condition, versus the Homicide Report, which states that the body was found in the bedroom "unconscious."

Unconsciousness and rigor mortis are at opposite ends of the physical spectrum: Rigor mortis is a stiffening condition that occurs after death; unconsciousness, a state in which a living body loses awareness. Bedroom and bathroom are two different places.

I am a compiler of information, not the creator of it. Other than detailing my reaction to the writing of the novel *Orion* and the strange circumstances that followed, the majority of the information, contradictions, and questions presented via *Is Elvis Alive?* was compiled from others' previously published material. It became a case of taking a multitude of flickering matchsticks in the darkness and putting them in a centralized location, the end result being a gigantic bonfire.

At no time have I presented myself as an investigative reporter or as some super-sleuth of this century. As I've often repeated, my husband has said, "Gail, you might be able to track down Elvis Presley, but you can't ever find your car keys." Thus, so much for any monumental "psychic" abilities I might have!

Although two national surveys showed that between 84 percent and 86 percent of the American people believe Elvis Presley is indeed alive, I have had more than my share of criticism for daring to ask that question. It's a case of the "Let's kill the messenger who brings the news" syndrome.

PEOPLE, AMONG THEM EVEN SOME ELVIS FAN CLUB MEMBERS, ALSO frequently tell me: "Your doing this is an exploitation of Elvis Presley."

My answers: What about the facts? Is searching for the truth considered "exploitation"? How do you explain Elvis' middle name being misspelled on his grave at Graceland?

And, to continue:

- What about the contradictions in the many documents, such as the Medical Examiner's report, which listed Elvis' body weight as 170 pounds when it was in reality closer to 250?
- What about the tape—authenticated—that was sent to a top voice-identification expert, on which Elvis talked about things that did not occur before August 1977?
- What about the mind-boggling picture taken in the poolhouse behind Graceland's Meditation Gardens four months after the death of Presley and showing a man seated who looked exactly like Elvis?
- What about the life insurance, and no one's making claims on it?
- What about the sightings, many by very credible people?

The list of questions goes on and on. Strangely, those who accuse me of exploitation never answer them. Facts seem irrelevant—too confusing? Those who accuse me of putting all of this together in a book and selling it forget that Elvis Presley never gave away his albums, not did he give concerts free. His estate was valued at around $4 million on August 16, 1977. Today it is reportedly valued at over $100 million. And why? Because the fans and the media have kept Elvis alive. It is a hand-in-glove operation. Elvis would not be a star if no one received and noted his "light." And, also, why is it all right for the fan periodicals (which are not given away free) to ask the same questions I ask, and escape any charges of "exploitation"?

I posed this question to my friend Maria Columbus, president of one of the oldest-established Elvis Presley fan clubs.

"Gail, I've asked myself the same question," Maria responded. "Since Day One, we've asked the questions you're asking—through our *The Elvis Special* newsletters. I think one of the reasons you're receiving some heat from a few of the other fan clubs is because you stated you had never been a fan of Elvis Presley's. That makes you an outsider, so how *dare* an outsider ask such questions, cause so much commotion. Also, there are a lot of fans who swear, 'Elvis wouldn't do this to his fans. He loved them too much.' "

"On the telemarketing show *Breakthrough* I recall your reply to that accusation," I said.

"'I've always replied, 'Why *wouldn't* Elvis do it? After all, we put him there!' " said Maria.

THE POLICE AND OTHER DOCUMENTATION QUESTIONED IN *IS ELVIS Alive?* remains unexplained and has given birth to new questions, new evidence. Time has *not* removed the sting of the contradictions, mystery, missing documents, false information; but, rather, the fires have been flamed to yet another plateau.

So, yes, I am about to "face the heat by going back into the kitchen." The possibility of Elvis Presley's being alive is greater now than it was a year ago, two years ago. And I am not alone in this belief. Several national surveys state that approximately 85 percent of the American people believe Presley lives. You be the judge.

"I may not look good tonight, but I'll look good in my coffin," said Presley on his last concert tour, 1977.

"If I should return you would not recognize me" is underlined in one of Elvis' favorite books.

"I Am and I Was" are words spoken onstage by Presley during his last concert tour, 1977.

1977 IS TODAY MORE THAN A DECADE AGO, AND A NEW GENERATION OF Americans has come of age who never knew Elvis, who never read or heard the details of his "demise." Even older Americans may by now have forgotten the events of August 16, 1977. To refresh our memories, it will be well to relate *what the public was told happened,* August 15–18, thirteen years ago:

August 15, 1977
- Elvis was preparing for a twelve-day concert tour that was to begin in Portland, Maine, on the following day.
- Because his daughter, Lisa – who by now lived with Priscilla Presley in California – was at Graceland on an extended vacation, Elvis spent much of his time that day (as well as before) with her. They rode golf carts, and planned to watch the movie *MacArthur* that night on the home screen (because of

the projectionist's inability to work late that night, the plan was scrapped).

- Sometime during the evening, Elvis telephoned to his dentist, Dr. Lester Hofman, asking if he would open his office for an emergency appointment. (Elvis, we were told, suddenly decided that he needed his teeth cleaned, as well as some other dental work.) Along with his cousin Billy Smith, friend Charlie Hodge, and girlfriend Ginger Alden, Elvis – wearing his blue DEA (Drug Enforcement Agency; see File Cases Nos. 1 and 2) jogging suit – headed out for a 10:30 P.M. appointment with dentist Hofman.

August 16, 1977
- Elvis was back at Graceland somewhere between 12:30 and 1:30 A.M. He was reported to be energetic, optimistic, good-humored, and full of plans for the future.
- At 4:00 A.M., Elvis called Billy Smith and Billy's wife, Jo, to join him and Ginger on the raquetball court for an hour's play.
- At 5:00 A.M., after raquetball, Elvis played the piano and sang some songs.
- At 6:00 A.M., Elvis and Ginger went up to his bedroom, where he changed into pajamas and then, alternately, watched television and read.
- At 8:00 A.M., Elvis told Ginger that he was going into the bathroom – which served, in addition, as a large, comfortable lounge – in order to continue reading. (This bathroom/lounge had its own back entrance.)
- For the next six hours, according to original reports, no one saw or talked with Elvis.*
- At 2:00 P.M., Ginger Alden discovered Elvis' body in the bathroom/lounge on the floor in front of his chair, where he had been reading. She called downstairs to Al Strada, Elvis' friend/employee, who was in the kitchen. Al rushed upstairs, then called downstairs for Joe Esposito, another Elvis friend and employee. Elvis' family doctor, George Nichopoulos ("Dr. Nick"), was telephoned. Noticing that rigor mortis had set in, Joe called Unit Six of the Memphis Fire Department.
- At 2:33 P.M., the Memphis Fire Department unit arrived. Despite the fact that the body was in rigor mortis, paramedics had been called, and gave CPR.
- At 2:48 P.M., the body was taken to Baptist Memorial Hospital.

---

*New evidence indicates that Elvis left the bathroom and went downstairs, where he signed for a special-delivery letter at 9:30 A.M. (see File Case No. 16).

- At 3:00 P.M., to family and friends Elvis was pronounced dead. The public was given a death time of 3:30 P.M.
- At 8:00 P.M., Dr. Nichopoulos and Dr. Jerry Francisco, the Medical Examiner, were interviewed in a press conference at the hospital.

August 17, 1977
- At noonday, the body was returned to Graceland for private family viewing.
- From 3:00 to 6:30 P.M., the public viewed the body at Graceland.

August 18, 1977
- By order of the Governor of Tennessee, Ray Blanton, flags were flown at half-mast for the funeral procession. At midday, the gates of Graceland swung open and a white Cadillac hearse drove through them, trailed by sixteen white Cadillac limousines.

Gail Brewer-Giorgio
Gainesville, Georgia
August 1990

There are two ways to slide easily through life: to believe everything or to doubt everything;. both ways save us from thinking.
—ALFRED KORZYBSKI

Men become civilized, not in proportion to their willingness to believe, but in proportion to their readiness to doubt.
—H. L. MENCKEN

One's friends are the part of the human race with which one can be human.
—GEORGE SANTAYANA

If you look back on my life, you will see I have not had as much to say about the way I live as most men do. My life was run by my fans. I'm not complaining. I did want it. People have written that I am a bad influence. That hurt me bad at first. I'd think what do they want from this kid from Memphis? I was but myself. I've got to be Elvis. I'm going to live the way I have to live, and if something should ever happen to me, I hope they remember I was not afraid. . . . .There might even be somebody who would say, "If Elvis had lived, he would have made a nice old man."

ELVIS PRESLEY,
in *Modern Screen,* 1966

The question of Elvis' death has always been a hard one for me. And it hasn't become the least bit easier in seven-plus years. I honestly can't remember when Elvis wasn't a part of my life. I got my first album at age seven ("King Creole"), and it's been only Elvis ever since. . . . .I have heard (and read) all of the arguments, both pro and con, since his death, and if I were to weigh it all into one thought, it would be this: "I have been waiting since August 17, 1984, for the announcement that Elvis is still alive." Enough said.

MARK K.,
in *The Elvis Special*
(January/March 1985)

No. 1

DEA Agent Elvis Presley

The price of greatness is responsibility.
—WINSTON CHURCHILL

Question: Was Elvis Presley really a Federal Agent?
Answer: Because Elvis Presley was a collector of law-enforcement badges, the debate over whether Elvis' federal badge was real or honorary continues. Most of those who followed Elvis remember the story of his December 1970 visit with President Richard Nixon at the White House. Witnessing the historic meeting were Jerry Schilling and Sonny West; both worked for Elvis.

The majority of biographers state that the badge was real and that the purpose of Elvis' trip was to obtain a real, not an honorary badge, as well as to offer his services in drug enforcement. The badge was presented. A White House photographer snapped over two dozen pictures of the meeting. In the spring of 1988 the government offered the pictures for sale to the public, and they immediately became the most sought-after photographs in the history of the National Archives.

This is part of the Nixon Presidential Materials Project. As a matter of information for those wishing to purchase 8x10, 11x14, 16x20, or 20x24 prints, you can write to the government and receive ordering information along with numbered photocopies to help make your selection.

All of the details of the Nixon–Presley meeting are not known, although the National Archives and Records Administration has

more than 40 million pages of documents of the Nixon Administration as well as documents regarding Elvis' visits to the Oval
Office. Further, the U.S. Department of Justice's Federal Bureau
of Investigation in Washington confirmed in a letter to Maria
Columbus, president of The Elvis Special fan club, that Presley
visited FBI headquarters on December 31, 1970. Although J. Edgar
Hoover was not available to meet with Elvis, the entertainer and
his group (which included William N. Morris, former sheriff of
Shelby County, Tennessee, and six others) were given a tour of FBI
facilities.

The letter states that during this visit Elvis Presley indicated
that President Nixon had presented him with a Federal Agent's
badge of the Bureau of Narcotics and Dangerous Drugs, which
was at that time part of the Drug Enforcement Administration.
Elvis displayed the badge during this meeting. What I find strange
about this letter to Maria, dated September 30, 1982, was a pas-
sage clearly stating that it was not known whether Nixon made
a *personal* presentation of the badge.

Why would the FBI not know that President Nixon did indeed
make a personal presentation when, only a few years later,
pictures of his meeting with Elvis were made available by the
government?

According to the letter, there is no indication that Elvis had an
FBI badge or FBI credentials—which is different than a badge from
the DEA. Less than a week after Elvis' visit with the FBI, Elvis
received a personal letter from J. Edgar Hoover thanking him for
the offer of the confidential assistance Elvis had extended to the
bureau. Whether the FBI took Elvis up is not on public record. But
then, if Elvis did work in a confidential manner, it seems reasonable to assume that such public information would not be readily
available.

However, another picture* has come to my attention taken of
Elvis not too long before August 16, 1977. Elvis is boarding an
airplane with who appears to be Ginger Alden behind him. Elvis
has a book in his hand and is waving. On his jacket appears the
emblem: DEA Staff.

In *Elvis, My Brother*, Billy Stanley noted that Elvis was wearing a jogging suit with the DEA logo during the early morning
hours of August 16, 1977. Monte Nicholson, a 19-year veteran with

---

*There is a picture of Elvis in DEA Staff jacket in Sean Shaver's *Elvis Presley, Softly
I Must Leave You;* also in *The Life of Elvis Presley,* by Sean Shaver and Hal Noland,
is a picture taken in June 1977, approximately six weeks before August 16.

the Los Angeles Sheriff's Department writes in his novel *The Presley Arrangement* about a government helicopter hovering over Graceland, and finally landing in the back. Nicholson was informed there were pictures of Elvis getting on the helicopter during the early afternoon of August 16. Others report seeing a helicopter(s) – including Larry Geller in his book *If I Can Dream: Elvis' Own Story*, who says he saw from his window at Howard Johnson's helicopters hovering over Graceland.

THERE ARE VARIOUS VERSIONS OF HOW THE MEETING BETWEEN PRESIdent Nixon and Elvis came to be. Timing may have had a great deal to do with Elvis' becoming a Federal Agent with the DEA. For one, Elvis had, prior to his December 21, 1970, meeting in the Oval Office, been nominated by the U.S. Jaycees as one of America's Ten Most Outstanding Young Men for his work in drug enforcement. He was a bonded deputy with the Memphis Police and was known to don disguises and go out on narc busts. Two months prior to meeting with President Nixon, Elvis was presented with a CNOA Membership Certificate that reads: *This is to certify that Elvis A. Presley is a member in good standing of the California Narcotic Officers Association.*

He had badges from many law enforcement agencies – some honorary, others not. For instance, in his wallet he carried a badge from the Memphis Police. An article appeared around 1975 that stated, "If Elvis ever decides to quit as a singer he'd make an excellent law enforcement officer." This quote has been attributed to Sheriff Roy Nixon. He presented Elvis with a deputy sheriff badge only after Elvis had passed a rigid firearms qualification test with flying colors. Elvis needed a score of 70 out of 100 to qualify on the firing range. On the second series of shots, he reportedly made 95 out of 100. Before being sworn in, Elvis was required to attend multiple hour training sessions in firearms, which permitted him to carry a gun. Elvis declared that only in the case of extreme emergency would he exercise his power as deputy sheriff to make a legal arrest.

In the first of the following four photos, we see a formal pose – Nixon shaking Elvis' hand. (Another version of this photo is on the book jacket.) In another photo the President examines the singer's cuff link; at right stands presidential aide Bud Krogh. In another photo Nixon chats with Elvis and his friends Sonny West (left) and Jerry Schilling (right).

Several biographies tell of the time Elvis used his federal narcotics badge to stop a commercial airplane at the Las Vegas airport.
Elvis was after a man accused of stealing from him. Elvis raced out
on the tarmac as the plane was taxiing and flashed his badge up
to the pilot in the cockpit. The pilot immediately recognized the
badge – as well as Presley. He lowered the gangplank and allowed
Elvis on board. After checking out the passengers and discovering
the guilty man was not among them, Elvis waved the pilot on.

TO BE NOMINATED AS ONE OF THE TEN MOST OUTSTANDING YOUNG MEN
in America in 1970, Elvis must have been involved in undercover
work on a local level that is not known. However, by 1970 Nixon
had launched his own national crusade against drugs, which most
certainly fired up Elvis. Nixon and Elvis called drugs "America's
number one problem." To this end the President was planning to
set up a massive and powerful drug enforcement agency model-
ed after the FBI and CIA. It was to become one of the most
prestigious arms of the government.

Elvis offered his services as an agent – as an informer, a
dangerous offer at the very least. The DEA was formed and Elvis
Presley was there at the beginning.

Although this was a bounty for President Nixon, it does appear
by some of the correspondence that Elvis' commitment was not
taken as too serious. But Elvis took it as serious, and in the end I
believe that is what counted. Elvis Presley was the great hero, the
number-one entertainer, the idol of millions of American youth.
They would listen to what he had to say. Obviously he was
dedicated to law enforcement, and although his work with the
DEA may reveal some hypocrisy since he took too much prescribed medication, we should remember that a president's wife
also found herself in similar trouble at one point. Human nature
is strange: There is the "Do as I say" syndrome versus "Not as I do"
truth.

Be that as it may, Elvis received a complete set of credentials
and a badge.

At this point, it would be well advised to study some of the correspondence from the White House in order to get a clearer picture of what transpired. Remember, President Nixon did not have
the Oval Office wired until the following year, thus the correspondence and personal witnessing is all we have to go on.

It begins with a six-page letter written on American Airlines
stationery:

AmericanAirlines

In Flight...

Altitude:

Location:

Dear Mr. President.

First I would like to introduce myself.
I am Elvis Presley and admire you
and Have Great Respect for your
office. I talked to Vice President
agnew in Palm Springs 3 weeks and
expressed my concern for our country.
The Drug Culture, the Hippie Elements,
the SDS, Black Panthers, etc do not
consider me as their enemy or as they
call it the Establishment. I call it america and

AmericanAirlines

In Flight...

Altitude; ②

Location;

I Love it . Sir I can and will
be of any service that I can to help
the country out. I have no concern
or motives other than helping the
country out. So I wish not to be
given a title or an appointed portion, I can
and will do more good if I were
made a Federal agent at large, and
I will help out by doing it my
way through my communications with people
of all ages. First and Foremost I am an
entertainer but all I need is the Federal
credentials. I am on this Plane with

AmericanAirlines

In Flight...

Altitude;   ③

Location;

Sen. George Murphy and Will
have been discussing the problems
that our Country is faced with.
So I am Staying at the Washington
hotel Room 505-506-507. I have
2 men who work with me by the
name of Jerry Schilling and Sonny
west. I am registered under the name
of Jon Burrows. I will be here
for as long as it takes to get
the credentials of a Federal Agent.
I have done an in depth study of
Drug Abuse and Communist Brainwashing

AmericanAirlines

In Flight...

Altitude;

Location;

4

---

techniques and I am right in the middle of the whole thing, where I can and will do the most good. I am Glad to help just so long as it is kept very Private. you can have your staff or whomever call me anytime today tonight or Tomorrow I was nominated tha coming year one of america's Ten most outstanding young men. That will be in January 18 in My Home Town of Memphis Tenn. I am sending you the about autobiography about myself so you can better understand this

AmericanAirlines

In Flight...

Altitude:

Location: 5

~~approach~~

approval. I would love to
meet you just to say hello if
you're not to Busy.

Respectfully

Elvis Presley

P.S. I believe that you Sir
were one of the Top Ten outstanding men
of America also.

I have a personal gift for you also
which I would like to present to you
and you can accept it or I will keep it
for you until you can take it.

The sixth page of the letter contained personal telephone numbers at which Elvis could be reached (Beverly Hills, Palm Springs, Memphis, a Washington hotel) under the name "Jon Burrows."

A December 21, 1970, White House memo was sent to H. R. Haldeman from presidential assistant Dwight L. Chapin. As you will note, it was decided that Presley was important enough not to be "pushed off on the Vice President" and that no one disagreed that it would be a bad idea for Elvis to become a "Federal agent at large" and that "Presley might be a perfect one to start with." Chapin also notes: "Presley was voted one of the ten outstanding young men for next year and this was based upon his work in the field of drugs."* (Again, we do not know how much and how often, or what, Elvis did in the field of drugs to earn this nomination.)

However, if we note on the second page of the memo Haldeman's response in pen was "You must be kidding," it would appear that Haldeman was not as enthusiastic as President Nixon and his assistant. However, Haldeman did sign his initial on the approval line.

During the meeting, Bud Krogh took notes, which he compiled into another memorandum. It is interesting to note that Elvis told President Nixon that he had been "studying the drug culture for over ten years." Elvis also indicated that he could get into any cultural group easily and be "accepted." According to Krogh: "The President mentioned that he thought Presley could reach young people, and that it was important for Presley to retain his credibility. Presley responded that he did his thing by 'just singing.' He said that he could not get to the kids if he made a speech on the stage...The President nodded in agreement."

Another interesting note from Krogh:

> Presley indicated to the President in a very emotional manner that he was "on your side." Presley kept repeating that he wanted to be helpful, that he wanted to restore some respect for the flag which was being lost. He mentioned that he was just a poor boy from Tennessee who had gotten a lot from his country, which in some way he wanted to repay. . . . At the conclusion of the meeting, Presley again told the President how much he supported him, and then, in a surprising, spontaneous gesture, put his left arm around the President and hugged him.

---

*Elvis received this award on January 18, 1971, in Memphis.

MEMORANDUM

THE WHITE HOUSE
WASHINGTON

December 21, 1970

MEMORANDUM FOR: MR. H. R. HALDEMAN

FROM: DWIGHT L. CHAPIN

SUBJECT: Elvis Presley

Attached you will find a letter to the President from Elvis Presley.
As you are aware, Presley showed up here this morning and has
requested an appointment with the President. He states that he knows
the President is very busy, but he would just like to say hello and
present the President with a gift.

As you are well aware, Presley was voted one of the ten outstanding
young men for next year and this was based upon his work in the
field of drugs. The thrust of Presley's letter is that he wants to become
a "Federal agent at large" to work against the drug problem by com-
municating with people of all ages. He says that he is not a member
of the establishment and that drug culture types, the hippie elements,
the SDS, and the Black Panthers are people with whom he can communicate since he is not part of the establishment.

I suggest that we do the following:

This morning Bud Krogh will have Mr. Presley in and talk
to him about drugs and about what Presley can do. Bud will
also check to see if there is some kind of an honorary agent
at large or credential of some sort that we can provide
for Presley. After Bud has met with Presley, it is recom-
mended that we have Bud bring Presley in during the Open
Hour to meet briefly with the President. You know that
several people have mentioned over the past few months that
Presley is very pro the President. He wants to keep everything
private and I think we should honor his request.

I have talked to Bud Korgh about this whole matter, and we both think
that it would be wrong to push Presley off on the Vice President since
it will take very little of the President's time and it can be extremely
beneficial for the President to build some rapport with Presley.

In addition, if the President wants to meet with some bright young
people outside of the Government, Presley might be a perfect one to
start with.

Approve Presley coming in at end of Open Hour_____

Disapprove_____

A second memorandum was prepared establishing a meeting of Presley on December 21, 1970, at 12:30 P.M. with President Nixon and a member of his staff, Bud Krogh. The purpose was to accept Elvis' offer and ask him to help with the drug epidemic:

EXECUTIVE
HE 5-1
PR 7-1/p

THE WHITE HOUSE

WASHINGTON

December 21, 1970

A

MEMORANDUM FOR: THE PRESIDENT

SUBJECT: Meeting with Elvis Presley
                                      December 21, 1970
                                      12:30 p. m.

I.   PURPOSE

   To thank Elvis Presley for his offer to help in trying to stop
   the drug epidemic in the country, and to ask him to work with
   us in bringing a more positive attitude to young people throughout the country.

   In his letter to you, Elvis Presley offered to help as much as
   possible with the growing drug problem. He requested the
   meeting with you this morning when he presented himself to
   the guard at the Northwest Gate bearing a letter.

II.   PARTICIPANTS

   Elvis Presley

   Bud Krogh (staff)

III.   TALKING POINTS

   A.   We have asked the entertainment industry - both television
         and radio - to assist us in our drug fight.

   B.   You are aware that the average American family has 4 radio
         sets; 98% of the young people between 12 and 17 listen to
         radio. Between the time a child is born and he leaves high
         school, it is estimated he watches between 15, 000 and
         20, 000 hours of television. That is more time than he spend
         in the classroom.

C.   The problem is critical: As of December 14, 1970, 1,022
     people died this year in New York alone from just narcotic
     related deaths. 208 of these were teenagers.

D.   Two of youth's folk heroes, Jimi Hendrix and Janis Joplin,
     recently died within a period of two weeks reportedly from
     drug-related causes. Their deaths are a sharp reminder
     of how the rock music culture has been linked to the drug
     sub-culture. If our youth are going to emulate the rock
     music stars, from now on let those stars affirm their con-
     viction that true and lasting talent is the result of self
     motivation and discipline and not artificial chemical euphoria.

E.   Suggestions for Presley activities:

     1. Work with White House Staff

     2. Cooperate with and encourage the creation of an hour
         Television Special in which Presley narrates as stars
         such as himself sing popular songs and interpret them
         for parents in order to show drug and other anti-estab-
         lishment themes in rock music.

     3. Encourage fellow artists to develop a new rock musical
         theme, ''Get High on Life.''

     4. Record an album with the theme ''Get High on Life!'' at
         the federal narcotic rehabilitation and research facility
         at Lexington, Kentucky.

     5. Be a consultant to the Advertising Council on how to
         communicate anti-drug messages to youth.

Some food for thought: Many DEA agents appear to be "drug
users" and "pushers" in order to do their undercover work. It's not
unusual to find undercover agents who look very young taking on
the role of high school or college student in order to get the goods
on the "big guys."

There is little doubt that Elvis Presley could get to anyone at
any time, especially if he gave the appearance of a "user." This falls
in line with what was stated in *Elvis: What Happened?* when one
of the guys wondered if Elvis was ever as whacked out as he appeared? Maybe he was the ultimate actor, after all.

Not long ago, I was told by a law enforcement official that Elvis
did indeed get into trouble because he had been responsible for the
gathering of drug information concerning a major drug bust involving a big-time drug dealer. This information was used to put

the big-timer behind bars. Death threats were issued against Elvis
and/or his family, and those intent upon carrying out the threats
got as close to Elvis and his family as having broken into
Graceland. Other biographies ascertain *more* death threats, with
the FBI being called. Something was happening.

"PRESLEY GETS NARCOTICS BUREAU BADGE" WERE THE HEADLINES OF
Jack Anderson's article in the *Washington Post*. According to this article, Deputy Narcotics Director John Finlator sought to enlist
Presley in the anti-drug fight. "Finlator invited the singer to the
Narcotics Bureau for a quiet visit and arranged for the guards to
admit him under the pseudonym 'John Burroughs,'" wrote Anderson. Elvis was happy to help, although Finlator did not want to give
him a narcotics badge. Finlator's decision was reversed by the
President. "When Finlator finally handed Presley the badge and
promised to issue him consultant credentials, the singer was over-
come with emotion, and his eyes became misty."
     Ten days later Elvis Presley met with the FBI.
     That same day President Nixon wrote Elvis a thank-you note.
     A memorandum from Bud Krogh, dated January 27, 1972,
regarding Anderson's column in the *Post,* supported Presley's
desire to fight drug abuse.
     According to an interview by syndicated columnist Bob
Greene with Richard McNeill, the archives specialist in charge of
the Nixon–Presley photos, the thing that surprised McNeill the
most was the quality of Americans requesting the pictures:
Doctors, lawyers, registered nurses. . .
     Although the Nixon–Presley pictures have been available from
the government for many years, only recently have they been
made so public. They are available from:

> Richard E. McNeill,
> Archives Specialist
> Nixon Presidential Materials Project
> National Archives and Records Administration
> Washington, DC 20408

Send no money to this address. Ordering information, and an
address for purchase of the photos, will be given by Mr. McNeill.
     Many of the fan clubs focused upon them, biographers to
some extent have, Bob Greene has, and to a small extent *Is Elvis
Alive?* did. Richard McNeill reported that until recently there had
been only about a dozen requests per month versus today's
thousands per day. According to Bob Greene there will be a delay,

because employees of the National Archives have been instructed to devote only two hours per day to the Nixon– Presley pictures since they have other business to attend to.

Although perhaps at first the government may have looked upon Elvis' desire to be a federal narcotics agent with a tongue-in-cheek attitude, it is clear that Elvis' romance with law and order ran deep. In his heart he was a dedicated American. It is very possible, *probable* perhaps, that Elvis agented with the same zest and "take it to the max" commitment he once held toward entertaining. The American Hero now became an expert in self-defense: He learned karate and became a sharpshooter.

"I can and will do more good," Elvis wrote the President, "if I were made a Federal Agent at large, and I will help out by doing it my way. . . . "

THERE ARE THOSE WHO INSIST THEY WERE AWARE OF EVERY BREATHing moment of Elvis' life – knew exactly what he was doing, what he was thinking. Yet many of these same people relate how Elvis would become a recluse in his bedroom for weeks, seeing no one. It is nonsense to believe any one person was around Elvis twenty-four hours a day, day after day, nonstop. They had families of their own.

In Elvis' friend and spiritual advisor Larry Geller's book *If I Can Dream* we read about how scared the singer was after being visited by some "businessmen," who met privately with him on one occasion. After the meeting, Elvis inferred that the men, although they *appeared* legitimate, were not, and he expressed the thought that the universe was "very dangerous." What had the men said to Elvis to frighten him so?

There was a back staircase at Graceland. Certainly a man with the skills of Elvis could play games – "Now you see me, now you don't." Recall: Elvis Presley managed to sneak out of Graceland undetected, go to the airport, purchase a ticket on a commercial airline to Washington, D.C., book himself into a hotel, go to the White House and make contact with the President of the United States!

For a man known not to carry cash, some planning must have occurred days prior. Elvis was known as a master planner. His whereabouts were unknown by those who state they knew his every move, every thought. I wonder how many other moves and decisions Elvis made that people are unaware of? Logic states that if one such monumental incident happened, others did. The problem is that only Elvis knew/knows the "whens and wheres."

Ask yourself these questions:

- Do I believe Elvis Presley's dedication to his country and to law and order were sincere?
- Do I believe Elvis Presley took his Federal Agent position with the DEA seriously?
- Realizing that one of the tasks of the DEA is to gather information on major drug dealers, do I believe that if the opportunity presented itself to Elvis he would have turned over such information to the DEA?
- Do I believe Elvis would have put himself in a dangerous situation in order to pay allegiance to both his country and the DEA?
- Do I believe Elvis Presley could get into places and groups that others could not?
- Do I believe Elvis was both clever enough and adept enough to pull off the task of being an undercover agent with the DEA?
- Have I ever heard of DEA agents getting into trouble and having the finger of death pointed their way (A contract on their life)?
- Have I heard of the government's protection plan for its agents? Have I ever heard of agents "disappearing" or being thought "dead" in order to fool those issuing the "contract"?
- If Elvis did what DEA agents do (gathering drug information on the "big guys" for prosecution) and his role as the DEA informant was discovered – resulting in a "contract" out on his life and the life of his little girl – would Elvis have done just about anything (especially if there was a break-in at Graceland) to save their lives?
- Would the DEA give Federal Agent Presley the same protection they would give any other agent? (A new identity? new passport? protection?)

HOW BETTER TO CANCEL OUT A "CONTRACT" THAN TO HAVE THE "victim" appear dead?

The majority of people I've talked to say, "Of course I've heard of things such as the government witness protection plan. Of course, agents get in trouble! But Elvis Presley? He was just an entertainer, wasn't he? I mean, who would ever suspect Elvis Presley?"

That's the point: Who would suspect Elvis Presley?

It does appear that Elvis Presley was a Federal Agent with the

Drug Enforcement Agency. "By Presidential dictum," Jack Anderson wrote in the *Washington Post* on January 27, 1972, "Elvis Presley, the swivel hipped singer, has been issued a federal narcotics badge."

Elvis' Role of Undercover Agent

> *The only thing necessary for the triumph*
> *of evil is for good men to do nothing.*
> — EDMUND BURKE

Question: What is the role of an undercover agent?
Answer: The reading of New American Library's *Donnie Brasco: My Undercover Life in the Mafia* (New York, 1989), by Joseph D. Pistone with Richard Woodley, gives insight and understanding as to the role federal undercover agents play, zeroing in on the fact that Pistone was an unlikely candidate who became a Federal Agent *by accident.* He was not the type to be suspected.

It is obvious that the most effective agent is the one least suspected, one who has a legitimate "other job" (entertainer?), and, as in the case of Elvis, a person who could get to the kind of people and places others could not. This is precisely the service offered to President Nixon in December 1970. We also know by other biographies, including *If I Can Dream: Elvis' Own Story,* that in June 1977 during Elvis' last concert tour, Larry Geller was with Elvis in the Netherland Hilton in Cincinnati, where Elvis showed him a small black book issued each year from the U.S. Justice Department listing the names of all narcotics agents – a book that only agents who are listed are given. Excitedly, Elvis talked about his love of America and his willingness to help in any way possible.

Some months earlier, December 31, 1976, Geller was also witness to a telephone call Elvis received from President-Elect

Jimmy Carter – a call lasting about ten minutes. Elvis told Larry that President Carter had asked for a meeting with him at the White House after the Inauguration, with the President planning to appoint Elvis as Special Advisor to him on the youth of America, the music scene, and "other projects." "President Carter is planning to create a special post for me," Elvis said to Larry and to others. "And I promised him I would serve my country and use whatever influence I had, especially with the war on drugs."

Records attest to this truth: From 1970 to 1977, Elvis Presley was connected to two United States presidents, both wanting this entertainer's services to help with the drug war and its horrendous influence on the youth of America. We also know by a letter written November 29, 1982, to Maria Columbus, president of The Elvis Special from the Department of the Treasury's Bob Pritchett that during the years 1974, 1975, and 1976, "Mr. Presley provided one of our undercover agents, who was a musician, a job cover."

Although this letter was focused upon in *Is Elvis Alive?*, I believe it essential to zero in on the fact that for several years an undercover agent was being provided cover by Elvis Presley, himself an agent. We're not talking months, we're talking years, and as I pointed out, undercover agents appear to have other occupations. They are not lurking beneath lampposts clad in trench coats. In this case the undercover agent was a musician. The letter also states the belief that "President Nixon recognized Mr. Presley's contribution and assistance to the Drug Enforcement Agency."

The Elvis Special fan newsletter makes a valid point in stating: "It is obvious to us that no one in Elvis' group of 'friends' knew of this special undercover agent and the role Elvis played in setting up his cover. Since Elvis had an undercover agent in this group from 1974–76 when did he find the time to do drugs himself?" (Apparently Elvis was very good at keeping secrets and of living a "double life.")

Although it is clear by the government's correspondence with Maria Columbus that the undercover agent's identity had to remain secret, it is interesting to note – in a second, December 22, 1982, letter to Columbus from Pritchett – that the "files are Criminal Investigative files."

Which should mean a criminal investigation was taking place over approximately a three-year period and that Elvis was at least involved to the point of "providing cover" for this agent. Since the government with good reason could not expose the nature of this criminal investigation, nor the agent's identity – even if Elvis was assisting beyond providing "cover" – would it not be reasonable to assume that this would be confidential information?

In a letter from Pritchett to an Elvis fan as late as August 15, 1988, he again insists that "our undercover agent. . .does not want his name made known to the public."

I would also like to point out that of the 663 FBI pages on Elvis, much of the material consists of files dated after August 1977. What I am discovering is mind-boggling and far too cumbersome for this book. However, I will try to touch upon certain elements in a later chapter. Because so many of the file reports are blacked out (for security reasons?), putting all the pieces together is impossible.

Having waded through 663 FBI documents on Elvis Presley, as well as analyzing other data, I find that it is quite obvious Elvis Aron Presley was not just an honorary agent-at-large with the DEA, nor did Elvis view his association with drug enforcement as less than serious – nor did two United States Presidents. Those who are set on portraying Elvis as little more than an over-the-hill rock 'n' roller will not want to embrace this possibility. However, there is far too much here to chalk it up as coincidences, or as mere trophies for a bored entertainer.

These same 663 documents attest to the truth that Elvis Presley's life was threatened seriously and that the FBI had been called in.

Because this book cannot accommodate so much data, if the reader wishes to peruse the documents personally, he may write:

Freedom of Information – Privacy Acts Section
Records Management Division
U.S. Dept. of Justice
Federal Bureau of Investigation
Washington, DC 20535

Subject requested: Elvis Aron Presley

Freedom of Information Act (Title 5, U.S. Code, Section 552)

The government charges copying costs somewhere between $50 and $60.

ELVIS WAS LONG INTERESTED IN LAW ENFORCEMENT: HE HAD LONG associations with the Shelby County Sheriff's Department. I include here the final page of Elvis' November 1974 application for

Shelby County Special Deputy, as well as the complete document of his appointment as Deputy Sheriff in September 1976:

19. To what extent do you drink?___DON'T DRINK-_____

20. List three (3) business firms as credit references:

  1._____Active_____

  2._____Active_____

  3._____Active_____

21. Hand Gun Information: Make S-W Model 6/6 Caliber 357 _____

   Serial Number_____Blue____Nickel____Stainless Steel_X_____

   This weapon owned by_____

   HAND GUN MUST BE APPROVED BY SHERIFF'S DEPARTMENT

   PLEASE READ BEFORE SIGNING:

   I hereby state that the information entered here is complete and true to the best of my knowledge. Any false statement, knowingly or willfully made will be reason to reject my application. I further agree to abide by the regulations and restrictions established governing this commission. This signature is to authorize a complete background investigation.

   _____
   (Signature)

   ___11/20/74_____
   (Date)

A TWENTY-FIVE ($25.00) NON-REFUNDABLE FEE MUST ACCOMPANY THIS APPLICATION IF WEAPON IS CALIBER .38 SPECIAL. THIRTY-FIVE ($35.00) IF WEAPON IS ANY OTHER CALIBER.

NOTE: If this application is rejected for insufficient references or any other reason, and the applicant wishes to re-submit, an additional charge of twenty-five ($25.00) will be required

Elvis was also a member of the National Sheriffs' Association, headquartered in Washington, D.C.

We know that Elvis was a visiting guest at FBI headquarters in late 1970. Although Jimmy Carter was not President-Elect until November 1976, Elvis' connection went as far back as at least 1973, when Carter was Governor of Georgia. A well-known photograph shows him with the Governor and Mrs. Carter. Governor Carter subsequently proclaimed January 8, 1974, as "Elvis Presley Day in Georgia."

There is no doubt that both President Nixon and President Carter held a great deal of respect for Elvis Presley; more than one book reports that both presidents spoke with Elvis shortly before August 16, 1977. In fact, Elvis spoke with President Carter two weeks prior, his wish to converse privately with the President delivered via *an agent of the FBI*. (Records indicate that Elvis' con-

OFFICE OF

SHERIFF OF SHELBY COUNTY

COUNTY OF SHELBY,
State of Tennessee }

    By virtue of authority of law in me vested, I do hereby *appoint and constitute*................Elvis Aron Presley................, *a Deputy Sheriff* under me, in and for the said County of Shelby, to do and perform such duties as are prescribed by law.

    This *commission* to continue at my will.

    Given under my hand, at office, in the Court House, in the City of Memphis, this the ....1........day of........Sept.........19 76

Gene Barksdale
Sheriff of Shelby County.

STATE OF TENNESSEE,
County of Shelby }

    I do solemnly swear that I will support the Constitution of the United States, and the Constitution and Laws of the State of Tennessee; and that I will discharge the duties of the office of DEPUTY SHERIFF OF SHELBY COUNTY, TENNESSEE, to which I have been appointed, and which I am about to assume; and that I have not given, accepted, or knowingly carried a challenge, in writing or otherwise, to any person being a citizen of the State, or aided or abetted therein, since the adoption of the Constitution in 1835 and that I will not be guilty of either of these acts during my continuance in office: So help me God.

Elvis Presley

Sworn to and subscribed before me, this........................day of........................19 ......

........................Clerk.

........................D. C.

versation with the President revolved around aid to a friend.)

Two weeks after this private conversation—August 16, 1977—President Carter issued this tribute:

> Elvis Presley's death deprives our country of a part of itself. He was unique; and irreplaceable. More than twenty years ago he burst upon the scene with an impact that was unprecedented and will probably never be equaled. His music and his personality, fusing the styles of white country and black rhythm and blues, permanently changed the face of American popular culture. His following was immense and he was a symbol to people the world over, of the vitality, rebelliousness, and good humor of his country.

Many journalists noted this tribute, noting also that although it was not unusual for local leaders to comment on a celebrity's death, for the President of the United States to issue a formal statement was unusual.

Thus, one obvious question arises: Since Elvis was an agent-at-large of the DEA and was at least involved in providing cover, for three years, for another undercover agent together with his ongoing associations with at least two United States presidents—both of whom he spoke with shortly prior to August 16, 1977—is it possible that Elvis became the target of some drug dealers who were the focus of the 1974–76 criminal investigations? If you can at least fathom that possibility, then the next question would be: If Elvis and his family were under *serious* death threats due to his DEA involvement, could Elvis turn to that same government for protection?

We know he told friends and family about how dangerous the universe was, even inferring that "the mob" could cause him danger. An interview with karate master Ed Parker, who was confidant and bodyguard to Elvis, in the September 1988 issue of *American Karate* magazine describes a time in Florida when a terrorist group threatened Elvis' life in order to make him an example of how they could get to famous people—thus blackmailing them into contributing to their causes. "We will plant a bomb in one of the gifts offered Elvis at a concert," was the threat. Police authorities were summoned and whatever threat there was never materialized. Still, living under such constant threats had to take its toll on the singer. As long as he was "alive," he and his family would be targets.

But dead? Hard to kill the hen who lays the golden eggs if it has already expired.

ONCE ELVIS WAS A DEA AGENT, IT APPEARED HE BEGAN TO SURROUND himself with law enforcement officials such as John O'Grady, who had earlier been in charge of the Narcotics Division of the Los Angeles Police Department. Also around the time he became commited to law enforcement he hired Dick Grob, formerly a fighter pilot with the U.S. Air Force and a sergeant with the Palm Springs Police. Thereby we now have a picture of Elvis in the 1970s: an undercover agent acting as a musician in his traveling band and surrounded by two lawmen in top security positions.

Yet Elvis remained in danger. If he wanted higher protection could he, for instance, call the FBI? the President of the United States?

Are *other* agents protected? Would the FBI and/or the President of the United States care enough? And...was Elvis Presley frightened *enough* to plea for help?

In his book *If I Can Dream*, during Larry Geller's telling of Elvis' government role, he reports that Presley fell asleep only to awake mumbling his daughter's name, warning her to stay away from a trap. When Larry asked Elvis what was frightening him, Elvis was evasive, ending with the statement that he wanted Lisa at Graceland as soon as the tour was completed.

"I read in one book that J. D. Sumner [friend and backup for Elvis] was always afraid someone would try to kidnap Lisa Marie and even warned Elvis," wrote a reader. "Elvis saw to it Lisa did not fly commercial. If this is true, why was Lisa still at Graceland on August 16, 1977, not back on the West Coast with her mother? Since Elvis was leaving that day for an extended concert tour, how was Lisa to return?"

Many have raised such questions. Under normal circumstances, Elvis would have had Lisa flown home on August 15 via the *Lisa Marie*, so that the plane would be available for the upcoming tour. One report states that an Elvis staff member planned to escort Lisa back to the West Coast on a commercial flight – again strange in view of Elvis' deep, deep concern for his nine-year-old daughter's safety. Why hadn't he sent her back the day before? Surely it was not to keep her an extra day, because Elvis had instructed what staff remained not to waken him until later that afternoon. The question is: Were there any plans to send Lisa home? Was there another reason why Elvis wanted his little girl close by?

Mary Jenkins, Elvis' personal cook, in her book *Elvis the Way I Knew Him* reports that, around two in the morning of August 16, Elvis called down on the house phone asking that she come upstairs to straighten his bed. When she arrived, the room was quiet and empty. All the television sets were off—which she found strange, since Elvis was known to keep a television on at all times. Thinking he was in the bathroom, she changed the bed, then took his water bottle to Lisa's bedroom in order to fill it in her bathroom. Since no lights were on, Mary flipped the switch. She stepped back, startled: Elvis and Ginger Alden were sitting on the side of Lisa's bed in the darkened room, whispering. Mary said it was all so strange . . . so unlike Elvis.

Obvious questions: Where was Lisa Marie? Nine years old, two in the morning. . . . Was something about to happen?

Had threats against Elvis and his family escalated to a point where Lisa was not in her bedroom for security reasons? Having been informed by more than one law enforcement official that a break-in had occurred earlier on, that items had been taken from Lisa's bedroom and mailed back to Elvis as proof of how close "they" could get to him and his daughter, it is understandable how terrified Elvis was.

Could the reason be that Mary was called upstairs to get her out of the kitchen (from which a back staircase led to Elvis' bedroom)?

Accepting that both Elvis and Priscilla were cautious about family security—Lisa's, in particular—then the fact that Priscilla wrote in her book *Elvis and Me* that upon arriving at Graceland in the wee morning hours of August 17, finding Lisa outside riding around in her golf cart makes even less sense. Remember, there were journalists and thousands of screaming fans clamoring at the gates. Under sane conditions the safety of any nine-year-old at three in the morning would be suspect. But *this* child?

Then, Priscilla writes, she hugged Lisa and left her outside while she went inside to comfort the grieving family. No child, under most circumstances, would be outside at that hour, especially the daughter of Elvis Presley, who only twelve hours earlier supposedly "died."

I have the greatest respect in the world for Priscilla Presley. I doubt that I could have created Danielle in my novel *Orion* without her commentary.

Yet we must evaluate her story:

- She says she heard the news around noon in L.A.
- She says she sent for the plane *Lisa Marie*, which was in Memphis; she boarded at 9:00 P.M. L.A. time (which is 11:00 P.M. Memphis time). Consider an approximate four-

hour flight time and you have her arriving in Memphis around
3:00 A.M.
- She was sped in a waiting limo to Graceland. (With all those
people? Elvis' Uncle Vester told me it took an hour to go four
blocks.)
- She says that nine-year-old Lisa was outside riding around in
a golf cart.
- There are thousands of fans and media, but Priscilla leaves
her outside.

In her film adaptation of her book, Priscilla plays the arrival
completely opposite, showing it to be in broad daylight. It could
not have been the afternoon of August 16, 1977, because Elvis'
body was not discovered until around two that afternoon and
Priscilla was in California, according to her own book.

Was she already there, having perhaps arrived at least the day
prior to August 16? In February 1989, I appeared as a guest on the
Geraldo show with Joe Esposito, Elvis' friend and road manager.
Geraldo Rivera asked Joe about his initial reaction to the news
about Elvis. (Joe was in Memphis at the time.) I had several friends
in the audience, as well as a friend from the media and a
distributor from my publishing house. All distinctly heard Joe reply that he was concerned about Lisa *and Priscilla at the house!*

At the house? We know Lisa was at the house, having been
with her father on an extended visit to Graceland, but Priscilla in
her own words states she was in California. All of my people at
the *Geraldo* show were front row; one of them taped the show, and
she was so shocked at what Joe said that she reacted verbally, saying, ". . .at the house?!" Over and over I have listened to the tape:
". . .at the house" was clear.

This may explain the contradictions in Priscilla's story. It
appears highly possible that Priscilla had arrived at least the day
before. But then, even if she had, why would she relate it other-
wise? After all, she had a good-enough excuse: Her daughter was
there; Elvis was leaving on tour; she would escort Lisa back home.
Seems reasonable. Only that is not what she said.

Is it because there had to be a reason for the plane *Lisa Marie*
to fly *from Memphis to Los Angeles?* The reason given was to pick
her up. But what if Priscilla was already at Graceland and Elvis
was on board the *Lisa Marie.* What if he needed to be flown to the
coast, deboard, and be flown privately out of the States, or to an
island (Hawaii?) as the Mystery Tape with *Is Elvis Alive?* states?
The *Lisa Marie* arrives in L.A. in plenty of time to refuel. Then it

waits for Jerry Schilling (close friend of both Elvis and Priscilla; Jerry now handles some business for the estate) to board. Joan Esposito, who was married to Joe, boards. Priscilla's immediate family boards. The *Lisa Marie* flies back to Memphis, leaving at 9:00 P.M. L.A. time. There were some hurt feelings on the part of some others on the coast who were close to Elvis. They asked to fly back on the *Lisa Marie* too, but were denied. Was that because they would have known Priscilla was not on board? Perhaps only a few "trusted" were to know.

In light of what Priscilla has described and what Joe has said, this possibility has substance. Further, I have been told that helicopters (some say government) were seen at Graceland shortly prior to the two-o'clock hour. Since Elvis was a Federal Agent with the DEA, could he have been assisted in his escape from serious death threats? Would the government do this for any DEA agent, whether it were Elvis Presley or not?

While we are on the subject of "time," as well as Joe and the *Geraldo* show (taped on February 27, 1989), Priscilla also states in *Elvis and Me* that she was on her way to a noon meeting with her sister Michelle. Remember that noon is 2:00 P.M. Memphis time; this was before noon. Upon Priscilla's arriving, Michelle tells her that Joe Esposito has been frantically trying to reach her. Priscilla calls Joe and Joe tells her, "Elvis is dead."

Yet according to Joe's story, Al Strada was the first called by Ginger Alden that Elvis was on the floor. This was reportedly around 2:00 P.M. Al rushes up, tries to revive Elvis, calls down to Joe. Joe has just arrived from the Howard Johnson Hotel. Joe goes upstairs, sees that Elvis is in a rigor-mortised condition but tries to give mouth-to-mouth anyway. Paramedics are called. Joe, I assume, continues to work on Elvis—says it took a long time for them to arrive. Paramedics arrive, work on Elvis. Others come into the room, are shooed away. Finally Elvis is put into an ambulance after Dr. Nick (George Nichopoulos) has arrived. Hospital. At 3:00 P.M., Elvis is pronounced dead to family and friends. Now, when did Joe have time to call Priscilla at the time Priscilla says he called her? After all, if he had actually been attempting to reach Priscilla pre-noon, that means he was trying to tell her Elvis was dead *before* the body was discovered! When I asked Joe about this on *Geraldo,* his answer was that he had not read Priscilla's book.

Lisa meant more to Elvis than life itself. I doubt that Elvis would want to "live" under such terror, and if such threats were a result of his involvement with gathering drug information for the DEA, then it is reasonable to assume Elvis would have asked for

foolproof protection from that same government and, knowing
how far "up" his connections went, I cannot believe he would have
been refused. Still, a paradox looms: Is it possible that a man
rumored to be addicted to pharmaceutical drugs worked diligently
gathering drug information on behalf of our government? (If you
cannot relate the two, may I remind you of *how* and *why* the Betty
Ford Center came into being?)

Will history prove Elvis Aron Presley an American hero
beyond being an American entertainer?

Possibly.

WILLIAM "BILL" MORRIS, SHELBY COUNTY SHERIFF, PRESENTED ELVIS
with his identification card as a law officer. In published interviews Morris stated that Elvis was very vocal about situations that
were anti-law enforcement. For instance, there was a *Laugh-In*
program on cable TV featuring a Keystone Cop image hitting
someone over the head with a club. Elvis thought this mocked law
enforcement and was instrumental in getting it changed from the
series. Elvis also played a major role in getting drug abuse centers
established in Denver and Los Angeles. Morris says that a program had been discussed where all of the law enforcement agencies throughout the United States would develop a program for
older scouts called the Elvis Presley Law Enforcement Specialty
Post, funded by the Elvis Presley Foundation – one purpose being
to help young people establish positive attitudes toward law enforcement. It is clear that law enforcement and fighting drug
abuse held top priorities with Elvis. If he could help youth respect
the law, his job fighting the war on drugs would be easier.

Sheriff Morris accompanied Elvis to FBI headquarters in late
1970 and was instrumental in Elvis' being named by the Jaycees
one of the Ten Most Outstanding Young Men in the United States
in January 1971. Elvis did not go in for awards in general, but it was
brought out in an interview with Sheriff Morris that Elvis believed
that the Junior Chamber of Commerce was one of the most involved groups of men in the free world. Normally when a selection is made, the honor goes to a scholar, scientist, politician. Elvis
was the first entertainer to receive such a high award – an award
he coveted and accepted with pride, saying it was one of the great
achievements of his life. "I learned very early in life that without
a song the day would never end," Elvis said when accepting the
award, reading a portion of the lyrics to *Without a Song*. "Without
a song a man ain't got a friend; without a song . . ."

Law and order and a fight against drugs was a declaration

Elvis made time and again to friends and family, his stepbrothers, saying that one of his dreams was to expose drug dealers, clean up Memphis. It was an offer he made to two United States Presidents, both of whom were ready to establish government posts, one who made him agent-at-large with the DEA: President Richard Nixon, President Jimmy Carter.

George Bush? George Bush and Elvis Presley?

Keep in mind that President Bush's number-one priority is a War on Drugs. But a connection with Elvis? Consider the following, which appeared in a Memphis newspaper in January 1971:

> A hectic day of Jaycee activities yesterday was highlighted by a luncheon speech from United Nations Ambassador-Appointee George Bush and last by the organizations awards ceremony honoring the Ten Outstanding Young Men in America. He praised his audience as "men who have thought new thoughts and rejected old dogmas. But to guarantee this country never accepts the violent answer our people must be willing to work within the system." He complimented the Jaycees on their Top Ten selection and told Memphis to "watch out if Elvis Presley ever decided to enter politics. They would have to regroup their forces," he said.
>
> Mr. Bush earlier praised Presley's comments at a morning forum which was closed to the press where Mr. Presley commented that "God is a living presence in all of us."

Thus, Elvis Presley had connections with at least three United States powers, each of whom either was or became U.S. President.

Beyond Elvis' native intelligence, he was a man with vision. He himself stated as much in his acceptance speech to the Jaycees:

> I've always been a dreamer. I read comic books and I was the hero of the comic book. I saw movies and I was the hero in the movie. So every dream that I ever dreamed has come true a hundred times. These gentlemen over here, you see, these type of people who care, are dedicated, you realize, is it not possible that they might be building the Kingdom of Heaven? It's not too far-fetched from reality.
>
> I'd like to say that I learned very early in life that without a song the day would never end, without a song a man ain't got a friend, without a song the road would never bend, without a song. So I'll keep singing a song.

. . . And the man is the father of the child. If Elvis is alive, I believe he still holds this dream. Perhaps he is disguised as a comic book hero and is out talking to youth about the dangers of drugs and is working with the government doing what he can in guiding the youth to respect the law? Too far-fetched?

FILE CASE No. 3

Elvis' Intelligence and Character

> Intelligence appears to be the thing that enables a man to get along without education. Education enables a man to get along without the use of his intelligence.
> —ALBERT EDWARD WIGGAM

Questions: Was Elvis intelligent enough to pull off something so bizarre as a "death" hoax? And would his character traits have allowed/induced him to do so?

Answers: I recall Larry King's making a comment on his show equating Elvis' intelligence with "only having a high school education" and my reply that I felt Elvis Presley was very intelligent. Further studies of Elvis prove he was amazingly intelligent. And I offer, in this chapter, an analysis of his character that sheds light on what he was capable of.

If we apply to Elvis the definitions of the word "intelligence" itself – "the ability to learn or to understand or to deal with new or trying situations," "the skilled use of reason," "the ability to apply knowledge to manipulate one's environment or to think abstractly as measured by objective criteria," "mental acuteness," "the basic eternal quality of divine Mind" – our answer to the first question asked must be "Yes." From Day One, Elvis dealt with new and trying situations and triumphed magnificently. His reasoning was outstanding: Be different to stand out. No one has manipulated the environment better than Elvis. His difference has become the most imitated uniqueness on this planet! His mental

45

acuteness in making career judgments and changes goes without elaboration. Divine Mind? Jesus was called King. Elvis was called "the King." No one can deny Elvis' very special presence.

If Webster is correct, then Elvis Presley was/is a genius!

However, on a more basic level, everyone who knew Elvis spoke of how truly an intelligent man Elvis was, how deep was his thinking, how intense were his private studies into religions, philosophies, history. Not only was he an avid reader but, according to singer T. G. Sheppard, Elvis had an amazing memory.

I am frequently asked whether this statement isn't in conflict with those who say that toward the end Elvis often forgot lyrics to familiar songs? I can only answer that toward the "end" Elvis' health had deteriorated. He suffered from glaucoma, which is a disease of the eyes marked by increased pressure within the eyeballs and damage to the optic disks. With glaucoma there is always the threat of gradual loss of vision. The hot lights of performing, the sweat in the eyes added to that danger. Elvis told people he might have to cease performing for that reason alone. Other health problems caused him great pain, such as colon and stomach ailments. He was on various prescribed drugs, all of which would have dulled his memory.

Most who knew him agree that Elvis did not take street drugs but that he did overindulge in prescription drugs. Still, Elvis *knew* his drugs, knew which one mixed with another. He was also known to have taken prescribed sedatives for sleep. There were times when Elvis performed while sick, one time with the flu, other times with a temperature. Most of his tours were grueling to the point of exhaustion. I personally doubt he could have stood on his feet if he were as drugged-out as rumored.

"Last week I was sick for a day. I had 102 temperature. I had the flu and missed two shows," Elvis said during one performance. "They said I hadn't been sick but that I was strung out on drugs. I heard from three different sources that I am dependent on heroin. Never in my life have I been strung out. They don't give a black belt if you're on drugs. Reports like these hurt my daughter, my family, everyone . . ."

Elvis then displayed a certificate to the audience. "This is from the International Narcotics Enforcement Association. This certificate gives me special honors and a lifelong membership. I've been wearing a federal narcotics badge for six years. They don't give you that if you're strung out."

Further proof of Elvis' intelligence comes from Marty Allen via a guest spot on KGO Talk Radio in San Francisco: "Elvis was one of the nicest men I knew. He was the kind of man who could find humor in anything. I asked him once how he could do that in sad situations and he told me that if he didn't, then he would not be able to cope," Marty said, adding: "Elvis also had this ability to read lips, and he would be listening to you and talking and also reading the conversation across the room! He often shocked people by knowing what was going on all around him. He used to play down his intelligence, preferring that people did not know how smart he really was."

Although Elvis' face was/is one of the most recognizable in the world, he could indeed "go underground." For one, there are hundreds of Elvis lookalikes, and if Elvis desired, he could actually walk around looking like the "image" of an Elvis Presley and get away with it—i.e., long dark hair with the famous sideburns, sunglasses, dressed in a typical Elvis costume. However, the most reliable reports say that Elvis allowed his gray hair to grow, grew a beard and a mustache that were also gray, and cut the sideburns. Many times he wore sunglasses and hats. His clothing was described as "understated and average." Nothing that would stand out. Plus, who would be looking for him since he was "dead"?

THE LATE ABBIE HOFFMAN PROBABLY HAD A TOUGHER GO OF IT THAN Elvis might have, during those six years when Abbie disappeared and went underground. Recall that in 1974 Hoffman's withdrawal from the world began when, facing 15 years to life for arranging the sale of three pounds of cocaine to undercover cops, he skipped bail and also the country. He left his family and friends behind and was lying low in such places as Mexico and Canada.

Remember, this was a man *known* to be alive, a famous face, who not only managed to elude legal authorities but who eventually settled in Fineview, New York, on the St. Lawrence River under the name of Barry Freed. And, while in hiding, he actually became the respected leader of the Save the River movement, which successfully opposed a dredging project!

Some say that Hoffman's most solid political work was done during his six years of hiding. He could have remained in hiding longer, had he not chosen to surface in 1980 to face cocaine charges. He served only eleven months after a plea bargain.

If Hoffman—an outlaw if you may, a man known to be alive, a man with limited financial resources—could accomplish so daring a feat, how more so could Elvis Presley, a Federal Agent with the DEA, a man who was part of the law, a man with unlimited financial resources, a man *not* being hunted because he no longer existed, have accomplished the same?

As for those who say Elvis never went out in disguise, there are an equal number of close friends who say Elvis did don disguises. And since the act of disguising in itself means to change appearance and identity – secrecy – then it is highly possible Elvis disguised himself more often than anyone was aware. After all, if Elvis could sneak away from family and friends and go to Washington, D.C., to make an appointment with the President of the United States, certainly lesser "outings" were possible! (Perhaps those times he was reclused in his room with the "Do Not Disturb" dictum were more than they appeared?)

Would this type of "game playing" fall in line with the psyche of Elvis Presley? Was he that clever? It seems so. In fact, if you recall in the book *Elvis: What Happened?*, by Sonny and Red West and Dave Hebler (all close to Elvis), incidences involving Elvis' faking his death are reported. Elvis pulled one off so efficiently that he was actually taken to the hospital! That book also made the statement, in regard to drugs, that there were suspicions about whether Elvis was ever as "whacked out" as he seemed.

Obviously Elvis Presley was a magnificent actor, no matter what.

One of Elvis' aides, close friend and singer Charlie Hodge is quoted in a fan periodical about the time Elvis tried unsuccessfully to convince a throng of people outside a Memphis club that he was really Elvis Presley! No one believed that Elvis would even be out in public – which goes to show you. Another incident involves the Colonel hunting all over for a "disappearing" Elvis. They were at the airport waiting to board a plane to Denver. Finally found, Elvis was down on his hands and knees pitching pennies with a taxi driver.

Several people write about the time Elvis was convinced to go out on a Las Vegas street midday with the bet that no one would make a big deal of it. Elvis did. He stood for some time leaning against a building. People walked by. Some looked. Others did not. Those who did a double-take paused but then continued on, probably thinking, "Nah. Can't be."

WE HAVE ALL READ OF INCIDENCES WHEN ELVIS WENT OUT ON DRUG busts in disguises.

My point is that Elvis' cleverness is underlined. If he managed to go unnoticed pre-1977, it is reasonable to assume that *if* he is still alive it would be easier. The letters I've received reporting sightings may be only the tip of the iceberg. In most cases it may be another, "Nah. Can't be."

Another disguise occurred in Denver. Elvis was looking to

purchase a home in Vail and wore a ski mask and jumpsuit while making an offer. (The bid was rejected by the owner, who was unaware of Elvis' identity.)

People ask me whether Elvis went out in disguises often. I can only reply that how often is up for grabs. However, he was known to don disguises now and then. Several times, he wore police uniforms in public – once to a restaurant. He was recognized, but brushed it aside when asked if he was Elvis, saying, "Nah. Everyone gets me confused with him." Another incident is reported where he wore a blond wig.

The most famous incident was told in the book *Elvis: What Happened?* It involved an evening when Elvis went out on a drug bust with a Memphis narcotics officer. In order to disguise himself, Elvis put on a jumpsuit. Over the jumpsuit he put on a snowsuit. Over his face he put on a ski mask. On top of that he put on a hat. They say he stood out like a neon sign!

One of the fan newsletters states that several police uniforms were delivered to Graceland on August 15, 1977.

Kelly Burgess, a former editor with the *Detroit News*, wrote me of interviewing a woman whose husband sang. She had been in a club some years ago where her husband was rehearsing. The club was closed. In a dark corner at a table sat a monk with a grayish beard. When she approached the monk to say the club was closed, he silently rose to walk away, his face carefully hidden beneath a hood. However, she managed a glimpse and felt a shock: It struck her it might have been Elvis Presley. I also spoke to this woman, and although she wishes to remain unidentified, the club was a Memphis club owned by a friend of Elvis Presley.

What is significant about this sighting is that Larry Geller in his book *If I Can Dream* says Elvis told him he wanted to become a monk.

Elvis told Larry and others that the life he was leading had to end, that it had gone on far too long. He talked often, especially to Larry, of seeking that higher purpose: of doing more with his life. He never felt his destiny had been met. When he expressed a desire to go into the ministry, he was told that that was silly. After all, he was Elvis Presley, "the King."

One fact comes across clearly: If Elvis Presley wanted to do something, no one talked him out of it; eventually he did it; and when he did, he took it to the max. He was said to be a master planner, a genius at detail. He may have been "the King," but his desires were loftier: He appears to have wanted to represent the one true king, Jesus Christ. He had stated his desire to go away to hibernate and study—to find solace and harmony in the peace of a monastery. So perhaps. . .?

The ultimate disguise, however, was when Elvis disguised himself as Elvis Presley.

The story goes that before 1977 there was an audition for an "Elvis lookalike, soundalike" at a Memphis theater. Elvis got a kick out of it and decided to put on his best "Elvis outfit"; he strolled nonchalantly into the theater and openly mingled with his clones, doing his best "Hey, baby. . ." Afterwards, Elvis came back to Graceland laughing. He had tried out and lost! He found it hilarious.

SO MUCH FOR ELVIS' INTELLIGENCE. AS IMPORTANT A PART OF THE profile as it may be, so too is character. Rather than extracting material from Priscilla Presley's remembrances, or from friends' —such as Joe Esposito or even Muhammad Ali—I've chosen the following "analyses" of Elvis' character and personality.

The first is by Dr. Raymond A. Moody, author in the mid-1970s of the acclaimed seminal work *Life After Life* and, later, the book *Elvis After Life* (1987). In his Introduction to the Elvis work, he explained, "Over the past nine years, I have gathered numerous cases of unusual psychic experiences involving Elvis Presley," meaning, of course, experiences *of* Elvis by others. "As a doctor of medicine and a psychiatrist, I am intrigued by these accounts. . .They interest me for what they reveal about the human mind and spirit. They tell us a lot, I believe, about the psychological aspects of what it means to be a devoted fan, about the nature of our relationship with celebrities, and about some of the less well understood manifestations of the human process of mourning."

In his "investigation" of "Elvis experiences" he also learned much about the singer. He found

> no fewer than fifteen characteristics were attributed to Elvis Presley by the persons whom I interviewed. These characteristics were (1) kindness, warmth and sincerity ("He was a sweet person, very nice."); (2) generosity ("He was always giving cars to people he met on the street."); (3) success ("He was a poor boy who made good."); (4) material wealth (He "was rich," "had a palace," "had a fleet of cars," "could get all the money he wanted," etc.); (5) being a good son ("He was real close to his mother." "I hear he hired his father to be his business manager."); (6) humor ("He was funny on stage." "He could laugh at himself."); (7) sadness ("He got into trouble with drugs." "He couldn't handle it when his mother died."); (8) macho ("I read where

he broke up a fight at a filling station once." "He was good at karate."); (9) fun-loving ("He knew how to have a good time."); (10) a great entertainer ("He had a wonderful voice." "He put on a good show."); (11) influence on others ("None of this, the Beatles, rock music, generally, could have gone anywhere without him."); (12) loyalty to his friends ("I hear he took good care of his friends."); (13) sex appeal ("When I think of Elvis, I think of sex."); (14) law and order ("He was all in favor of America, I know that." "I believe President Nixon made him an officer for drug enforcement."); and (15) strong religious faith ("He was a convinced Christian." "I like his gospel songs best. You can tell he sang them from the heart.").

"As a people and as a culture," asserts Moody, "we can't let go of Elvis. He lives on and on in the thoughts and memories and dreams of his fans. He lives on, also, as the ostensible central figure of fascinating and occasionally baffling psychic experiences – reported paranormal events and mental states – which tantalize us, and which reveal, again and again, the depth of the affection which his fans hold for him."*

The second character analysis falls somewhat in line with the entertainer's astrological and numerological leanings, and would please him, I believe. It is a graphoanalysis by California-based Master Certified Graphoanalyst/Certified Document Examiner Paul R. Weast. (We will meet Mr. Weast again in File Case No. 16, which contains perhaps the book's biggest surprises!)

In an April 16, 1990, graphoanalysis of Elvis' handwriting, Weast admitted that his "interest in Elvis Presley came [only] after I was asked to examine some handwriting to determine if it could have actually been written by Elvis." He examined "several pages of handwriting, from different points in time." The examination revealed that

Elvis Presley was, or still is, an extremely emotionally responsive person. Nearly every experience he has is an emotional experience: This man is ruled by his heart, not by his head. He will be very sympathetic, very caring. His heartfelt feelings will have him reaching out to others and trying to help in any way that he is able. Elvis' renowned generosity attests to his strong emotional feelings for others. He has a strong need to be with people. They stimulate him to respond and "feel." In turn, he needs people to respond to him. Emotional interplay is very important to him. All of his emotions are on the surface and all of his feelings are keen. He laughs more readily and cries more easily [than others]. Anger will be shown

*From *Elvis After Life,* © 1987 Raymond A. Moody, Jr., Peachtree Publishers, Ltd.

more vividly, despair more completely, and joy more delightedly.
Responsiveness is demonstrated in every aspect of his functioning.
The people close to him are always on his mind. He likes to be
asked about the well-being of his loved ones—people as well as pets.
In all of his relationships, personal and business, he wants to be
shown that people are compassionate and that they care.

Elvis is intelligent but not a sharp or keen-minded person. This
graphologist has no idea of the extent of Elvis' formal education. I
suspect it was rather limited. His mental processes show that he
probably was not thought of as a great student. His is the slower,
more methodical method of processing information. He needs time
to think over the available facts, mulling them over and slowly
reaching conclusions. In school . . . he wasn't the first to raise his
hand when the teacher asked a question.

This does not mean that he was not smart. He just was not quick.
When he had thoroughly digested the facts, he was in a better position to answer correctly than were the quick thinkers who often
were in error because they answered too soon.

Elvis does like to learn, and will seek information, investigating
into areas of interest. The information he uncovers will be carefully
analyzed to enable him to understand thoroughly. He has a decided
interest in the mysteries of life. There is abstract imagination, which
indicates an interest in philosophical thought. He searches into the
mental realms, into theory. Quite possibly, he has an interest in
religion. He is an ethical man and will devote a great deal of time
and effort to the ethical approach to daily living.

A decided interest in the mental realms is very evident. He will
explore into the abstract. His imagination is at work in the philosophical, the theoretical, the paranormal. He probably has studied
in areas considered metaphysical and has taken time to learn all he
could of these mysterious concepts.

Elvis' analytical mind is quite strong. Too much analysis can make
a person critical, because he tends to analyze everything and thus
is able to find the flaws. It is quite possible that Elvis is critical.
On the other hand, he could take personal criticism of himself,
[because] it just did not bother him.

This is a very thorough man. He looks after the details and keeps
things as well organized as possible. Impulsiveness may detract
from the more positive traits, and Elvis could be very impulsive.
The stories of his generous gift-giving certainly show an impulsive
nature. But although impulsive, he is firm. Decisions are readily
made, and he sticks with his decisions. In fact, he may often
demonstrate a stubborn nature. His beliefs are strong and his loyalty
to his beliefs are firm. Whatever he believes to be right he will cling
to and show determined loyalty to it.

While Elvis is reasonably ambitious, his goals are really very practical. Perhaps at the time he wrote the handwriting examined he felt that he had already reached his goals and did not need to aim higher.

His letter written to President Nixon in 1970 shows this practical aim in life. He expresses his desire to be helpful to his country. He was very sincere, and there is nothing to indicate that this could have been an ego trip or only wishful thinking. He sincerely believed he could be useful in fighting the drug problem, and his request that President Nixon appoint him as an undercover Federal Agent was serious. He meant it, and he had the will to go into this work with a firm sense of purpose supported by enduring determination.

The Nixon letter shows some evidence of his physical deterioration that continued to progress until his reported death in 1977. An earlier letter, written in 1963, shows a very different penmanship. The personality traits were about the same. The decisiveness was as strong, and so were the purpose and determination. The obstinance didn't show as much in 1963, [but] his practical goals, concern for others, and impulsiveness were very much in evidence.

This is a courageous man. The fears we might expect to show are just not there. There is no compelling desire for attention that is so often seen in the handwriting of celebrities. Probably by this time he had had all the attention he could stomach. There is no sensitiveness to criticism – a trait often found in entertainers. There is a little jealousy, but it is not very strong. There is repression: He does not reveal everything about himself and does not want everyone to see how he really feels. He is self-conscious. With all of the showmanship demonstrated on the stage, he really is rather shy. Even though he was not physically well [in some of the handwriting examined], and was said to be under a lot of medication, he was nevertheless rather well adjusted.

Looking for resistance traits that would help him to cope with his problems, I find he is remarkably free of such traits. He is a bit aggressive. *This* is a resistance, but comes under the sphere of "a good offense is more effective than a good defense." But even the aggressiveness is not a strong trait. He probably did not argue, was not greatly irritable, and shows no inclination for a temper. Really a rather sweet kind of guy.

He doesn't use any of the escape traits except one. And this one is revealing: He is secretive. He certainly has demonstrated that he can keep a secret. There is no evidence of intentional deceit, evasiveness, or self-deceit. He is an open and truthful person; his integrity is intact; he can be trusted; and he is loyal. If he has indeed been engaged in undercover work in a super-secretive manner for several years, his personality attests to his ability to be successful in this regard.

Finally, Weast confesses: "The critics will not believe me. The believers will believe me." And he adds that his "analysis may not be 100 percent accurate. Graphoanalysts do not claim to be any more than 85 percent accurate"; and that, although graphoanalysis has been used extensively in Europe for many years, "Americans are very quick to debunk that which they do not understand."

The Spelling on the Gravestone: Aaron vs. Aron

A self-made man may prefer a self-made name.
—JUDGE LEARNED HAND

Question: Is it really so important that Elvis' middle name is misspelled on his gravestone?
Answer: The conflict continues. There are some who think that many of the fans, the media, and particularly this writer are making too much of the fact that Elvis' middle name is misspelled on the gravestone at Graceland. Others do not think it is incorrect. I disagree on both counts and thus will touch upon it again in this update. Graceland, with *Aron,* underscores the truth that Elvis' middle name was spelled with the single *a* and that his name was of paramount importance to his parents and to him.

A ccording to biographers, there are two birth certificates. The first was erroneously filled out by the attending physician, who used the traditional biblical double-*a* spelling. However, it was Gladys and Vernon, Elvis' parents, who dictated that Elvis' middle name be spelled with a single *a* because of a dead twin, Jesse Garon. Thus Elvis would always know by looking at "Aron" that he was a part of "Garon."

A second birth certificate, with "Aron," appeared, and it is the second version that is sold as a souvenir. This is the spelling Elvis himself chose when signing his name: Elvis Aron Presley. Who should know better than Elvis which spelling is correct?

Patsy Guy Hammontree, Assistant Professor of English at the University of Tennessee, in her extensive researched work *Elvis Presley: A Bio-Bibliography,* states Elvis' middle name as being spelled "Aron," with his twin brother's name spelled Jesse Garon. More about Jesse momentarily.

The majority of the fan publications use the "Aron" spelling and a few in particular, *Elvis Now* and *The Elvis Special,* have pictured a full shot of Elvis' signature: Elvis Aron Presley. Sue Wiegert, president of The Blue Hawaiians for Elvis fan club, relates in her book *Elvis: For the Good Times* that once, when she asked the singer to autograph a book, he told her personally that he spelled his middle name with the single *a,* admitting also that there were those who mistakenly used the biblical spelling.

I strongly underline this fact: Elvis *Aron.*

Even the Tennessee Historical Commission states that Elvis' middle name was Aron. The Elvis Presley International Memorial Foundation purchased the marker, which was authorized by the Tennessee Historical Commission, the mounting done by the Shelby County Historical Society. This marker was presented five years after the "death" of Elvis, on August 16, 1982, negating the rumor that Elvis may have legally changed his middle name somewhere down the line. Surely that type of documentation would have surfaced. As it is, the historical marker outside the walls of Graceland reads: Elvis Aron Presley.

Also, had Elvis legally changed his middle name to Aaron, why would Elvis' family have sent out a note of appreciation to the fans and media after Elvis' "death," stating, "The family of Elvis Aron Presley. . . "? Secondly, why would Elvis want to change the spelling of the name his parents chose, particularly his mother, with whom he was so close? Elvis was attracted to the metaphysical, to numbers, to the meaning of letters and names. He felt deeply attached to his own destiny. It would seem out of line with his way of thinking that he would interfere with original dictates.

As outlined in *Is Elvis Alive?,* legal documents such as his high school diploma, Army induction and discharge papers, and marriage license all use the single *a* spelling. For the most part such legal documents are based upon the birth certificate. Some of these certificates are found in various publications, such as *The*

Elvis Catalog, by Lee Cotten, a noted Elvis scholar. The multitude of official Collector's Magazine Editions list him as Elvis Aron Presley and his twin brother as Jesse Garon, featuring full-page tributes with:

In Memoriam

Elvis Aron Presley

The All Children's Hospital in St. Petersburg, Florida, features "The Elvis Aron Presley Examining Room," which is a special project of the Elvis Forever TCB* FC Club Presidents. And as Maria Columbus, president of The Elvis Special, has said, "If you want to know anything about Elvis, check with the fans." She further stated, "He spelled his middle name Aron, not Aaron."

Upon studying RCA's albums and sets, we see: "Elvis Aron Presley 8 LP Box Set" with his signature, "Elvis Aron Presley." It's known as the "Elvis Aron Presley–Forever" album.

Whenever RCA used Elvis' middle name, they used "Aron." One number-one Elvis fan has named his two sons Elvis and Aron. Fans, family, friends, biographers, documents, RCA, and Elvis himself, all attest to the truth that Elvis' middle name was "Aron." Then *why* is Elvis' middle name misspelled on all of the gravestones at Graceland – not only Elvis' gravestone but his mother's as well? Was this an accidental mistake? Something too expensive to change? (Graceland took in $15 million last year alone, and the estate has reportedly grown from between $1 million and $4 million to over $100 million.)

Again, why would the most famous entertainer in history have as his final tribute a stone with a misspelled name? And why would Vernon Presley purposely do this? While I was on a Memphis radio station discussing *Is Elvis Alive?* a gentleman called in, identified himself by name, and said he was the one who engraved the stones – with instructions from Elvis' father to spell it with two *a*'s.

WHEN *THE COMMERCIAL APPEAL,* ELVIS' HOMETOWN MEMPHIS NEWSpaper, wrote about Elvis and his brother, it stated on Wednesday morning, August 17, 1977, in a historical recollection of the city's most famous son: "'We matched their names,' his mother recalled

*Taking Care of Business.

later, 'Jesse Garon and Elvis Aron. Jesse died at birth. Maybe that is why Elvis is so dear to us.'"

Friends in their biographies, including friends from high school, write: "Elvis Aron Presley."

The *Elvis Presley Memorial Edition* magazine (Ideal Publishing Company, 1977) states: "Gladys Smith Presley bore twins in Tupelo, Mississippi, on January 8, 1935. One boy, Jesse Garon, would die in infancy. The other child, Elvis Aron, would grow up loved not only for himself but for the brother with whom he entered this world."

In *Elvis: The King Lives On* magazine (Tempo Publishing, December 1987), we read: "'We matched their names to rhyme,' said Gladys Presley. 'We named them Jesse Garon and Elvis Aron.' Whether the Aron was purposeful misspelling of Aaron or just an uneducated mistake on the birth certificate was never made clear. Jesse Garon was buried the following day in an unmarked grave on a hill overlooking the town. Elvis Aron never had any other brothers and sisters."

In *The Illustrated Elvis*, by W. A. Harbinson, can be found: "About a year after the birth of Elvis Aron Presley and the almost simultaneous death of his brother Jesse Garon . . ."

Fans have named their sons with the misspelled middle name. One such fan is Paul MacLeod, a Mississippian, an Elvis collector with over 15,000 articles on the entertainer.

At least one Graceland portrait names him "Elvis Aron Presley."

On Marriage Certificate No. A 175632, State of Nevada, we see: "This is to certify that the undersigned Justice David Zenoff did on the 1st day of May 1967 join in lawful wedlock Elvis Aron Presley of Memphis, Tennessee, and Priscilla Ann Beaulieu . . ."

On his Memphis City Schools diploma, Humes High School, is inscribed: "This is to certify that Elvis Aron Presley . . ."

Elvis' Social Security card, on display at Graceland, has his name as "Elvis Aron Presley."

A *Star-Ledger* (Newark, New Jersey) headline, January 7, 1984, reads: "In Memory ELVIS ARON PRESLEY."

Following his "death," the Medical Examiner's Report of Investigation of it read: "Elvis Aron Presley."

On his Army induction and discharge papers we find: "Elvis Aron Presley." (Elvis Presley entered the Army on March 24, 1958, and was honorably discharged on March 5, 1960.)

Elvis' Bible, on display at Graceland, is inscribed: "Elvis Aron Presley."

BOOK 248   **405254**

Marriage Certificate

State of Nevada ss.   No. A 175632
County of Clark.

This is to Certify that the undersigned __JUSTICE DAVID ZENOFF__
did on the ___1st___ day of ___May___ A.D. 196_7_ join in lawful
Wedlock ___ELVIS ARON PRESLEY___
of ___MEMPHIS___   **State of** ___TENNESSEE___
and ___PRISCILLA ANN BEAULIEU___
of ___SHELBY___   **State of** ___TENNESSEE___
with their mutual consent, in the presence of _____
and _____ who were witnesses.
Recorded at the Request of David Zenoff
        Date   MAY 5 1967
In Book of Marriages, Clark County, Nevada,
Records, Paul E. Horn, Recorder.   JUSTICE, SUPREME COURT OF NEVADA
Fee $1.00 Indexed   , Deputy.   (Sign this in official capacity.)

Elvis' Army duffel bag, on display at Graceland, reads: "Elvis
Aron Presley."

Every memorial magazine I've perused, all legal documents
and biographies, and Elvis' own handwritten signature read: "Elvis
Aron Presley."

Yet, on the graves at Graceland we see: Elvis *Aaron. Why?* But
so what? What's in a name?

Larry Geller's *If I Can Dream* says that Elvis was indeed intrigued by names and name combinations, Elvis being quick to
note that the anagram for "Elvis" was "lives." Elvis was also pleased
to discover that the word *El* means God to the Jews and *vis* is a
power of God.

ONE NATIONAL POLL HAS STATED THAT "ELVIS" IS THE SECOND-MOST-
recognizable name in the world. ("Coke" took the number-one
position.)

Historians write that the name "Elvis" is probably derived
from ancient Norse mythology, "alvis" meaning "all wise." In
Hebrew, Aron may mean "to teach" or "to sing" whereas its Arabic
meaning is "messenger." "Priestly" gave birth to "Presley." Studying
the meaning possibilities of his name, Elvis often told people he
felt destined and that God had chosen him for a specific purpose,
that purpose perhaps being a "messenger of God."

When I spoke with Elvis' Uncle Vester and asked him how Elvis spelled his middle name, he said, "A-R-O-N." Yet there are others who have said Elvis felt he held a dual destiny, that of both "Aaron" (the older brother of Moses and his spokesperson) and of "Aron" (the singer who shone). He felt that since there were two birth certificates, he was meant to live as two persons: first, as Aron-the-singer; second, as Aaron-the-spokesperson-for-God. It is said he instructed his father to be sure and put "Aaron" on the grave.

Now think about this: Why would Elvis instruct his father, who was very ill, weak, and years older, as to what to put on his tombstone unless Elvis knew he would "die" very soon. Just some sort of psychic whim? And if he truly wanted to depart as "Aaron," why didn't he use that spelling while "alive"? Or is it possible that the singer Aron departed on August 16, 1977, while the messenger-of-God Aaron was given "new life"?

Far-fetched? Not when you study Elvis' spirituality and his intense interest in the science of numbers, numerology. In fact, File Case No. 6, involving Elvis and Hugh Schonfield's 1966 novel *The Passover Plot,* is perhaps the most important part of this book, for it explains on a higher level *why* Elvis may have hoaxed his death, *why* he had to be born "anew" in order to fulfill the role God had chosen for him.

Keep in mind that if Elvis added another letter to his name it would change the power of his numbers, particularly if Aron became Aaron, which would change Elvis' soul number, three, giving to him a personal self. Again, I'll go into this more in the next File Case. My point now is this: Elvis was an identical twin. He said he always felt a part of "himself" missing, that his brother had died so that he could live. "I feel because identical twins come from one egg they share a twin soul," Elvis said. A call I have received elaborated: "If one twin dies at birth, his soul goes back into the living twin—therefore twice the power, twice the fame; twice the sorrow, twice the pain..."

Therefore, if Elvis added another letter to his name to change his soul number, would he not have to add another letter to his dead twin's name? How could the same soul be split? Although this may seem irrelevant to those who know very little about Elvis' spirituality, together with his cosmic studies, those who do know Elvis and who have perused his studies know this would be in line with his thinking.

Remember, all historical documentation states that Elvis' twin was named Jesse Garon. It's spelled that way everyplace *except on the stone(s) at Graceland!* The Memorial Plaque at Graceland reads:

In Memory Of

JESSIE GARON PRESLEY

Gladys' Graceland stone reads:

Gladys Love Smith Presley

Mother of

Elvis Aaron Presley

and

Jessie Garon Presley

Elvis' twin soul was in alignment. He added another letter to his name and his brother's name, on the graves. Would his sick, ailing, elderly father have been so cosmic-conscious to have thought this out on his own? I cannot fathom it.

No. Elvis was the one "taking care of business." And that business was related to the cosmic.

And here is more about the grave. An August 12, 1978, news article in the *Windsor* (Ontario) *Star* stated: "Graceland was zoned R1. In R1 zones burials were not among approved uses. Variance was permitted." It continued: "Within a week of Elvis' funeral workmen disinterred the body of Elvis' mother and moved her from her hillside grave into the crypt to lie beside Elvis. Permit to move the body was applied for retroactively." And it tells that "a few days later attorneys for the Presley estate applied for a zoning variance to allow the bodies of both Elvis and his mother to be moved, this time to a gravesite at Graceland."

If the above is correct, then it makes one question why the move was later blamed on three men attempting to break into the crypt. They were charged with attempted "bodynapping," but Vernon dropped the charges; one local official stated: "If the truth ever came out it would open a can of worms. . ." And in effect it would have shocked the entire world. Apparently the move to Graceland was planned as early as August, not October.

INTRIGUE HAS ALWAYS SURROUNDED THE DEATH OF JESSE GARON, buried in an unmarked grave in Priceville Cemetery in Tupelo, Mississippi. Elvis often mentioned that Jesse's death was a "mystery" and felt a sense of profound loss—which leads one to wonder why, after making his fortune, Elvis never had a memorial placed at Priceville Cemetery? If it were for security reasons—bodynappers—then that reasoning should carry over to his mother's grave, the original at Forest Hill Cemetery in Memphis, where an elaborate memorial was erected in her honor. Other avenues of thought suggest that no one is buried at Graceland, that Elvis' grandmother, father, and mother are in the mausoleum, where it is reported a sealed-off room exists, its door several inches above ground so that one can peek beneath. Some who have peeked wrote to question why a single rose is seen in there on Mother's Day and on August 14 (the day Gladys Presley died). But again, this does not necessarily mean that Elvis is alive, only that no one is buried at Graceland—again, for security reasons: bodynappers.

"Elvis loved his mother very much and always said he would be buried beside her," many fans have noted. So why is he buried between his father and grandmother? they ask. There is no reason for it. After all, he and his mother were there first. Another clue?

"I've never really let my mother go," Elvis said. "She's in my heart. She always will be."

With deliberation and thought, Elvis had the Star of David and the Christian cross added to his mother's Forest Hill memorial plaque. One reason was that Elvis' spiritual studies embraced a universal god. He, too, wore the Star of David and a cross. Those who knew of his spiritual quests knew he believed he came from the House of David, which was Jesus' lineage, and other biographies state that he was pleased to learn he had Jewish blood on his mother's side – lineage again to Jesus, whom Elvis called the true "King." When asked about the Star of David together with a cross, Elvis kiddingly said he didn't want to take any chances about getting into heaven on a technicality. Knowing this, fans have again questioned why the Star of David is missing from Gladys' Graceland plaque as well as Elvis', and why the "TCB" appears (on Elvis').

"Taking care of business"? Is that what he's doing?

"My husband and I have been to Graceland and visited Elvis' grave," wrote a fan from Illinois. "We do not believe Elvis or family members are buried there, because I have been taught you bury a human body facing east and west according to the Bible. Elvis and his family members' headstones are facing *north* and *south*."

According to the Bible, one should have their head in the west, feet in the east, facing east; thus, when Resurrection Day comes, the Departed will face the face of God. I called several mortuaries and they said it is traditional to bury facing east, especially in the South. "I don't know of any church cemetery not burying facing east; even Memorial Parks try to hold to this tradition," was their response.

Elvis and his family read the Bible religiously, studied it. They were fundamentalists. Why are the graves the opposite of Biblical declaratives? (Gladys' original grave in Forest Hill did face east.) Another clue?

Those knowing the Bible and those knowing Elvis and his family's respect for it say this is definitely another clue that *no one* is buried at Graceland – which brings me full circle to stating that that does not necessarily mean Elvis is alive, just that no one is there. (Which then means that Vernon must have been the genius behind all of this. Does it sound like Vernon?)

Or does it sound more like Elvis?

I received an interesting letter from a woman who said she and her friend attended the 10th Anniversary Tribute Week in Memphis, arriving a few days prior to August 16 for sightseeing. Forest Hill Cemetery was on their tour. It was early morning and they wandered about. A man walked toward them wearing a baseball cap and sunglasses, with gray hair, no sideburns, normal clothing, head down. They nodded, but then as the man passed, they suddenly stopped and stared at each other in shock. "It was Elvis Presley, I swear it," the woman wrote. "But we talked ourselves out of it, thinking: No, it's impossible. So we continued on, only to learn that we were heading in the direction of where Elvis' mother had been buried. It was the morning of August 14, 1987. August 14th is the day Elvis Presley's mother died.

"Could it be possible...?"

I HAVE NEVER SEEN ONE CROSSWORD PUZZLE USE "AARON." ON THE following page is a sample of a puzzle that appeared in *Globe* (Boca Raton, Florida) on June 14, 1988.

Note: 172 Across: Elvis _____ Presley. Four letters: ARON.

Again a letter regarding "Aron" versus "Aaron" reached me, this past January. Here are some interesting extracts from it:

> The two birth certificates, the first with the name Elvis Aaron Presley, is dated January 10, 1935,* but the second one was dated only two days after the first, being January 12, 1935. The name was changed to Elvis Aron Presley. This tells me that Elvis' parents had to have changed the name, and not Elvis later in life as so many are saying.... I think it was on the *Larry King Live* show that a caller called-in and pointed out that later on in life Elvis did drop one of the *a*'s and just use one. But as of January 12, 1935, it was Elvis Aron Presley—and not someplace down the road in life.... Again, on Major Bill Smith's cassette "Elvis Lives" he stresses the middle name as being "Aaron," because his beloved mother gave Elvis that name. I wonder if Mr. Smith has taken the time to read the dates on the two certificates.

Documents such as both birth certificates, the will listing Aron Music, Inc., Elvis' marriage certificate, and Elvis' signature appear in *Is Elvis Alive?*, as well as in other books. For verification of documents using "Aron" mentioned in *The Elvis Files*, another source is the book *Elvis: His Life from A to Z*, by Fred L. Worth and Steve D. Tamerius.

SINCE *IS ELVIS ALIVE?* WAS RELEASED, I'VE RECEIVED THOUSANDS OF letters, a portion of one of which follows:

> I am the mother of two sons—my youngest, Dan, became a very good friend of one of the Presley cousins. Now, the Presley cousins trust few people, usually because someone always wanted something. They were used. But my son became close to all the remaining Presleys, particularly Jimmy Gamble. He is Vester Presley's grandson. Patsy Gamble worked as Elvis' secretary and did many other things. She was always at the mansion; so was Vester, as he

---

*The actual birth date of the twins was January 8. This date is that of the filling out of the certificate.

GIGANTIC PUZZLE

BIG-X America's biggest crossword

ACROSS

1. Chide
5. Manta
9. Perch
12. Less
16. Overturn
20. Chem. suffix
21. Nuptial response
22. 1/1000 inch
23. Lubricate
24. Kilmer poem
26. Citrine
28. Humorous
30. Jockey's uniform
32. Kind of recall
35. Meal
36. Roman magistrate
37. Acrylic fiber
38. Titans' father
41. Hebrew prophet
43. Dotted with stars
46. Asian grappler
48. S.A. rodent
50. Hindu social group
51. Bet
52. Agile animal
53. Threefold
54. Pinto
55. Roman river
56. ___ fixe
59. Moose org. (abbr.)
60. British princess
63. Christmas
64. With fiddle or base
65. Moisten
66. A Carter
68. Free
69. Sun orbiter
71. Comment
74. Like a slalom
77. Call for help
79. Common sense (sl.)
82. Farrow member
86. Hustler's game
88. Kadiddlehopper
90. Field sport
92. Ennead
94. Got up
95. Swiss capital
96. Glower
97. Like an avian
98. Water (comb. form)
99. "R U R" character
100. Prefix for god
103. Garfield's pal
104. Tiny arachnid
107. One-___ sale
108. Safe
111. Obelisk
114. Navigation system
117. Schooled
120. Hebrew measure
121. Tonsorial concern
122. Helpmate
126. Surgeonfish
127. Model Macpherson
129. Bob of folk-rock
130. Run over
131. Survive
132. Former SAG

147. Yalie
148. From ___ to stern
151. Attempt
155. Toddler
157. Accountant
158. King or queen
161. Mercurial
165. Track has-been
166. Fear
167. 1985 Nelligan film
168. One of the Judds
169. Ferber novel
170. Olympic sled
172. Elvis ___ Presley
173. Idea
176. Cupid
178. Hide
180. Gal Friday
182. Actress Hunt
184. Home at Fenway
185. Soften
189. Chem. compound
191. Grating
194. Capone ID mark
196. Russian sea
198. Louvre locale
199. Bolt
200. Room at a spa
201. Earthling
202. Godliness
203. Heel
204. Sphagnum
207. Knotted
208. Secondhand
211. Early US satellite
212. Lentil, e.g.
213. Cricket-team no.
214. Newt
216. See 173-A
217. Demean
219. Isthmus
222. Third-stringers
225. Astral altar
227. Published
230. Make friendly
234. Prison (sl.)
236. Attention getter
238. Kilted one
240. Hula Bowl team
242. Kind of power
243. Manifest
244. Canes locale
245. Daughter of 3-D
246. Salt's "stop!"
247. Nimble
248. Actor Richard
251. Superdome sounds
252. Ancient Syria
255. Soon
256. Scrivener
259. Silly
262. Hit the ___ button
265. Teachable
268. Raring
269. Wiper
270. Roman-fleuve
273. Grudge
274. Busy airport
275. Arikara
276. Hindu weight

7. Come clean
8. Alpaca
10. Japanese singer
11. ___ Lanka
13. Arabian VIP
14. Candyman Wonka
15. Nevada city
17. Broke
18. Ravi's instrument
19. Sparkle
24. Proctor's concern
25. Shore

45. Ms. Bombeck
46. Tarry
47. Valuable vase
49. So-so mark
57. Virtuous
58. Greek letter
61. Nativity bird
62. Tropical fruit
67. Bovine sound
70. Sleuth Sam
71. Library and study
72. Borden cow

89. Susan I
91. Martini
93. ___ se
101. "Camill playwri
102. Steal
105. Reckle
106. City on Arkans
109. A Porte
110. Budget
112. Tobacc

once was a guard at the gate. My son played touch football on the grounds of Graceland, swam in the pool. . . . Gail, you talk about Elvis' middle name being misspelled on the gravestone. You ask why? I know why. He (Jimmy) told my son that Elvis was not buried there. My son looked at him and said, "Well, if not there, where?" He said, "Oh, well, only the family knows."

Regarding the coffin, according to the *Commercial Appeal,* Memphis, Sunday, August 16, 1987: "Hahn-Cook Funeral Home in Oklahoma City had a large silver-plated National Seamless casket flown into Memphis by private plane. The casket arrived about 11:15 P.M."

Elvis-in-the-coffin appeared on the front of the *National Enquirer,* taken by relative Bobby Mann. What surprised everyone was how "pugged"* Elvis' nose was. Response from family and friends about this oddity — since Elvis had a beautiful, classic nose — was that he fell on his face because he had a heart attack. Most people do fall forward, but the body's weight does not rest on the nose like a spinning top. If that were the case, people who sleep on their faces should have pugged noses.

In Bill Burk's book *Elvis Through My Eyes,* he writes about Alanna Nash, formerly of the *Louisville Courier-Journal* (and author of the bestseller *Golden Girl*), who viewed the body in the casket twice and commented on how wax-like it looked, ending with her belief that the whole thing was a hoax and Elvis would eventually show up. (Alanna was a guest on *Geraldo* and said that although that is what she originally thought, and said, she has changed her mind. Hmmm?)

The following quote came from *The Elvis Special* by LaCosta, sister of Tanya Tucker: "We were right up to his casket and stood there, and God, I couldn't believe it. He looked just like a piece of plastic laying there. He didn't look like him at all. . .he looked more like a dummy than a real person. You know a lot of people think it was a dummy. They don't think he's dead."

I received a note from Betty W., an Elvis fan, in 1989 that said: "I would love to tell you the name of the mortician who worked on the 'dummy' for over a year, but I promised not to. He said he would give his life before he revealed E.P.'s main home. Maybe it won't be long till this whole mystery is solved."

"If Elvis wanted to escape, why couldn't there have been a plane crash and a closed coffin so as not to arouse suspicion?" is

---

*Larry Geller supposedly said he knew every part of Elvis' body, and his nose never turned up.

a frequent question – with this answer: If *no* body had been put on public view, people might not have believed Elvis was dead. As it was, even a "body" was not convincing to many. Knowing how Elvis felt about Gladys' funeral turning into a circus, one wonders why Vernon allowed his son's to turn into a media fiasco – unless it was because Elvis' life was truly in danger and it was essential to convince *someone* that Elvis Presley was dead. Dead. Dead.

Thus the questions continue: *Who* or *what* was in the coffin. . . .Or, as Elvis said only weeks before, "I know I look fat now and I'll look terrible for my TV special coming up. But I'll tell you this: *"I'll look good in my casket."*

Elvis was pronounced "dead" approximately eight hours earlier, although the official announcement did not come until 3:30 P.M. Since the body was to be on display the next day, August 17, and the funeral on August 18, Vernon Presley had to do quite a bit – especially trying for a sick man, which indeed he was. Yet the speed with which all arrangements were made is mind-boggling, particularly when one considers that an autopsy and embalming were completed, that the body was back at Memphis Funeral Home around 8:00 P.M., that sixteen white limousines were ordered, that a white Cadillac hearse was readied, that a specially designed casket was ordered and flown in, that a casket blanket of 500 red roses was made, that security and police were ordered, that the tour was canceled, that personal calls were made by Vernon to fan club presidents asking that they not attend, that clothing was chosen, songs were chosen, ministers contacted, the procession planned, and the body put on private display by 11:30 the next morning. The planned public viewing by the press and crying fans would take place a few hours later.

The casket was moved from the living room to the foyer of the front entrance of Graceland. At 3:00 P.M., according to Memphis' *The Commercial Appeal*, "the floodgates at the end of the long driveway were opened to the thousands who flowed like a river past the lifeless body. . . ." At 6:30, the gates were closed.

Elvis fan Kim S. has written the following: "I personally know the man who made Elvis' coffin. He said it was really bizarre. It was a rush order, it was copper, but it had three lids! The first that would go over was double, then there was another single one piece that went over that, and finally a single copper to go over everything! He also said that there was no way Elvis' body weight and the weight of the coffin* was 900 lbs. Something else was in

*By all reports, the coffin weighed close to 900 lbs.

it. He did say it was big enough to put an air-conditioner in it. . . ." (Silver or copper? The majority of the reports say "copper.")

From Lynn G. in Ohio came these words: "I did some snooping on my own concerning the casket and corpse. I got into a really detailed discussion about copper caskets. The absolute best copper casket would be what he called 48-ounce. Then there is also a 32-ounce. I asked him how much a 48-ounce casket would weigh empty and he said around 375 pounds."

Add that weight to the 250 pounds Elvis was supposed to have weighed and you have a discrepancy of around 250 to 275 pounds, the weight of a small air conditioner. Wax dummy? Something cool to keep the wax from beading up?

Except that at times there *were* beads of "something" on the body in the coffin! When I was on the *Larry King* show in August 1988, Joe Esposito, Elvis' friend and road manager, was also a guest. I asked Joe about viewers reporting "beads of sweat" on the body in the coffin and he said that was true, that everyone was sweating because the air conditioner had broken down. Except that *dead* bodies do not sweat.

"It looks like a wax dummy," was the comment many made about the public viewing. Larry Geller commented that Elvis looked like a piece of clay, attributing it to makeup. He also talked about a full half-inch of white roots showing in Elvis' hair and/or sideburns, although a picture taken during the wee hours of August 16 shows no white hair.

Elvis and
The Passover Plot

Prayer is not asking. It is a longing of the soul.
— MOHANDAS GANDHI

Question: Since the book *The Passover Plot* is on display at Graceland — a book about Jesus' hoaxing of his death — is this a possible clue left by Elvis?
Answer: Many have made connections between Hugh Schonfield's bestseller and the possible hoaxing of Elvis' own death, his Exodus, as it were.

A lthough Elvis' interest in law and order was intense and sincere, his spirituality was really what he was all about. I cannot fathom that the most total stranger to the life of Elvis should not be aware of this. The majority of biographies have made pointed references to Elvis' spiritual quests, some more than others.

One of the most important mental journeys taken in compiling *The Elvis Files* was to read Elvis' favorite books — through his eyes. Not only has *The Passover Plot* (New York: Bernard Geis, 1966) been on display at the museum at Graceland, but so have others as well, such as Joseph F. Benner's *The Impersonal Life* (Marina Del Rey, CA: Devorss & Co., 1941); Paramahansa Yogananda's *Autobiography of a Yogi* (Self-Realization, 1974; the Holy Bible; and the works of Kahlil Gibran (*The Prophet*, etc.). My Elvis studies included two of his other favorites: Cyril Scott's *The Initiate* (York Beach, ME: Samuel Weiser, Inc., 1920) and Morton Cooper's *The King* (New York: Bernard Geis, 1967). By the time

I was finished, I not only had a deeper understanding of who *Elvis* was/is but I know who I am/was. To verbally portray what I learned is impossible – an entire book could be dedicated to Elvis-the-spiritual-man. Perhaps someday, when my studies have been concluded, such a portrait will be possible.

Before investigating the very possible effects of *The Passover Plot* on Elvis, there are three other novels that have dealt, like it, with a faked death that should be mentioned.

We know that Elvis read Morton Cooper's *The King*. The book made quite an impression on Linda S., of Maiden, North Carolina, who saw it at Graceland and secured a copy. She wrote me:

> It is about a forty-four-year-old singer who is "the King." He has decided to leave his way of life and go to work in the President's administration. . . .
> The character does not resemble Elvis too much in his background – but the description of the man's charisma, talent, and the public's adoration is classically "Elvis." The book is really eerie in that it was published in 1967 but so closely describes events that took place in Elvis' life in the 1970s.
> There is a Madison Square Garden performance that is to be his *last* and is telecast by CBS. . . . He studies medical books when he cannot sleep. He has a longtime good friend who is his doctor. He has become friends with the President. He also acts in movies. He owns his own production company. The description of his performances will just blow your mind: The book describes Elvis' stage presence, style, type of songs, etc., to the letter. Now, this was written in the 1960s, before Elvis even started his concert tours.
> He is divorced but has never stopped loving his first wife. . . . He gives generously to needy or sick individuals and to charities anonymously. . . . [It] reminds me so much of your Orion. . . .
> Here is a quote from the jacket of the book: "In the posh Manhattan hotel suite of President Joseph Haywood, Orlando brushed off the fawning hangers-on and left for Madison Square Garden . . . And as he sang, he said a silent good-bye to it all, because he had decided to get off the dizzy merry-go-round of his life, to trade it all for a job in President Haywood's administration. . . . [It would give him] a last chance to do something that would make him proud to look the world in the eye."

An anonymous novel was copyrighted in 1985 by a German-titled company, Bringes ans Licht (which means "Bring It to Light" or "Reveal It"). This mysterious book, published in England as *Fairytale,* has raised many eyebrows. It is the story of a rock star named Aaron Wade, whose death is questionable. The book has a Joe Esposito–like character who, with Aaron himself, is planning the "death"; the book has a "to be continued"-type ending.* Fans have pointed out that "Fairytale" was also a song, one of Elvis' favorites; the song told, in effect, the story of a life (a man packs up his things and walks away, feeling that his life would only get worse if he stayed saying his life is only a dream, a "fairytale"). The color of the book–blue–was Elvis' favorite color. The name "Wade" was somewhat significant in that Elvis played Jess Wade in the non-singing movie *Charro* (1969). (Priscilla Presley played Jenna Wade on CBS' *Dallas*.)

Finally, there is a highly recommendable novel, *The Presley Arrangement,* written by Monte Nicholson, a nineteen-year veteran of the Los Angeles Sheriff's Department.† The novel, partly based on fact, depicts the possible hoaxing of the death of Elvis. Like my own 1977/78 novel, *Orion, The Presley Arrangement* disappeared from bookstores almost as soon as it had been stocked – and this *not* by individual, interested purchasers.

Nicholson's story is of a body that is autopsied – a man resembling Elvis who had died of cancer. The body is later returned, for private burial, to the man's own family, and they are paid a great sum of money to remain silent about the affair. "If it is true that Elvis Presley is alive," says Nicholson, "my book would be pretty close to the truth of how it was done."

Nicholson also describes a governmental connection in the novel, and stated during one 1989 radio interview that even if he knew there was an FBI connection and was told not to say anything, he *could* not say anything.

WITH AS MUCH INTEGRITY AS IS HUMANLY POSSIBLE, I HAVE DELIBERately tried to "walk a mile" in Elvis' spiritual shoes, each step taken bringing me closer to the "Light." Strangely, this journey was familiar, and it felt so comfortable. Every word of enlightenment became thoughts already present. How can I accurately explain? Try explaining the scent of a rose to someone who has never seen a rose, or express the nectar of a pear to one who has never tasted such.

*At one point, the novel could be ordered from Fairytale, Heanor Record Center Limited, 41/47 Derby Road, Heanor, Derbyshire, DE7 7QH, England. It was a blue hardback with no dust jacket but simply an etching of someone resembling Elvis, and was probably a private printing.

†Nicholson, who co-wrote the Foreword to *The Elvis Files,* has a degree in police science. During the 1968 Tet Offensive, he served in the 27th Marine Infantry Regiment and received the Vietnam Cross of Gallantry.

Does this make sense? To "know" one must already *know.*

Thus, for *The Elvis Files* I must condense, fully knowing that to do so is like running a race with a broken leg: I am in the race, but at best I will finish last. However, before this file is considered foolish and "beside the point," I suggest the reading of at least the books mentioned as well as *Cheiro's Book of Numbers,* keeping in mind at all times that these were Elvis' favorite books – books he carried with him on tour, some copies of which are on display in the museums at Graceland. (Both Elvis' Bible and *Cheiro's* were missing from Elvis' nightstand on August 16, 1977!)

One of those who knew Elvis' spirituality best and who played an important role in directing Elvis' reading eyes was Larry Geller, his close friend and spiritual advisor. I highly recommend the reading of Mr. Geller's book *If I Can Dream: Elvis' Own Story,* co-written with Joel Spector and Patricia Romanowski. Points elaborated upon by Mr. Geller include these:

- Elvis had a desert vision where he saw himself as the Christ. (Keep in mind that Jesus' last name was not Christ, that Christ is from Christus/Christos, meaning "appointed one or messiah," which also means "annointed one and/or expected king and deliverer of the Jews." In order to ward off charges of blasphemy against him, Elvis' love for Jesus was paramount, and when he saw God/Christ/Jesus within him, he was touching with that basic truth taught us: that we are indeed created in the image of our Maker – God.)
- Elvis believed that his true mission was "God and the Brotherhood. . ." (Keep in mind the word "Brotherhood.")
- Elvis told Larry he had given his life over to the Lord, that he had meditated, prayed, asked God how "Elvis" fit into the universal picture.
- Elvis was deeply concerned about people's suffering; he wanted to bring happiness into their lives and believed that his mission in life was to "uplift." He was grateful for his talents, but he was questioning the position he was in and what further role God intended him, feeling deeply that God wanted to use him in a bigger way.

"From the House of David will come the messiah" is a Jewish prophecy. The fact that Nashville – the music capital – is in Davidson County held symbolic significance for Elvis. Elvis wore the Star of David along with the Cross. According to at least one biographer, Elvis was proud there was Jewish blood on his mother's side of the family. He had both the Cross and the Star of

David placed on her headstone at Forest Hill Cemetery. Elvis
believed in a Universal God of Love; he considered Jesus the real
King, not himself. He had grown far beyond the confines of sec-
tarianism, seeing bigotry as a limit of one's "God-soul," or the God
that is in all of us; and he felt that the hellfire-and-brimstone
teachings of some churches was morally wrong, that God should
be loved, not feared.

Elvis was not upset about Christianity or the Bible, but with
differences of interpretation that infringed upon another's rights.
Elvis' belief in God ran far deeper than church walls, choirs, and
icons. The "God-breath" within his soul wanted to emulate what
Jesus taught: love, charity, relief of others' suffering, the abandon
of material trappings, healing, helping. . . .

Yet Elvis also possessed great wisdom and insight. He knew
that if Elvis Presley the rock 'n' roller were to "wear the robes,"
there would be many who would crucify him with:

> Elvis Presley! How can a man with the name of Elvis Presley repre-
> sent the word of God? He's a lowly man born in the backwoods of
> Mississippi, born in a simple shack, hardly wore shoes or had fine
> clothing or college teachings! And look at the mistakes he made. . . .
> I mean he was human far too often and, granted, he gave often to
> the poor and his love for humanity was quite apparent – but Elvis!
> Nah. . . . Look at the way he dressed sometimes and look at some
> of the people he hung out with and those showgirls – harlots, all of
> them! Well, of course, God came first in his life, we all know that.
> And, yeah, we all know how he honored his mother and father, and
> of course when he sang "How Great Thou Art" it brought tears to the
> eyes and even the soul of man to its knees; and true, he was more
> generous than most. But still, what would God want with the likes
> of an Elvis? Just the name alone, for God's sake!

Elvis was a Christian in that his belief in Jesus was steadfast,
yet he never closed his mind to the belief that God could work and
might work through any others of us or at least those who took the
time to become enlightened. Religion, soul-searching, or rather
finding the "God-Within," was never a fad for Elvis but rather a
search that began from infancy, a search that proved to him how
much there was to know. His deep faith did not outlaw studies and
questions.

Elvis noted, early on, the "Missing years of Jesus" – those years
(some say sixteen*) when Jesus was supposedly involved in spiri-

---

*If sixteen, and if Elvis is alive, the year 1993 could be significant. It would mean
sixteen "missing" years. 1993 was the original year set for Lisa to inherit estate.
And Elvis left on a sixteenth day.

tual studies, perhaps traveling to discover the truth in various other teachings and philosophies. (There is more evidence than not that the teachings of Jesus – now called Christianity – were indeed influenced by age-old teachings such as Buddhism or Taoism, the bottom line being: God is Love. . . Do unto others. . .Whatsoever you sow, so shall you reap. . .the law of Karma. . .the law of sequence and consequence.) When Jesus said, "Ye are gods. . ." Elvis knew it meant that Jesus was talkng about the god-love within all of us, that presence we are taught to bring to the surface so that we can act in a "godly" way. Elvis also remarked that to believe one has been born many times (reincarnation) was no more ridiculous than to believe that man was born once. Above all, Elvis believed the relationship between man and God was a personal journey traveled at one's own speed. His quest to understand the God-Within was total and sincere; he *knew* he was chosen, yet he had not defined for *what?*

When Larry Geller talked about how hard it was for Elvis to reconcile how God could both bless and punish with the same hand, I was amazed because when I wrote the novel *Orion* back in 1977 (copyrighted 1978), one of the basic problems facing the work (a singer who fakes his death) was the "blessings/punishment" thesis, something Orion had to work through. (One twin lives, one dies. . .fortune/fame = power/pain. . .height of joy/loss of mother, etc.)

The greatest minds to walk this universe held a common denominator: one's personal quest for self and for the God-Within.

Realizing – via only a brief view – Elvis' Jesus connection (i.e., Elvis' desire to live and do as Jesus taught), the fact that *The Passover Plot* is prominently on display at Graceland's museum is worthy of examination, particularly because it deals with the possibility of Jesus' hoaxing his death. (This file is not a presumption on the part of the author one way or another, nor is author Schonfield's treatise something I wish to debate; I am simply telling you about a book Elvis Presley considered important as well as some amazing parallels.)

Knowing also that there are those who will be offended by this file case, in that some of the thinking presented does not match their own, I suggest not reading this portion. (I actually encountered someone who said Jesus could not be a Jew because why is the Pope Catholic?!)

ELVIS TOLD MANY AROUND HIM: "THIS LIFE I AM LEADING CANNOT GO ON much longer. . ." In a low voice, he spoke these words during his last concert: "I am, and I was."

As with all his favorite books, Elvis read *The Passover Plot* many times over. It seemed he saw something of himself in every page despite the fact that the book is about the life of Jesus, not Elvis. I had long known that this book was a favorite of Elvis' and ironically it played a role when I created the novel *Orion,* the novel that started everything, climaxing with *Is Elvis Alive?* What I have not until now focused upon was *how* startling the similarities are – especially when one attempts to read *The Passover Plot* through Elvis' eyes!

Others besides the *Los Angeles Herald Examiner's* Mitchell Fink have noted the possibility of Elvis' using *The Passover Plot* as a roadmap of what he did: like Jesus, hoaxed his death. Note the following extracts I've made from a fan, Fern B., of Mentor, Ohio, sent to me on October 16, 1989:

> A man looking for the reasons for who he was and why he was put on this earth to be what he had become might feel that the answers to all his questions could be found in the Bible or other books. . . . We find in [Jesus] the symbol both of the martyrdom and the aspirations of man, and therefore we must cling to him as the embodiment of an assurance that our life has a meaning and a purpose. . . .
>
> I believe that after reading *The Passover Plot,* it could plant in some people's minds a way of removing themselves without actually removing them at all. The perfect plan! . . .
>
> I found the dates of Jesus' crucifixion similar to those of Elvis' death, and the times of Jesus' death and His Resurrection similar to the time that some say Elvis died and when he was found. And to read that Jesus had been taken to the Garden Gethsemane after his death caught my attention. Naturally, Elvis read this. . .so now all close family members are buried in Gracelands' Meditation Gardens. . . .
>
> Schonfield states that Jesus would have used only close friends (a few) and family to help him to fake his own death. Like the Beloved Disciple (who was he? not even the Bible tells us), was Dr. Nick Elvis' Beloved Disciple?
>
> And no one reading *The Passover Plot* can not stop when reading that maybe Jesus used drugs to make himself look dead. I do not believe this – but for someone looking for answers, as Elvis was, this would have helped in his plan for death: to cheat death, to give the appearance of death.
>
> Jesus stayed in the public eye before his death, as did Elvis himself. . . .
>
> [According to Schonfield], if Jesus was alive, who could tell how

or when he would appear, what he would look like. Had not Elijah been revealed in the guise of John the Baptist?

Did Elvis, after reading these same words, use the name John or John Burrows because it was done in the Bible? The word "burrow" means to hide (oneself) in a burrow or a place of refuge. Strange!!

Fern's letter concerning *Elvis and the Passover Plot* was not the only one I've received. Moreover, a very tattered copy of a January 1977 edition of *The Passover Plot* (paperback) arrived in the mail. There was no note, no reference as to who sent it, and because of the amount of mail, clippings, books, and so on coming into this office, the best I can do is say the envelope may have had an Ohio postmark. Because I did not know the significance behind the arrival of the book, the envelope went into the trash can with other envelopes; I had to rummage around in order to find the one I believe it arrived in. The book's significance was in some of its underlinings, such as:

• "The root of Jesse." (Elvis' twin was Jesse, his root.)
• Jesus' death at around 41 or under 50. (Elvis' "death" was at 42.)
• Free the mind of preconceived ideas.
• Destroy an illusion and the man behind the myth.
• King of the line of David.
• Jesus was taunted with being a demon-possessed Samaritan. (Elvis, although generous, was also said to be demon/devil-possessed.)
• A call to office.
• Killed and be raised again the third day.
• Jesus was the eldest of a fairly large family and brought up in humble circumstances. (Although Elvis was an only child, he came from a large extended family.)
• He saw himself acting out the prophecies.
• It was from the banks of Jordan that Elijah had been taken up to Heaven, and now in the guise of John, as it could be thought, he had come back as foretold. (Reincarnation.)
• Jesus was not alone in supposing that John was Elijah returned. (Reincarnation again.)
• Jesus and his psychic experience.

Those are some of the underlinings, and my (parenthetical) commentary.

Another letter writer pointed out the following from *The Passover Plot* – about Jesus. Amazingly, the observations fit Elvis as well, and thus one can appreciate why Elvis placed the book in high esteem:

1. This child was to prove to be no ordinary boy, for he was destined to play a unique part in history. This is how we must understand him as the one above all others who showed mankind *how to make their dreams come true.*

2. His disciples became familiar with his spells of silence, which they feared to break. They would be walking with him, talking animately among themselves, even arguing heatedly, virtually ignoring his presence. Suddenly he would say something, either at the time or later, which showed that he was not wholly inattentive and had heard their conversation.

3. He says and does things quite unexpected by his intimate associates, which takes them by surprise or which they are unable to fathom. They may like to think they are wholly in his confidence, and even that he will do what they have in mind for him. But he baffles and defeats them, and makes arrangements of which they have not been cognizant, to secure his objectives.

4. The effects of all he may have endured as he contemplated what was to come, and dared not betray his secret, were bound to take their toll and show themselves in his physical appearance.

5. Rapidly, his fame spread far and wide, and his name became a legend overnight. Nothing was too impossible to be credited to him. There were those, on the other hand, who were scandalized by his teaching and behavior, particularly members of the Pharisee fraternity, who considered themselves to be the custodians of the nation's moral and spiritual instruction. The more straitlaced of them winced at some of the things he said and were offended by the freedom of his conduct.

Like a man who has experienced what is called conversion, he felt in himself that he was a new being, and this feeling would have been stimulated by his sudden emancipation from the tension engendered by the long years of waiting, by the knowledge that he had liberty to speak and act now instead of having everything pent up inside him.

6. Jesus had now to prepare for the most difficult and dangerous part of his present mission, which demanded the utmost caution and the most careful organization and timing. He could not look to his disciples to assist him directly in the arrangements for his coming ordeal.

7. He dies about 3:00 P.M. [at about age forty-one].

8. Two things, however, were indispensable to the success of a rescue operation. The first was to administer a drug to give the

impression of premature death, and the second was the speedy delivery of the body to Joseph. [Could "Joseph" equate to "Joe Esposito"?]

9. If he was to cheat death, it was essential that well in advance of time, *he would have to give every appearance of being dead.* Further, help must speedily be forthcoming. Unless his body came into possession of friendly hands, there would be no possibility of his recovery—we would have to imagine how Jesus contrived to give the impression of death, and suggest a way in which his body could have been secured by his friends. We have only to allow that in this as in other instances Jesus made private arrangements with someone he could trust, who would be in a position to accomplish his design.

10. When stripped of supernaturalism, the empty tomb may point rather to a removal of the body from the place where the women had seen it laid and its burial elsewhere. But if the body of Jesus was taken from the tomb by his friends on Saturday night, we should be ready to agree with the Gospels that the immediate disciples of Jesus knew nothing about this, and they would be quite sincere in indignantly repudiating any contention that they had been guilty of perpetuating a fraud [the hoaxing of a death].

11. If Jesus was alive, who could tell how or when he would appear, what he would look like.

12. Again, an important ingredient is the failure to identify Jesus —this time by his own relatives.

13. Neither had there been any fraud on the part of Jesus himself. He had schemed in faith for his physical recovery.

14. When the few saw him, they were in awe; but some doubted.

15. The special conditions that produced him at a peculiar and pregnant moment in history are never likely to occur again.

Since I am always interesed in what Elvis fans have to say— they being the backbone of the Elvis phenomenon—some of the following offer insight.

The following letter is a fun game of substitutions of today's names for yesterday's. And it offers some material for thinking. By the way, the page numbers from Audrey N's letter probably come from the hardback edition of *The Passover Plot.*

These are a few excerpts from the book with *Elvis'* name in the place of *Jesus'*:

Elvis made private arrangements with someone he could trust, who would be in a position to accomplish this design (page 163).

Was this person a member of the family or a friend? After the task, this person disappears completely from view. Afterwards, there is no indication of association with Elvis. Elvis plotted and schemed with utmost skill, making secret arrangements, taking advantage of every circumstance conducive to the attainment of his objectives. It is difficult to credit that he had neglected to do anything about the supreme crisis of his career, when it was imperative that he should outwit the forces arrayed against him and wrest victory from the very jaws of death (page 163).

Elvis would have to give every appearance of being dead. Further help must speedily be forthcoming. Unless his body came into possession of friendly hands, there would be no possibility of his recovery. Elvis contrived to give the impression of death, and suggest a way in which his body could have been secured by his friend (page 163).

Considerations of safety and secrecy will have dictated that as few people as possible should be in the know or involved, and these would not have included any of the Memphis Mafia [the letter writer's substitution for "disciples"?], to whom he never confided his plans. His was the mastermind, and the ones to whom he gave his instructions neither worked together nor were acquainted with more than their specific function (pages 166–67).

The Memphis Mafia knew nothing and would be quite sincere in indignantly repudiating any contention that they had been guilty of perpetrating a fraud (page 172).

Elvis may not have overlooked that he might taste death in spite of the measure he had secretly taken for his survival. He knew, however, that his fans [followers?] would be in anguish (page 173).

Clearly, some did not recognize the man they [later] saw as Elvis. Some rushed to tell of having seen Elvis. Another ingredient was added to the Myth (page 176).

If Elvis is alive, who could tell how or when or where he would appear, what he would look like? Cheered by the strange discourses, the fans were soon telling each other that the man seen must be Elvis (page 177).

When the few saw him, they were in awe, but some doubted (page 179).

Neither had there been any fraud on the part of Elvis himself. He had schemed in faith for his physical recovery (page 168).

The special conditions which produced him at a peculiar and pregnant moment in history are never likely to occur again (page 181).

What I have found interesting in the many letters I received regarding Elvis and *The Passover Plot* is how similar the analyses have been. Here are extracts from one from Joan G., of Portage, Indiana:

(Page 132) . . . the destined road led to torture – But these things had to come about in the manner predicted and after preliminaries entailing the most careful scheming and plotting to produce them. *Moves and situations had to be anticipated, rulers and associates had to perform their functions without realizing that they were being used.* [The italics are Joan G.'s.]

(Page 166) Two things, however, were indispensable to the success of a rescue operation. First, administer a drug to give the impression of a premature death and, second, obtaining the speedy delivery of the body (to whoever was in on it). [Here Joan is paraphrasing the book.]

From Marcella B., of Belleville, Illinois, came the following note: "In *The Passover Plot,* I find most interesting the following passages: '. . .people struggling frantically to reach him, to touch even the sacred fringe of his robe as he passed, by the end of most days he was utterly exhausted. . .he could not get away' and 'He himself saw to it that he would not be forgotten, that he would be continually pestering and challenging us. In spite of everything done to stop him in his own time and since. . .he has continued to come through.'"

One of the words underlined in the copy of *The Passover Plot* sent me was the word "atonement," which brought an interesting observation from Linda S., of Maiden, N.C.: "In looking in a Nave's Topical Bible under 'Atonement,' I found that so many of the scriptures pertaining to atonement mention Aaron. Check it out—Lev. 16:1–35; Num. 8:21; Ex. 30:7–10; Num. 16:46–50; Heb. 5:1–4; Heb. 9:1–7; Lev. 9:7. Maybe this is the reason Day of Atonement was underlined in your copy—because looking for that in the Bible would take us to the name Aaron. I don't know what it means—but found it interesting."

REPETITIOUS AS HAVE BEEN THE HUNDREDS OF LETTERS, THE POINT OF the repetition is to illustrate the similarities that Elvis must have found in *The Passover Plot.* Knowing Elvis' deep spiritual connection with Jesus, one cannot help but wonder that *if* Elvis hoaxed his death, did he use the book as a spiritual roadmap?

Faye H. of Tulsa, Oklahoma, wrote: "I have read and studied *The Passover Plot* and find it very interesting. One thing I found fascinating and almost a dead (oops) giveaway was the 'shedding of the [Jesus'] white clothes and leaving them neatly folded in the tomb.' When did anyone ever change clothes on a corpse, yet on page 439 (paperback) of *Elvis, We Love You Tender,* Dee [Presley's stepmother] described Elvis as dressed in a white suit looking 'frighteningly different.' Then on page 440 she says he was changed into a pale blue suit, which Vernon had given him for Christmas. Were the cheap white clothes used to show our humble Saviour?"

...Or, as another writer observed, "Was the changing of the clothes symbolic of the changing of Jesus' 'death' robes?"

If *The Passover Plot* was not on display, perhaps others – notably, Mitchell Fink of the *Los Angeles Herald Examiner* – would wonder whether the book wasn't a clue. (Even with an amusing eye, it does make one wonder!) The fact is, *The Passover Plot* was a favorite of Elvis', a book that describes step-by-step that Jesus was no milk-and-water Messiah but, rather, one Who was master of His own destiny – including His "death."

Larry Geller said Elvis asked that he bring to him the book *The Shroud of Turin,** among others, with, according to what Charlie Hodge wrote, the additive that "Elvis was expecting to find something in its reading." It was the last book found beside the "body" – a book concerning a shroud bearing what is thought to be the image of Jesus – an image thought to be the result of some cosmic force "that brought Jesus back to life," while other scholars and experts think the shroud is a "hoax."

Recall that in both the Bible and in *The Passover Plot* Jesus' tomb was found empty, except for the shroud.

Is Elvis' tomb likewise empty?

Many of the letters I've received ask the following question, in these or other words: "I saw a letter on display at the Million Dollar Museum, which outlined some of Elvis' beliefs. One part struck me deeply. Elvis wrote: 'You are soon recognizing a brighter light within yourself. The sharing of that light with others and feeling the importance of stressing and/or distributing the love and will of God . . .' Do you think it possible that in order for Elvis to reach God he may have had to give up the 'life' he was leading? That to share his light he had to use the cloak of darkness?"

My answer will draw, largely, on Larry Geller's book. According to Geller's *If I Can Dream,* the entertainer said that the life he was leading had gone on far too long. And Elvis shared other intimate thoughts that were of a spiritual nature:

- He (Elvis) had a *mission,* and wanted to know if Geller was behind him? He explained that this mission had to do with a secret spiritual life. He said that changes would occur – soon – for he felt it was going to happen.

---

*Although Geller probably means the Doubleday *Shroud,* it was not released until 1978. Elvis may possibly have wanted the Werner Bulst *Shroud,* published in Milwaukee in 1957.

- Elvis told Geller that he believed that when one twin died, the other inherited his qualities. Recall, in *Is Elvis Alive?*, the strange telephone call I received after August 16, 1977, from a man sounding like Elvis and saying almost the same thing. Remember also that I could not have copied such a statement from Larry's book, because Geller's book was released after my own.

- As Elvis' studies deepened, he became fascinated with numbers, letters, and symbols as they related to the universe: Its systematic order was a source of enlightenment to him.

- Elvis discovered that the Bible was full of "hidden meanings," codes, mystical revelations. (If Elvis were to abandon one life for another, it would fall into his psyche to leave clues, codes, hidden meanings.)

- Elvis discovered that in Judaism rabbis changed people's names according to the principles of numerology. (In other words, Elvis may have changed his middle name from Aron to Aaron – as Geller said he did indeed do – so that the resulting numbers or combination of numbers would better interpret his character or fate.)

- Elvis, after hearing the explanation of the Hebrew word *chai*, meaning life, began wearing the symbol for it.

- Geller underlines that Elvis was one of the brightest, most intelligent of men, devouring books, not simply reading them but absorbing them, writing his thoughts in the margin, underlining – and most of the books dealt with spiritual quests, with "opening up."

- Elvis had a major religious experience in the desert – as did Jesus. It was a revelation: It underlined the truth that God is Love.

- Elvis told Geller he wanted to become a monk and join a monastery. (Doesn't this mean giving one's life to God, "dropping out" – giving up the material for the spiritual – to becoming "Christlike," as pure in soul as possible?) Do you believe that Elvis Presley had the depth of spirit to give up his fans, his wealth, his entertaining, for the love of God? Priscilla stated that he would not have done this to his fans, and I believe that is a true statement. But would he have done it for the love of God? "Yes" is also a true statement.

- Elvis told Geller he would never allow himself to degenerate into a fifty-year-old entertainer. Elvis told others this too, even saying he would not make it much past forty – which he didn't.

- Geller states that if Elvis had really contemplated his own death, it is conceivable he would have chosen to be buried in the Meditation Gardens at Graceland.

- The only thing Elvis ever mentioned to Geller about funeral or arrangements is that people shouldn't wear black. Remember, Geller's book was copyrighted in 1989. *Orion* was copyrighted in 1978. Yet read the following excerpt from *Orion:*

> As he stood beside the church organ and listened to Reverend Walker praise Esther Jackson, Orion's eyes wandered from one familiar face to another. The small church was packed; people were standing in the aisles and even lined up outside in the dark and cold. Reverend Walker had attached a loudspeaker to the front of the church so those outside would not miss his eulogy or the music. Orion had written a song that very afternoon. As his eyes traveled from face to face Orion wondered what they thought and what they did with those thoughts. He noticed most everyone was dressed in black; there seemed to be something incongruous about that. After all, God was life and light. One only met God through death, therefore why black? They should be dressed in white, the color of Jesus' robe. He had felt a tinge of remorse when he heard of Esther Jackson's passing, although he had never been as close to her as had Tuck. It seemed Tuck was always losing someone close. Well, one thing is for sure, promised Orion: When I die I shall be buried in white – pure white.

- Elvis was so anxious to attain higher knowledge that he wanted to take "shortcuts." Finally, he realized that there were no instant techniques but rather the dedication of years and years of study and practice. Higher knowledge was a secret revealed to only the learned. It was a moral transgression to seek it by "shortcut."
- A legitimate fear Elvis had was to be taken advantage of financially, once his quest for spiritual learning was known. In my opinion, for Elvis to study *as Elvis* would have been a disaster – the quiet solitude of mind and body would have been threatened. Even the knowledge that he could be located at any given moment would have taken its psychological toll, prohibiting him from truly learning. Elvis would always have had to be "looking over his shoulder." Further, once he completed his spiritual studies and attained his goals, how could an "Elvis Presley" go out into the world and walk among the common man? Who would listen to what he had to say? In fact, he had remarked more than once that no one, especially many of his fans, really ever listened to him. They were

caught up in the image, not the man. No. There is absolutely no way Elvis Presley could remain Elvis Presley and not be imprisoned in the image of a sexy rock 'n' roller with swivel hips. The imaged Elvis Presley would never have been taken seriously as Brother Presley. If Elvis did, indeed, hibernate and go into secret spiritual studies, only a select few could be allowed to know.

- Elvis admitted to Geller that his mission in life was to bring happiness into the lives of people, but that there might be something more in store for him, that he hoped God would use him in bigger ways.

- Elvis told Geller that he continually asked God to show him the way, to give him strength, to help him find his *true mission* in life.

- Elvis loved "plans and projects."

- When Vernon's marriage fell apart, Elvis saw that everything around him was breaking down. Apparently Elvis tried to break free. Later, Elvis would do and say things that suggested he might make some substantial move toward a change in life. Elvis spoke of sweeping changes, of making a new start.

- By 1976, Elvis was talking of going to Europe, of going to Japan. (This was impossible, though, due to the Colonel's citizenship status.* It was apparent that Elvis would never be allowed, as "Elvis," to see much of Planet Earth before his leaving of it . . . unless?)

- By April 1977, Geller says Elvis was on the brink of making major changes in his life. By the end of April, Elvis was talking about a secret spiritual life and a special mission. By the end of May he told Geller something described as "top secret." Basically, Elvis was going to "clean house," which included getting rid of the Colonel and the Memphis Mafia. He knew who his *real* friends were. He wanted to live a different life. The one he was living had gone on long enough.

- Further, Elvis told Geller, *that* different kind of life would occur by the end of the summer, and that it *would happen.*

---

*"The Colonel," Tom Parker's, influence over Elvis is well known to many. But for the less informed about the singer's life, I should explain that the Colonel's contracted control, as manager, over Elvis began early; and Elvis trusted in him. Parker was not a U.S. citizen, though he lived in this country as one. Since Parker could not get a passport to leave the United States, he would not allow "his boy" to go abroad either. Readers may want to refer to Dirk Vellenga's book *Elvis and the Colonel.*

• Less than three months later, on August 16, it did end. But, this writer questions, did it end the way we were told, or is it possible it ended the way Elvis planned it – *his* way?

Although fascinated with Jesus, Elvis, according to the biographies, did not think Jesus was the *only* Son of God, believing that all mankind had "God-Within." Elvis was heard making *other* comparisons with Jesus, saying, "This is the way Jesus did it. . ."
Many of those around Elvis said he had some ability to heal.
Elvis believed in the supernatural, such as telepathy, astral projection, and the learning of "the secrets of the Brotherhood."
His fascination with Paramahansa Yogananda extended to how the yogi was able to predict "the exact day of his own death." Elvis visited the Self-Realization Fellowship headed by Sri Daya Mata, a disciple of Paramahansa Yogananda, who gave Elvis secret manuscripts that might help him understand why God had chosen him to be Elvis Presley.

ABOUT THE "I AM AND I WAS" THAT ELVIS SAID DURING HIS LAST CONCERT tour. . .let's look at Revelations 1:8: "'I am the Alpha and the Omega,' says the Lord God, who is and who was and who is to come, the Almighty." And I have received, anonymously, from the xerox of a page of a religious booklet (unnamed), the following – which amounts to somewhat the same thing as the Revelations quote:

> The people of Yahweh always live between memory and hope, between their conviction that God has acted in the past and their assurance of God's redemptive presence in their future. Just as earthly life had a beginning, so will it have an ending; and Yahweh, whose name means "I Am," presides over both. The Being One is most fully revealed in the One "who is and who was and who is to come" . . .

The "I Am and I Was" words spoken by Elvis at "The End" are better understood by the reading of another of his favorite books, Joseph F. Benner's *The Impersonal Life,* whose first chapter is entitled "I Am." A few pages later, after "I Am" appears the "Always Was" idea. *The Impersonal Life* should be read at least three times to understand its full meaning. Basically, it is about the God-Power in us, the God-Power always in us. We were, are, and always have been – a philosophy Jesus taught, yet one not fully understood.
I would love to expand upon *The Impersonal Life,* having attempted to read it through Elvis' eyes, but, again, it would truly

take an entire book to interpret. I sincerely suggest that as many of you as possible read it, if not merely to understand the pinnacle of spiritual thinking arrived at by Elvis by August 16, 1977, then for your own spiritual awakening. *The Impersonal Life* seems an extension of the Biblical teachings that we are "created in the image of. . ." Thus, in my opinion, it awakens thinking and further enlightens. Of course, I have always believed that the God-power is in all living things–which explains why every living thing is totally unique or, to coin an old example, that "not even two snowflakes are the same."

Sometimes this belief is translated as the "I Am" consciousness, a consciousness that experiences, grows until the idea of Love, Compassion, Service to God *is* consciousness, that one *is* simply by *being*–or "A man is as he thinks."

Each man's spiritual awakening (or remembrance) travels at its own pace; to become a "master" (a master of one's own soul) depends on the individual. Just as no two children are equal in their intellectual capacity, thus no two adults are equal in their spiritual and/or "God-Awareness." Jesus, for instance, had attained a pinnacle of awareness of his "God-ness," and thereby was the Christ.

However, Jesus had to study, to meditate, to "disappear" for many years (sixteen)–during which "family and friends" did not know where he was, whether he was dead or alive–in order to totalize the I Am/I Was within, or the God-Within–I Was God, I Am God. Is this blasphemous? Is it irreverent for us to believe that indeed we can be like our Creator? But isn't that what we are taught to attain? Or why, then, Jesus? Why the great teachers? The majority of philosophies and religions, be they Christianity, Buddhism, Taoism, Islam, or Judaism, have a universal thread: God Is Love. They advocate that the more loving (compassionate, caring) we are, the more God-like (the God-likeness within) we are. God-likeness does not preclude joy, good humor, laughter, a happy countenance. A dour, see-me-in-church-on-my-knees countenance is not the God-Within coming forth.

Where in all this does Elvis fit? Why have so many millions related to him in a loving way? Is it because Elvis "exuded love"?

Magnetism, charm, charisma are adjectives used by those who were frequently in Elvis' presence. "I felt he was singing to me. . .alone," is a familiar comment. "Electric. . ." is another description of him.

Several philosophers have written words to the effect that "Elvis' soul was a follower of Jesus Christ. . . . He exuded a pres-

ence of 'goodness' and an 'inner knowledge' of the suffering of
mankind – and the pain of Calvary. Elvis, although a singer, was
truly a priest of the highest order." And that: "Elvis possessed
tremendous insight. Elvis gave unconditional love – not only with
physical gifts but by the giving of 'Self.'"

There is a family story concerning Elvis as a little boy. He had
wanted a tricycle for Christmas. His parents worked overtime in
order to get the money. Christmas morning arrived and Elvis was
elated. He took his tricycle out to ride, but soon came back
without it. His mother questioned him, and Elvis said he had
given it away to a little boy who had not gotten anything for
Christmas because he was "too poor." Everytime Gladys retriev-
ed the tricycle, Elvis gave it away again.

Others have written about how Elvis, by his mere presence,
turned their lives from ones of negative actions to positive, that
his presence made them feel "closer to God."

"Elvis' costumes appeared dull when on a hanger," said one
observer. "Yet walking onstage, he and his clothes radiated light.
Elvis' aura was so very visible – the Light of his Soul shone
through. He was not a closed soul and thus, being so open, was
also vulnerable to outside cruelties. Elvis could be hurt so very
deeply because he had never built walls, walls which could protect his soul – yet the same walls which would hide the Soul-Light."

Elvis, like Jesus, knew he would have his Judases – friends
who would sell him out for a "bag of gold." Knowing this, knowing about the Judases around him, he forgave them.

Another reaction oft repeated in meeting Elvis: "He was a phenomenon – he was electricity."

Elvis often spoke about the "Light of God." My friend, Dr. Raymond Moody, in his national bestseller *Life After Life,* (St. Simons-
Island, GA: Mockingbird Books, 1975), talks about the great white
light seen by those on the verge of death or who have had after-
life experiences. This light is like no other, its warmth one of love
and belonging to God, offering a Oneness with God, a total
recognition of "Self" in the highest spiritual sense. Those who have
witnessed the Light of God are never again the same; fear of death
is forever gone, for they know they are eternal: They "Are" and
"Have Always Been" and "Will Always Be" – "I Am" and "I Was," as
Elvis murmured at his last concert.

Elvis believed that our "Light" (soul) came from the Light of
God, but that that Light (once spiritual) was now confined in the
physical body – that same spiritual Light representing the sum
total of all knowledge. Realizing this and practicing this may ex-

plain why Elvis seemed to "glow" and why so many millions were and are attracted to this special man, how they automatically love him. Elvis' Jesus connection obviously embraced the Biblical "I am the way, the truth and the life: no man cometh unto the Father, but by me."

Because music is the international language – a language that often bypasses the physical senses – Elvis was able to reach the world. Gospel music was his first love and he said, according to the Presley fan magazine *Elvis World,* that he hoped one day he could devote the rest of his life to singing it. Gospel was his foundation stone, and when he sang hymns, his belief became ours, his splendor our splendor.

In his book *Elvis: Photographing the King,* Sean Shaver explains that no one watching Elvis could ever forget the electric energy flowing back and forth. Many reviewers have stated that when Elvis came onstage, something extraordinary occurred, something beyond control – magical – something beyond mortal definition, an energy emitted by Elvis alone. As Carl Wilson of the Beach Boys said, "His voice was a total miracle."

"Elvis looked different to anyone I've ever seen. He was beautiful," said Gordon Stoker, backup for Elvis in the 1950s and '60s. "He was more alive than anybody I've ever known, more of everything that a human being could be. He *lived* his faith," said Kathy Westmoreland, backup singer for Elvis in the 1970s.

Author Dave Marsh comments: "Elvis was more than anything a spiritual leader of our generation. There is no way to assess his importance." Said Patsy Guy Hammontree, author of *Elvis Presley: A Bio-Bibliography:* "In truth the man takes on mythic and archetypal dimensions such that for some fans only Christ is greater."

When asked who was most admired by Germans, a 1987 Hamburg poll revealed: One and Two, mother and father; three, Jesus Christ; four, Elvis Presley.

In 1984, via TV channel CNN, a seven-year-old boy was asked who his hero was. He replied with "Elvis," saying Elvis was an "angel who would take care of the world."

Larry Geller has talked about how, from their first meeting, he knew of Elvis' spiritual quality, that he could silence a room just by the power of his aura. Countless others have described Elvis' "overwhelming power of presence." Bob Green wrote in 1981 in his review of the *This Is Elvis* docudrama that when Elvis dominated the screen, the audience was silent, almost reverential.

Bernard Benson, author of *The Minstrel,* to explain Elvis' effect on the world, could only comment: "This great force cannot be explained." Dr. W. Herbert Brewster, a Baptist minister, saw this in Elvis: "Like most in the South and in whose soul God has pressed down a harp of a thousand strings, it only needed tuning. Elvis' voice was that kind of voice that agreed with a thought of Calvary."

In March 1979, Jeane Dixon wrote: "It was if his music opened up a window in the sky through which he could catch a glimpse of the peace denied him here on earth." And, on Elvis' awareness: "It is the sure sign that a person is fulfilling his or her calling. Like Elvis, they are shaping their future by keeping an eye on their past, never forgetting who they were at birth. That is the true pathway to greatness."

("I Am, and I Was"?)

When, on January 14, 1973, *Elvis: Aloha from Hawaii* was broadcast worldwide – witnessed by an audience of almost 2 billion – one religious figure noted: "There is a good man."

Obviously there is much more to both *The Impersonal Life* and *The Initiate* than given in my analyses; however, it would indeed take an entire treatise to dissect the books that had an effect on Elvis' spiritual life. However, there appears a common thread: We are born with the Light of God, and our role is to bring that Light forth (God = Love). There are masters among us, or those whose God-Light is far greater than average. Yet to find one's own mastership, light, soul, it is sometimes necessary to "go off from the world" to meditate, to study – which can only be accomplished by unshackling oneself from material trappings, and removing oneself from those around us who have no understanding of what "Truth" is, those who would mock, condemn – even crucify. When this initiation is complete, a "return" is possible. Underscored in one of Elvis' spiritualistic books are the words: *"Should I return, you would not recognize me."*

Early on in his career, Elvis received a copy of a short essay, "The Penalty of Leadership," written by Theodore F. MacManus. Upon reading it, Elvis said the author must have been thinking of *him* when he wrote it – even though it was written before Elvis was born. A framed copy hung in his office and is now on display in Graceland's Elvis – Up Close museum, along with his favorite books. Elvis said it was, in effect, about his own life:

> In every field of human endeavor, he who is first must perpetually live in the white light of publicity. Whether the leadership be vested in a man or in a manufactured product, emulation and envy are ever at work. In art, in literature, in music, in industry, the reward and the punishment are always the same. The reward is widespread recognition; the punishment fierce denial and detraction. When a

man's work becomes a standard for the whole world, it also becomes a target for the shafts of the envious few. If his work is merely mediocre, he will be left severely alone – if he achieves a masterpiece, it will set a million tongues a-wagging. Jealousy does not protrude its forked tongue at the artist who produces a commonplace painting. Whatsoever you write, or paint, or play, or sing, or build, no one will strive to surpass or to slander you, unless your work be stamped with the seal of genius. Long, long after a great work or a good work has been done, those who are disappointed or envious continue to cry out that it cannot be done. Spiteful little voices in the domain of art were raised against Whistler as a mountebank, long after the big world had acclaimed him its great genius. Multitudes flocked to Bayreuth to worship at the shrine of Wagner, while the little group of those whom he had dethroned and displaced argued angrily that he was no musician at all. The little world continued to protest that Fulton could not build a steamboat, while the big world flocked to the river to see his boat steam by. The leader is assailed because he is a leader, and the effort to equal him is merely added proof of that leadership. Failing to equal or to excel, the follower seeks to depreciate and to destroy – but only confirms once more the superiority of that which he strives to supplant. There is nothing new in this. It is as old as the world and as old as the human passions – envy, fear, greed, ambition, and the desire to surpass. And it all avails nothing. If the leader truly leads, he remains the leader. Master-poet, master-painter, master-workman, each in his turn is assailed, and each holds his laurels through the ages. That which is good or great makes itself known, no matter how loud the clamor of denial. That which deserves to live – *lives*.

To close this File Case, I would like to use the words from Elvis' song "The Impossible Dream": ". . . and the world will be better for this, that one man scorned and covered with scars, still strove with his last ounce of courage to reach the unreachable star."

Numerology and Astrology in Elvis' Life

The universe is but one vast Symbol of God.
                                                    —THOMAS CARLYLE

Question: Did Elvis play his life via numerology and/or astrology?
Answer: It is apparent that Elvis did often consult numerology and, at times, astrology in the making of important plans.

Wherever Elvis traveled, he always carried his Bible and *Cheiro's Book of Numbers,* two books that were always on his nightstand and were found missing from his nightstand only hours after his "death."

Numerology is the science of numbers as related to the occult, or "secret," patterns involving the universe—nature's calculations—which frequently relate to the spiritual side of things. This ancient study, for instance, was used by the Egyptians, who were considered absolute masters of the hidden meaning of numbers: their application to time and their relationship to human life.

Take the number seven as an illustration: Throughout the

Bible, as well as in other sacred books, the number seven always relates to the "God-Force":

- the seven days (or cycles) of Genesis' Creation
- the seven heavens
- the seven thrones
- the seven seals
- the seven churches
- the seventh day

The Bible speaks of the seven generations from David to the birth of Christ. Revelations speaks of the seven spirits of God sent forth into all the earth, while Ezekiel speaks of the seven angels of the Lord that go to and fro through the whole earth—a reference perhaps to the influences of the seven creative planets that radiate through the earth. Egyptian religion refers to seven spirits, as do other religions ranging from Hindu to Greek to Hebrew. All state that the number seven is the God-Force.

The number seven is the only number capable of dividing the number of eternity. The seven days of the week have been the outcome of the influence of the seven creative planets. To further understand the mystery of numbers, read (Count Louis Harmon) *Cheiro's Book of Numbers* (New York: Arco Publishing, 1964) or *Numerology and the Divine Triangle,* the latter by Faith Javane and Dusty Bunker. For this file, however, I will briefly zero in on Elvis' belief in numerology. According to the Javane/Bunker book, Elvis' life-lesson number was nine, the number for universal love and humanity. In *Cheiro's,* Elvis' name numbers equal nine, using "Elvis" and "Presley," which are both nines.* His compound number could change, depending upon whether he used "Aron" or "Aaron." By adding the second *a,* Elvis could have changed the vibrations of his numbers as well as his soul number. However, because this is a rather complicated and personal matter, it is best dealt with here only lightly—only pointing out that it was of intense interest to Elvis. August 16, 1977, adds up to 2001, the title of Elvis' theme song.† And as Tina G., of Defiance, Ohio, wrote: "The number six-

*In numerology each letter has an assigned number. E = 5, L = 3, V = 6, I = 1, and S = 3, totaling 18—but 18 is 1 + 8, or 9. Similarly, P = 8, R = 2, E = 5, S = 3, L = 3, E = 5, and Y = 1, totaling 27—but 27 is 2 + 7, or 9.

† Elvis would open his live performances with a taped version of Richard Strauss' *Also sprach Zarathustra,* one theme of which was used in the film *2001.*

teen is pictured by a Tower Struck by Lightning from which a man is falling with a Crown on his head. It is also called the Shattered Citadel. It gives warning of some strange fatality awaiting one, also defeat of one's plans. If it appears as a compound number relating to the future, it should be carefully noted and plans made in advance in an endeavor to avert its fatalistic tendency."

Tina further writes, "That description seems quite appropriate, whether he's dead or alive, don't you think? One more thing that I found interesting was the explanation for the number twenty, the name number for Priscilla Presley. Priscilla states in her book that at the funeral she placed a bracelet on Elvis' wrist depicting a mother and a child with their hands clasped. (This number is called the Awakening – also the Judgment. It is symbolized by the figure of a winged angel sounding a trumpet while from below a man, woman, and child are seen rising from a tomb with their hands clasped in prayer.)"

Tina wondered if there was a clue in any of this, especially since one of Elvis' favorite books was *Cheiro's,* and especially since he "died" on August 16th.

There is one more thing I want to share with you," Tina added, "regarding *Cheiro's.* I figured up the number for Elvis' name as it is spelled on the grave, just to see how it would come out. The compound number comes to twenty-five. Here is the explanation of that number: 'This number denotes strength gained through experience, and benefits obtained through observation of people and things. It is not deemed exactly lucky as its success is given through strife and trials in the earlier life. It is favorable only when it appears in regard to the future.'"

Another observer wrote:

Dear Gail,
Circle the date August 16, 1993, on your calendar! I believe that Elvis will return to the public on that date. All of this time I have been using the number eight for Elvis' numerology chart. For some reason, today I decided to sit down and read over what *Cheiro's* had to say about the number eight in more detail. Why I hadn't done this before, I don't know.

According to Cheiro, number-eight persons belong to a more fatalistic law of vibration and appear to be "children of fate," more than any other class. He suggests that to change from an unlucky number to a more fortunate one, you use the Zodiac period just opposite your own. December 21 to January 20 is the period of the positive eight. The Zodiac period opposite of this would be "the house of the moon," or the number seven. Sunday and Monday are the "lucky" days for this period, and the time from June 21 to July 20-27, and on to the end of August, is the "lucky" period for these people.

I am including a list of facts that pertain to the number seven and how Elvis might have used it, or even may use it in the future.

Interchangeable numbers with the number seven are: one, two, and four.

I think that there is an extremely good chance that many people will know what some of us have suspected: that Elvis Presley is not dead. Remember the date: August, 16 1993.

Recall that I said earlier that if Elvis is using Jesus as a guide, together with the fact that scholars believe there were sixteen missing years in the life of Jesus and that Elvis' March 1977 will stated Lisa would inherit the estate in 1993, this number may be significant. However, much also has changed in Elvis' family (the marriage of Lisa, the birth of a granddaughter, etc.), which could affect his own life readings, or the "signs of the times." Remember, we are not prisoners of the universe, and as certain influences occur, our readings can change – "flow with the tide."

A psychic by the name of Sara, from Maine, wrote:

No one, to date, understands the date chosen – name on tombstone, etc. Unless you are a student of numerology, the meanings of *all* remain hidden. However, it becomes very simple – when the instructions are given on how to interpret the questions that seem unable to be answered. For starters: Elvis chose August 16, 1977, because numerology is based on the Bible and the ancient Hebrew letters and number vibrations of each, especially $16 = 1 + 6 = 7$. A/a/r/o/n = 7 (Aaron falsified on purpose; real name Aron = 6). 1/1/2/7/5 = 16 (same on tombstone).

Name and date to coincide with $8/16/1977 = (8 + 7 + 6)$ 21 (2001). When you take the full date all together, $8/16/1977 = 21$, the number is called a compound # and its meaning is: This number is symbolized by the picture of "the universe" and it is also called "the Crown of the Magi." It is a number of advancement, honors, elevation in life, and general success. It means victory after a long fight, for "the Crown of the Magi" is only gained after long initiation and tests of determination. It is a fortunate number of promise if it appears in any connection with future events. . . .

Elvis rearranged the middle name on purpose. This is to indicate where he is living. His new name, John Burrows, has #1 vibrations, which is better for his original birth date; and because he was born a #8 – and was also born in a #8 period of the Zodiac – he needed to decrease the vibrations in order to have a happier life. Number-8 people "suffer the greatest losses," greater than any other numbers. His manager was also a #8, and when Elvis realized this he dissolved the business association. Number-8 people are generally misunderstood; they are very lonely people at heart, and because of this develop fears of mistrust and increase their potential of being used. Love is rarely given to a #8 individual in a pure form. It usually is given to a #8 for greed, lust, or advancement of self-gain. This is the biggest reason Elvis chose a life in exile. He wanted to study, meditate, educate his soul, learn, travel, and regain losses financially. Elvis' love is music. I predict he will return to the people and the public eye. He sings and feels from the soul, and the people will see him in a different light when he returns. His music will be better because he has become a better human being, has educated his soul. His music will reflect this.

He needs to return during this troubled time, and before the "years of peace," because the people will listen and learn. He is a teacher in his own right and has a lot of work left to do.

More clues. His age of leaving: $42 + 4 + 2 = 6$
Year $1977 = 1 + 9 + 7 + 7 = 24$
Correct name: Elvis = 9
Aron = 6
Presley = $\underline{9}$
24

. . . Elvis' desire to be accepted as a kind, loving, caring individual will be realized and respected. He gave a lot to many, and it shall be returned. He could have a big impact on the youth of today in relationship to drug problems – and get rid of the "bad music" that prompts suicide and drugs. I hope that soon he will return to the world.

I have received many letters concerning Elvis' "numbers," many of them focusing on the 2001 total, others noting that Lisa's wedding date of October 3, 1988, also equals 2001.

Although I do not totally understand numerology, I do accept its value to many believers. Since we obviously use numbers for daily calculations, as well as calendar numbers that relate to time and the universe, I have no problem accepting a systematic relationship between mankind/personality (or personhood) and a universal law or order, because numbers are order.

A numerology profile, by Widening Horizons, Inc.,* done on Elvis Aron Presley told of such traits as:

• devotion to people, innate love of mankind
• loving, giving

*Widening Horizons, Inc. (numerology profiles), 22665 Shady Grove, El Toro, CA 92630.

- philanthropist and humanitarian
- great compassion
- moodiness, when upset
- intensive feelings
- inspiration to others
- expresses himself via music
- ability to organize, analyze, and supervise (which make for a fine leader)
- demanding of himself, seeker of high standards
- uncomfortable dealing with finances

Three sections of the Widening Horizons profile are particularly interesting, since they deal with Elvis at midlife. Under "Re-evaluating Your Material Freedom," we find this advice:

Sometime in the middle of your life, most likely between the ages of thirty-five and fifty, you'll probably re-evaluate the satisfactions you've obtained with the material freedom and power which you've achieved. At that time, you'll probably focus on your current work and the potential you see for further development. You're likely to evaluate your career in terms of future financial and status possibilities. Because of this midlife appraisal, it wouldn't be surprising if you make some important alterations in your attitudes and actions in regard to your career in order to achieve greater satisfaction.

Under "Your Current Balanced Concern with Material Achievement," we discover:

The strain involved in striving for money, status, and success is likely to be substantially diminished with your current name. Although you are probably still interested in these matters, chances are that you have a better sense of proportion about them. You can now work on your material needs with considerable ease. You'll have far more pleasure from your accomplishments and advance a good deal further with a more reasonable expenditure of energy.

Finally, under "Your Current Feelings of Restriction," we read:

With your current name, you may feel boxed in and unable to change your course to a more productive direction. If you rationalize your uncomfortable position, your predicament isn't likely to change. Instead of accepting much needed help, you're apt to feel that friends who offer constructive comments don't understand the situation. The solution to your feeling of limitation often involves revising your viewpoint and adopting a lighter, more flexible approach. It will probably take a lot of effort to change your way of seeing things, but that is likely to be the best—possibly the only—way to ease your difficulties. If you choose not to change, or if you are lazy and indifferent, the pressures may intensify.

One cannot discuss Elvis and numerology without discussing astrology, the influence of the stars and planets on human affairs. The following letter, from "the King" himself, has been on display at the Million Dollar Museum in Memphis. Elvis entitles it, simply, "Astrology":

It is designed so as to expose the ultimate in height and depth. To relate the strength and weaknesses of those who are willing to accept and are seeking a closer relationship with the Divine. In order to recognize and correct one's faults and be in step. To be capable of understanding the necessity of the changing times. To participate, to create, to express, to appreciate, and to more fully understand his individual role in reaching the divine God. For man to more fully understand and to determine his own destiny. *The realization that divine God is life itself.* Upon being able to accept one's faults and weaknesses. To correct them in order to have a better understanding and to be capable of giving love and help to other human beings regardless of color or creed. To appreciate all people. The breaking down of barriers and recognizing individual traits. To be sincere in having the desire to show gratitude and appreciation for that which each individual has given to the world. You create a better understanding for yourself of life and the part you yourself and others play in this world. You are soon recognizing a brighter light within yourself. The sharing of that light with others and feeling the importance of stressing and/or distributing the love and will of God. For Christ, who gave life and hope and faith to the millions of people who have accepted his sacrifice and ray of life. He taught the love of God and the importance for the love of one another by keeping always the importance of expressing gratitude and respect for the greatest miracle of all—life itself!

It is always saddening to discover that much of what man does not understand he ridicules. So goes it with astrology and numerology, as we see at times with the book *What Does Joan Say?: My Seven Years as White House Astrologer to Nancy and Ronald Reagan,* by Joan Quigley (New York: Birch Lane Press, 1990).

I view it as ignorant *not* to use all that the universe offers in the making of decisions that could indeed affect not only the universe but one's personal life. Historians prove that more than one of our U.S. presidents used numerology and astrology as guides. Great philosophers and thinkers have used them as well. I have no doubt that there is proof that the moon affects mankind (moon = luna/tic). Ask any physician or policeman about the full moon and hemorrhaging and crime. This alone should make one think and investigate the possibilities. (I know many outward skeptics who read their horoscopes—which is why people such as Jeane Dixon are read by millions.)

Elvis Presley also understood.

However, we are entering a new age. Nancy R., of Carrollton, Texas, asked me if I knew that on August 17, 1987, the "Harmonic Convergence" took place, in which people all over the world celebrated the Coming of the New Age. "The day before [a decade earlier]—August 16, 1977—was when Elvis Presley potentially calculated his death date...Syncronicity?" asks Nancy.

We are also today on the threshold of the second millennium, said to usher in a thousand years of peace.

Teachers such as Joan Quigley can only smile and remain patient. Like a benevolent parent toward an unlearned child, they have to pull back and allow the child its continual crawl until "it dares" to walk. How childish remains so much of mankind that I often wonder how those who have mastered keep their good humor and patience. But, they *know*. . . .

Astrologically, August 16, 1977, was one of Elvis' most favorable days. Keep that in mind.

Another letter, from Debbie C., of Jackson, Tennessee, offered an astrological profile on Elvis Aron Presley. She pointed out fifty-four characteristics of people born between December 21 and January 19, Capricorns. Many of the characteristics do seem to describe Elvis: "ambitious," "inspires confidence and trust," "wins people over by charm," "tries to be fair-minded," "is generous with money," "goes out of his way to help someone in trouble," "gives way to depressed feelings," "likes prestige," "not afraid of hard work," "enjoys his home," "fond of music," "emotions run deep," "begins relationships with women by first being friends" . . .

Debbie goes, further, into the characteristics of individuals of the number eight:

- deep and very intense natures
- much misunderstood in life and intensely lonely at heart
- great strength of individuality
- generally play some important role on life's stage but one that is fatalistic
- fanatics in their zeal

- warm hearts toward the oppressed of all classes
- no happy medium, they are either great successes or great failures
- if ambitious they generally aim for public life, which involves great sacrifice
- are often called on to face the very greatest sorrows, losses, and humiliations
- represent two worlds, spiritual and material
- after their death, their work is praised and lasting tributes are offered to their memory.

He therefore entered his career in the month of the sun and left it in the month of the sun.

How amazing that a giant pyramid is now being built in Memphis, Tennessee, an $80 million shrine to the king of rock 'n' roll, where there will be a special Elvis section with a jukebox playing all of Elvis' No. 1 hits. The pyramid is scheduled to open in May 1991.

OPEN MINDS NOT AFRAID OF EMBRACING THE SECRETS OF THE UNIVERSE also accept the truth that there is more to man than the five physical senses, that indeed man has a sixth sense/psychic sense/intuition – whatever translation is comfortable. As numerology and astrology go hand-in-hand, thus do other ideas such as astral projection, psychic energy, the power of the pyramids, and so on. Elvis particularly felt a connection with the ancient capital of Egypt, Memphis, and he felt it was his destiny to play such an important role in Memphis, Tennessee. The sun figure plays a prominent role in Egyptology. The sun played an important role in Elvis' life: He recorded his first record at Sun Studios in August, the month of the sun. In 1977, the "sundial" suit was the only suit Elvis wore for his last two tours. Not long after, again in the month of the sun, Elvis made his exit.

Priscilla Presley has said: "People put him in a place he could not live up to; they just didn't understand that he wasn't a god – he was a man." However, according to Dr. Robert H. Crumby, of Nashville's Donelson Presbyterian Church: "It's not unusual that Elvis would be deified. The Romans made gods of their emperors, and great generals have been exalted. I think the loyal fans became enamored of Elvis long before they realized he had imperfections."

The cover of my novel, *Orion,* reads: ". . .When a man didn't

want to be a god anymore." And from that book, just before the singer "left the world":

> "The worst sin you've ever committed was to believe you held a monopoly on morality. You're human, Orion. And you've made a lot of mistakes, one *hell* of a lot. But that was yesterday. Forgive yourself, and say, 'I'm not such a bastard after all. I'm a man, not a god. I have every right to make mistakes. Let the gods lament and chastise themselves. I made mistakes yesterday, and I'll make more tomorrow. But that's okay. Because I am a man!'"
> "I am a man," Orion murmured.

From my own personal knowledge of the fans, most of them do not worship Elvis as they worship God but, rather, worship or are drawn to the "God-likeness" exuded by Elvis – the "Love" or "Light" or "Energy" – and God = Love.

Still, Elvis was (and is) a man. There are some theologians who fault Elvis for his loving nature, his charisma, as though he were the devil in disguise. Elvis did not ask for this worship, and those who give it do not fully understand why they are relating to him so profoundly. If they could simply accept his loving nature as a guide and use it to do good, rather than use it to imprison him, then what he gives would multiply a thousandfold over.

I have no problem accepting that Elvis was and will always be a special light in the universe – a gift from God. Yet I also know that there is a part of God in all (or most) of us. I know that when I created *Orion* I felt what Elvis must have suffered. In the following extract from the book, young Orion, with his childhood friend, Tuck, discuss their place in the universe. Here, Orion first voices his desire to be something special, or out of the ordinary, like the sun. When Tuck reminds him that the sun is just a star, Orion replies:

> "But it's not *just a star,*' Tuck! That's what I am trying to tell you. The sun is the king of stars. It's the grandest star of all, and its light is brighter and warmer. . . ."
> Tuck tried to comprehend what Orion was attempting to explain but his meaning was elusive. "So?"
> "So if a star burns out nobody much cares because there are so many more million stars burning and there are more being born. But if the sun burns out, well then, *everybody* notices. Even in an eclipse, when the sun is only black for a moment, people take notice and they worry. If the sun would die the whole universe would mourn." Orion lowered his eyes, pondering what he had said. Never had he become so deeply involved with life nor so anguished, and

even though he was only ten a sense of time and death took hold, a panic-stricken feeling that he was in a race with life itself.

More and more puzzled, Tuck said, "I don't know whether I would want that kind of responsibility. When the sun sets everyone expects it to rise in the morning. That's an awful responsibility, an awful lonely burden." Tuck shook his head. "No, Orion, if that's what you mean by being "something special", I wouldn't want no part of it. I'd rather be out there with all the other stars in the universe, shining when I want to shine, resting when I want to rest, with nobody expecting nothing of me."

Orion flushed with embarrassment. Who was he anyway to even dream of being the sun, the king of stars? He was as common as the moss he sat on. Reaching for the picnic basket, Orion wondered why his mama was constantly telling him, "Someday you'll be something special, Orion Eckley Darnell. You was born for it as sure as the sun rises and sets. God told me you was 'special' and you'll see – someday, you'll see."

Handing Tuck a slice of corn bread and a piece of sausage, Orion murmured, "I think every man should at least try to be the sun, even for a day – just to see what it's like."

Tuck broke off a corner of the bread and began chewing slowly. Orion was strange and complicated at times, but as Tuck looked at his friend's face, he now found it totally uncomplicated and serene. For a fleeting moment a thought took hold of Tuck: *Was it possible to be the king of stars for a day, and then return to being a common light in the universe?*

Further evidence of Elvis' psychic vibrations was brought out in a 1988 documented television interview on Las Vegas' *Billy Goodman* Show.* Goodman was spotlighting Brian Corelone:

B.G.   I'm Bill Goodman, I welcome you to the story behind the story. Today we're going to look into the possibility of Elvis Presley being alive. Some folks in Kalamazoo, Michigan, claim they have seen him driving around in a red Ferrari and with us is Brian Corelone, who is the Director of the Institute of Parapsychology in Las Vegas. Brian, you've met Elvis Presley and you were with him more than once. How about telling when you first met him, and the last time you saw him before his death.
B.C.:   Well, the first time I met Elvis was at a school dance. I was going to a private school with, I don't remember if it was his godson or nephew or something like that. Anyway, this classmate had said that Elvis might pop in to offer the graduating class his congratulations. And we were all out in the [inaudible] end of the ballroom waiting for him, and he did show up and when I shook hands with him, I was amazed at the . . . I

*For information on ordering a copy of the interview, contact RJD, P.O. Box 12239, Las Vegas, NV 89112.

mean people have described his personality as being electric and there really was some sort of electricity that felt, like, coming off of him. Then the last time I saw him was several years later at the Hilton, and I was as close to him as I am to you and the scarves that he used to throw at the audience were going over my head. And I felt that same charisma or electricity or vibration or whatever you want to call it. I've never felt since then anybody with such unique and dynamic vibrations.

B.G.:   What do you attribute that to?

B.C.:   Well, of course the first time I met him I had not really been into parapsychology as deeply as I am now. The only thing I can figure is, the man had a great deal of wonderful karma; he had so much within him that was dying to get out. I had once heard somebody say that, if Elvis Presley had ever really let go of everything that he had within him, there wouldn't have been billboards big enough or lights bright enough. And from what I felt coming off of him, I agree.

B.G.:   Repeat that again, people were saying that there wouldn't be lights bright enough if he were to give off his total energy.

B.C.:   Right. Very often he held a lot of his dynamicness (if that's the word) in. I never felt like he was really letting go, even with all the movement on stage there was something restrained in him.

B.G.:   So there was something different about these vibrations. They were so intense you would never forget them.

B.C.:   They were unmistakable and unforgettable.

B.G.:   Now, Brian, there came a time when a real ardent Elvis Presley fan asked you to go to Graceland to see for yourself because of your parapsychology background. To see if in fact, he was in that grave.

B.C.:   Well, she mainly wanted me to try to communicate with Elvis. Since the announcement of his death, I'd been invited to preside over several dark rooms, which is like a séance. Elvis is one of the few people I've never been able to raise. I was curious about that. She was frustrated about it, because usually she was the one who has to talk to Elvis in the dark rooms. So, we flew to Graceland, went on the tour, nobody knew who we were, just a couple hick tourists. When we went past the gravesite, I felt absolutely nothing. Now, part of my training in parapsychology was being taken through cemeteries. My teacher at the time was Richard King, and he'd point to a grave and say, "Tell me about the person buried here." He did this with maybe three to five hundred graves. I never really kept tab. One time he said, "Tell me what you feel from this one?" I felt nothing. As it turned out, it was a mock grave that had been used for a movie that had been filmed there, and there was never really anybody buried there. I felt that same nothingness from Elvis' grave.

B.G.:   Let's go back now. The vibrations you felt when he was alive at the Hilton. Would they have still been there with the body dead, as a dead body? I don't know anything about the vibrations.

B.C.:   The characteristics of the vibrations would have been the same. But the intensity would have been far less.

B.G.:   And they were not there.

B.C.:   Nothing.

B.G.:   Nothing.

B.C.:   I may as well have been standing in front of a hatbox.

B.G.:   So you can unequivocally say, as far as you're concerned, Elvis Presley's body was not in that grave.

B.C.:   Not a body as it was presented in the news: the human form in the glass-lidded coffin. If Elvis is in that grave in my opinion, either the body was later cremated or they must have put it in a lead casing, because lead is the only thing that will cut out any knd of electrical frequency. Human vibrations are a form of electricity.

B.G.:   So you're saying, once again, that unless he was encased in lead, or cremated, he definitely was not in that grave.

B.C.:   I tend to believe that he isn't in that grave.

B.G.:   Felt no vibrations.

B.C.:   Nothing whatsoever.

B.G.:   Did you at anytime feel any of his vibrations on the property at Graceland?

B.C.:   Yes, when we went on the tour of the mansion itself. There are doors that lead to what was known as the family wing. This is a part of the mansion reserved for the family and the caretakers and so on. The public was not admitted there. As we walked past those doors, I suddenly could not move. I was literally paralyzed with fear, because I felt the same vibrations I had felt when I shook hands with him, and when I saw him at the Hilton. I felt those exact same vibrations at the same intensity level, coming from the other side of those doors.

B.G.:   So, if I'm hearing you correctly, that means as far as you're concerned he was alive behind those doors. If it's the same intensity, and you only feel the same vibrations when they are alive, and they were the same.

B.C.:   Yes.

B.G.:   Then he was behind those doors as far as you're concerned.

B.C.:   He was alive in some sense. Now, I've heard a lot of people theorize that he was not dead when they found him, that he was in a coma, and that maybe he's on life-support systems, behind those doors. If that's the case, that would explain the intensity of the vibrations, because the consciousness of the soul, in the living being, is coupled with the life force – which gives off a double intensity of vibrations. When a person crosses over or dies, whatever you want to call it, the life force is no longer there. Only the consciousness. And without the life force to give it that extra energy, the intensity drops.

B.G.:   I understand that. But you're also saying that no matter what condition the body was in, he was alive.

B:C.:   Yes.

B.G.:   Behind those doors. Now, how many years ago was that?

B.C.:   That was about six years ago. Five or six years ago.

B.G.:   So six years ago, the man could still have been in a coma, could have been anywhere. But the vibrations were there and he was alive.

B.C.:   Yes.

B.G.:   And more recently he has been spotted in Kalamazoo, Michigan.

B.C.:   Right.

B.G.:   It's really becoming more and more fascinating with this man. You also mention the fact that you could not reach him during the dark room on the other side. Is that correct?

B.C.:   Right. Right, I have been asked to contact Mae West, W. C. Fields, some of the real old-timers, and they've always come through. But Elvis Presley. . . nothing comes through with Elvis Presley.

B.G.:   That's amazing, isn't it. Either he's not there or he doesn't want to come here.

B.C.:   Right. A spirit has the same thought patterns – if you want to call them that – as a living person. If a lot of living people don't want to be bothered on the telephone, they don't pick it up. If a spirit doesn't want to be bothered, it's not going to respond. I tend to believe that Elvis has not crossed over.

B.G.:   Which simply means that he's alive. Let's get right down to it.

B.C.:   In one form or another.

B.G.:   Right. He is laid up in a hospital bed or something of that nature, but alive.

B.C.:   Right, yes.

B.G.:   He could even be driving around in that red Ferrari.

B.C.:   Very possible.

B.G.:   Very possible. Brian Corelone is the Director of the Institute of Parapsychology, trained in this. He has no trouble reaching people on the other side. He cannot reach Elvis Presley on the other side. You did say one thing to me, Brian, and I think we should bring it up, that there's a middle place there too, which you never wanted to get involved with when you felt those vibrations down there at Graceland. You thought he could actually pull you through the door.

B.C.:   Yes. I felt like if I had reached out, he would have been able to grab hold of me.

B.G.:   And you wouldn't be here today.

B.C.:   Well, if he was on the other side – I tended to believe that that was his spirit – he could have sucked me right through the veil.

B.G.:   Ladies and gentlemen, you have heard it. Right here, on the story, behind the story, Elvis Presley could be alive. Brian, thank you very much for coming by.

B.C.:   Thank you.

B.G.:   And for enlightening us. And, boy, one question. Do you want to see him come back?

B.C.:   I would like to just know he's somewhere, and that he's happy and he's at peace with himself.

B.G.:   Do you think he would come back?

B.C.:   That's something only *he* could answer. I don't think so, though.

B.G.:   Let's leave it up to him.

B.C.:   Yeah.
B.G.:   "The King" himself.

In the journal *Tennessee Illustrated* of July/August 1989, the following appeared. It was entitled "Mere Coincidence?"

Just before Elvis died, he was reportedly reading a book entitled *A Scientific Search for the Face of Jesus,* whose subject was the Shroud of Turin.

In Hebrew the word *El* means God, and the Latin translation for *vis* is power. Each of Elvis's three primary homes contains *el* in its name—Tup*el*o, Grac*el*and, and B*el* Air, California.

Before becoming Elvis's Memphis residence, Graceland was a bona fide place of worship—Graceland Christian Church.*

According to one account, on the night Elvis died the lights in Graceland's Meditation Gardens inexplicably went out.

The month, day, and year of Elvis's death (8/16/77) add up to 2001, as do the day he was born (8), the day he died (16), his age at death (42), and the year of his birth (1935).

What's more, Elvis used the theme music from the film *2001: A Space Odyssey* as his introductory fanfare late in his career. That music was taken from Richard Strauss' tone poem *Also sprach Zarathustra,* which is based on a work by Nietzsche portraying the struggle of a mortal man to become a godlike superman.

Elvis has been called a "musical Messiah." Those psychics who believe Elvis to be alive—and there are many—declare that Elvis will soon resurface as a spiritual leader—that it was Elvis' deep spirituality that made him fake his death so that he would have the time and freedom to look deep within himself. The pulpit, the psychics believe, will be his new stage—he will lead a religious revival, teaching the truths he has learned, his magnetism drawing millions to him—in a good way, bringing them closer to God.

In 1990, the song "Black Velvet" hit the charts. Part of its lyrics ran: "Up in Memphis the music's like a heat wave. . . 'Love Me Tender' leaves 'em crying in the aisles, The way he moved, it was a sin. . ." The song is videoed in two versions, one by Alannah Myles, the second by Robin Lee, both of Atlantic Records, both focusing on Elvis Presley—and a new religion that will bring you to your knees. (The Robin Lee version ends with a shot of

---

*In 1989, Graceland purchased the Graceland Christian Church, located north of the mansion on 4.2 acres.

Graceland with boulder-like stones proclaiming, "Elvis Lives" and "Elvis Is Alive.")

Soon after came a letter from D'Lores G., of Olgilvie, Maryland, about the song/album:

> I haven't noticed anyone else writing to you about CMT videos, but the Elvis themes seem to be increasing, just as in every other area – movies, TV, etc. Up until now, I haven't thought too much about it, but the other night when I saw the video by Robin Lee of "Black Velvet," I really took notice of it. There seem to be a wealth of "messages" in that video. The lyrics themselves tell Elvis' story, but the line that really threw me was "a new religion that will bring you to your knees." What on earth is *that* supposed to mean??? Is someone trying to tell us that Elvis is a preacher? The video shows us not once, but *twice*, on the *stones* that "Elvis Lives"!! . . . I also noticed how much Robin Lee resembles Priscilla. Among the many things in the video that pertain to Elvis, there is the shot of Graceland, the Harley Davidson (license #10 0382; the state was too hard to read, but the name looked long . . . like it could read "Tennessee"); there's also the little boy on the porch of an old house – he looks to be about seven. . . . There's the "Elvis Aron Presley" plaque, a light *blue* Cadillac, instead of pink, and an old rundown alley. There's something about that empty Cadillac sitting in the alley. . . . There's nobody in it (like the grave?). And at the end of the video, the rider picks up the girl and just rides away, past the car, and doesn't look back! Doesn't all of this sound familiar? Even listening to the song without seeing the video, there's no way you wouldn't know it's about Elvis, even though his name is never mentioned (unless the person is from another planet!).

ELVIS SAID THAT PEOPLE NEVER LISTENED TO HIM, NEVER LISTENED TO the *lyrics* of his songs. Many have made mention of the song "Way Down" from the "Moody Blue" album – "Way Down" being Elvis' last No. 1 single. It was recorded at Graceland toward the end of his career, with the following credits listed on the record label: "Executive Producer: Elvis Presley."

The number AFL1-2428 on the back of the album has been puzzled over. The first number, 1, refers to the cut; the second, 2, to the side. "Do the 42 and the 8 signify forty-two years of age, eighth month?" one fan has asked. However, it was Elvis' change of the original lyrics written by L. Martine to "Fate is growing closer, and look at my resistance, found lying on the floor, taking me to places that I've never been before" that raised eyebrows. When he was asked about the change of the lyrics in "Way Down," Elvis replied, "Man, it just sounds better, it just sounds better. . ."

Others wonder, however, if this was a clue, whether perhaps Elvis already *knew* he would probably die of a heart attack and that his body would be found on the floor. A stretch of the imagination, maybe?

No. 7

The Mystery Tape

In music one must think with the heart and feel with the brain.
— GEORGE SZELL

Question: Is the voice on the tape with the book *Is Elvis Alive? really* Elvis'?
Answer: According to voice experts, the voice on the tape with the book *Is Elvis Alive?* and the voice of known interviews with Elvis Presley are "one and the same."

The following commentary by Gregory Sandow appeared in the *Los Angeles Herald Examiner* on Sunday, October 9, 1988:

Don't look at *me*: I don't know if Elvis is alive. But "The Elvis Tape" (included with Gail Brewer-Giorgio's breathless book *Is Elvis Alive?*) has to be pretty damn uncanny.

It's billed as Elvis, speaking a few years after — as we're supposed to believe — he faked his death. I guess I thought it would sound too dim to rank even as implausible. But not so. It's clear enough to draw qualified approval from a voiceprint expert, and easily clear enough for *me* to tell you that . . . well, it *could* be Elvis. Whoever's speaking hesitates just the way Elvis used to; that's what gets me.

What's Elvis supposed to be doing? You'll have to hear the tape yourself, but a short answer might be that he's thinking things through. And that's another reason not to toss the tape away. Would anyone faking this have resurrected an Elvis who sounds so unsure of himself?

In *DISCoveries* magazine, in December of the same year, appeared an item entitled "THE ELVIS TAPE: CON OR CONVINCING," written by Prewitt Rose, of Jamesport, New York:

> I recently bought the paperback *Is Elvis Alive?* by Gail Brewer-Giorgio, which included "The Elvis Tape." I wasn't very impressed by Gail's ramblings in her book, but the Elvis tape is an entirely different story. The voice on the tape is the voice of Elvis Presley. End of conversation!
>
> Did Elvis Presley actually die on August 16, 1977? He surely could have, but if he did then die, that would make me wrong about the voice on the tape.
>
> If the voice on the tape is not Presley's, then it is an absolutely perfect imitation, but such letter-perfect voice imitations have yet to be performed, so the burden of proof regarding the tape has to lie with those who say the tape is a fake. The voice on the tape is Presley's until somebody comes up with the guy who faked it.
>
> In my opinion, it would be much more difficult to fake the tape than it would be to fake a death. Maybe a person would have to be involved in recording to really understand just how difficult faking such a tape would be, but I'm not going into any detail about the tape. I have absolutely no question in mind about whose voice is on the Elvis tape. It is the voice of Elvis Presley.

The tape with *Is Elvis Alive?* was voice-authenticated by an expert with a major law enforcement agency in Texas; the Watergate methods were, in fact, used. The spectrographs are available on the video *Breakthrough* and have been available for perusing by anyone in doubt. The conclusion of the first official report states that "there is data indicating that the unknown and known speakers are the same with a moderate level of confidence."

These were the results of comparing the Mystery Tape (with *Is Elvis Alive?*) and known interviews with Elvis Presley. On the video the expert states that the voice on the tape and the known voice of Elvis Presley are "one and the same."

Taking into consideration the poor quality of the tape, since the original has never surfaced, and the fact that the one I had authenticated is many generations down, we were heading into the wind trying to get a definitive report. Still, the report stands, and until I see another that disputes mine I'll go with the one I have. Whenever I've been on talk shows, I've always stated, up front, that the tape is there for anyone to have officially voice-authenticated by a top expert—as I had done. If the experts dis-

agree, then they can have a "voice shoot-out at the O.K. corral."
At least one radio station took me up on the offer and contacted
two voice experts, whom they brought on air with me, this in
Michigan. The bottom line is: They basically concurred with the
report (by L. H. Williams).

Was the tape edited? Yes, in the sense that whoever the voice
was talking to was over the telephone; that voice was edited out
for whatever reasons – but not by me. It may have been done
when copying the original, in order that someone "in the know"
would not be involved in a cover-up conspiracy. The tape was sent
to a second expert, audio engineer Don Moran, of L.T.L. Enterprises; his report is also in *Is Elvis Alive?* The expert states that by
checking voice stress and background noise, the tape was not
edited from interviews. The conclusion of Mr. Moran's report:
"The tape is not a product of one or more interviews being edited
together, word by word. Simply, these sentences were spoken as
sentences, and if the voice print is true, then these were sentences
and topics spoken in their entirety by Elvis Presley."

Moran further concluded that because of the consistency of
the background noise it may be a product of poor recording
technique, "perhaps a suction cup microphone on telephone." He
states that the "noise by itself is proof that no editing was done
within sentences or topics."

Both pages-long reports are printed in total in *Is Elvis Alive?*

Although I did not gather a group of people in a room, ask
them to listen to the tape and take a poll in order to present a
report, the majority of mail I've received – thousands and thousands of letters – agrees it is Elvis Presley speaking. Some letters
have appeared in other publications such as *Elvis World*. It was entitled "Is Elvis Alive?" and came from a Peter Butler, in Denmark:

> I've heard fake tapes before and was really looking forward to pull-
> ing this one apart. I had a bloody pen and paper here to list all the
> faults as they came up. As soon as "Elvis" spoke those first words
> about where he's living, I very nearly hit the floor. It IS him!! Almost
> everything said by him pointed to his being alive in 1980-81. I've
> heard all the other fakes. I had never believed it possible that Elvis
> still lived in this world. I now strongly believe he is the man talking
> on this tape and that it dates from after 1977. Still, I'm not going all
> the way.

In my office are many letters that show how difficult it is for
some fans to voice their feelings that Elvis is alive, for fear of be-

ing laughed at. An extract from one 1989 letter must remain anonymous:

> Priscilla Presley said in an interview on National Television, when she was asked if that was Elvis Presley's voice on the Elvis Tape, that it was Elvis' voice on the tape; then she said that was just old past interviews spliced together. . . .
> I just can't believe that statement she made, because on the Elvis Tape, Elvis is talking about his life after August 16, 1977. I have listened to the tape and it truly sounds like Elvis Presley to me. I hope I'm not wrong.

In his syndicated column in the *Chicago Tribune* on May 3, 1988, writer Bob Greene admitted to writing too many articles about Elvis and suggested that my new book cited him as a believer that Elvis was alive. He mentioned the casket picture of a "pug-nosed" Elvis that was sold to the *National Enquirer* and quoted from the Mystery Tape. His tongue-in-cheek article, entitled "Funny, He Never Looked Jewish," went on:

> And every day, people are repeating the rumor. Elvis never died. He's alive. He's living in Michigan. In an old hotel he bought. He hangs out at Wendy's.
> Obviously preposterous. Yet the word is traveling from person to person. The other day my secretary said that a woman – a physician's wife – was on the phone with startling new information about Presley.
> I sighed. I knew what was coming.
> I picked up the phone.
> "I have to tell you the most amazing thing about Elvis," the doctor's wife said.
> "Go ahead," I said.
> "Elvis was Jewish," she said.
> I hesitated for only a moment.
> "*Is* Jewish," I said.

Mr. Greene's remarks engendered a spirited reply in a letter sent to the *Chicago Tribune* a few days later, by Thomas Sanocki. Among Mr. Sanocki's complaints: "You are *so* wrong. That tape was 'authenticated' by a voice analyst expert and verified as undoubtedly Elvis Presley. . . . [Gail Brewer-Giorgio] did not start the rumors about him being alive; they were started back in 1981, and Gail [then] had no knowledge of the tape."

A second letter from Sanocki to Greene, dated May 14, was even more informative:

> I have some proof besides what Gail has to believe that Elvis is in fact still alive. Back in the early 1980s, around 1981–82, I received many phone calls from a woman named Ellen Foster. Ms. Foster was a close friend of Elvis because she resembled Elvis' mother, Gladys, and Elvis took a fancy to her in 1977. In fact, Elvis was so close to her that he gave Ellen Foster a ring that had belonged to his mother.
>
> Ms. Foster died a couple of years ago, but I have some of the phone conversations on tape, and so does a friend of mine. We started getting phone calls in early 1981, because at the time I was the editor of an Elvis publication from a Chicago-based fan club, and my work was read throughout the Presley world. Ms. Foster told us many times that Elvis was still alive and that he called her on a weekly to biweekly basis. She used to tell us some of the things he told her, and most of the time it was quite fascinating. . . .

There is certainly reason to believe that it may have been Ellen Foster to whom the Elvis voice on the mystery tape was talking. Unable to speak, today, with Ms. Foster, we can only speculate.

FANS HAVE EXCELLENT EARS, PICKING UP ON HOW ELVIS PRONOUNCED – or mispronounced – certain words. In a letter from Carolyn K., of Erie, Pennsylvania, came the following information: "I heard, or read, of [Elvis'] saying, 'No one listens to my songs.' I, for one, listened to his songs, and while I was listening I looked at his face constantly. What a beautiful face! . . . Now let me get to the real reason I wrote you. I don't know if anyone has pointed this out or not: The way Elvis always said 'album' was 'alblum.' On his 'Elvis in Concert' album, side D of a two-record set, he pronounced the word 'alblum' and on the tape that was with your book it was also pronounced 'alblum.' I listened to the tape over and over again, and even had my son listen to it, and he agreed."

Carolyn K. was, of course, right about the mispronunciation on the tape – a mispronunciation made by Elvis Presley in several interviews during his career.

Two other words on the Mystery Tape are also mispronounced: "idea" as "idear." During the March 1960 interview with Elvis when he was discharged from the Army, the word "idea" is also pronounced "idear." Maria Columbus, president of The Elvis Special, said she received a call at work several years after the singer's death from a man sounding like Elvis. He called her "Marear" instead of "Maria"–which is the way Elvis had always pronounced Maria's name. It is reported that Elvis said "hep" instead of "help," at times, which is also on the Mystery Tape.

After reading the official authenticated reports on the tape, the question still remained: When was the tape done? It could have been recorded pre-1977. There are, however, many things said by "Elvis" on the tape that would indicate the message post-dates his "death": *"traveling all over the world"* . . . *"growing beards to keep from being recognized"* . . . *"going out to eat in Wiesbaden [West Germany]"* . . . *"foolish to go back into a life I just escaped from"* . . . *"people finding out"* . . . *"they wouldn't believe it anyway"* . . . *"I'm not completely in hiding"* . . . *"I'm hoping people aren't disappointed in me . . . I didn't mean to put anybody through any pain"* . . . *"I know there's a lot of movies that have come out in the past, the recent past, I haven't enjoyed at all . . . they try to make you a certain way"* . . . *"But just like the drug thing . . . not true"* . . . *"I'm looking forward to possibly seeing some people that are going to be shocked . . . I'm just hoping that these people I'm going to see won't be hurt, but I know they're going to be shocked"* . . . *"I know sometime the secret has got to be let out, and if it hadn't been for getting involved in what I'm involved in now, maybe it'd be different"* . . .

The entire text is published in *Is Elvis Alive?* Some of it (above) is reprinted here for those who didn't read the earlier book.

But there is much – besides Elvis' words – in the tape that does not relate to Elvis' life prior to August 16, 1977:

- Elvis never traveled around the world; the Colonel, his manager, would not allow him to perform outside the United States; during his Army years he was in Germany, did not go out, and only visited Paris briefly.
- During his Army discharge interview, Elvis said he never even went out to eat.
- Elvis was not known for going around wearing a beard.
- *When* did Elvis "escape" from his life?
- People "finding out" *what*? What wouldn't they believe?
- "Not completely in hiding"? He was walking around freely, but not before 1977.
- "Disappointed"? *Why*? Put *who* "through pain," and *why*?
- No movies were made about Elvis pre-1977.
- "The drug thing"? This was not made that public until after 1977, or at the very least only days before, via the book *Elvis: What Happened?*

- *Why* would people be shocked and hurt by seeing him?
- *What* secret?

If you'll peruse the complete text, I am sure you'll discover even more that could not have occurred before August 1977. Let me know your thoughts.

Because of the controversy the tape with *Is Elvis Alive?* caused, five people have claimed to be the "voice." However, when I ask them to be voice-authenticated by the police, they always back off. I most definitely am after the truth, as is Maria Columbus of The Elvis Special. As I mentioned earlier, to date I have no legal opposing reports to those of the voice-authentications published in *Is Elvis Alive?*

Who Is/Was Sivle?

I'll play it first and tell you what it is later.
— MILES DAVIS

Question: Who is/was Sivle Nora?
Answer: According to many who have listened to the singing and speaking voice of the mystery man identified either as "Sivle" or "Sivle Nora" (Elvis Aron spelled backwards), Sivle *is* Elvis Presley.

A man stood up in the audience more than halfway through a February 1989 *Geraldo* show and claimed to be the "voice" on the Mystery Tape I had included with *Is Elvis Alive?* On that show—to which Elvis' friend Joe Esposito, his stepmother Dee Presley, Major Bill Smith,* author Paul Licker, and Elvis Army buddy George Didevinzi, and myself were invited—and later, during a magazine interview with Bill Burk, publisher of *Elvis World* (No. 11, 1989), the man

- described himself as a "psychic entertainer" and later as a "spiritual entertainer"
- said he was paid $125 for a month's work; later, he said he was paid $125 a week for four weeks
- said the "clicks" on the tape occurred when he hit the "pause" button on the tape to gather his thoughts
- said he went into a "psychic trance" in order to bring Elvis' voice through (Then, what about pausing to gather one's thoughts?)

---

*A Fort Worth, Texas, record producer who claims to be an Elvis friend; also producer of platinum/gold hits "Hey, Baby" and "Hey, Paula."

- told Mr. Burk he was offered a million dollars to be the "voice" on the tape (. . .and then settled for $125?)
- said he was hired by the Eternally Elvis Fan Club in Florida (The Eternally Elvis club, presided over by June Poalillo, has never heard of this man – who did not give his real name.)
- showed Geraldo a contract dated 1981 and listing the names of the two men who hired him (Although Geraldo would not give me a copy of the contract, I found out via a Miami TV reporter that the names were "Chanzes" and "Crown.")
- said the background noise was a fan running (The same fan running for a month?)

When I was first invited to be a guest on this same *Geraldo,* by Vicki DeShazo, one of the producers, I agreed to appear under certain conditions:

- that Monte Nicholson, author of *The Presley Arrangement* and an almost twenty-year veteran with the Los Angeles Sheriff's Department, be present (Mr. Nicholson had evidence that Elvis Presley may be alive.)
- that L. H. Williams and other voice experts give their analyses and/or show the videoed spectrographs done on the Mystery Tape
- that Kelly Burgess, former associate editor of the *Detroit News* and current writer for magazines, appear to tell how she met and talked with Elvis Presley in Michigan in August 1988
- that Maria Columbus, president of The Elvis Special, appear to tell about the call she received at work several years after Elvis' death, and relate how Dee Stanley Presley (Elvis' step-mother) told her that she also received a call from someone sounding like Elvis, saying to her things only Elvis knew – this after 1977 (Dee also stated this on the air with me during a *People Are Talking* show in summer 1988 in Secaucus, New Jersey.)
- that the poolhouse pictures be shown, taken four months after Elvis' "death," clearly revealing a man identical to Elvis sitting behind the door to the poolhouse, and that negatives verified by Kodak Video be sent
- that I be able to show government documents and pictures of Elvis in his DEA staff jacket
- that there be no surprises (This, so I could have the proper data in order for proper rebuttal.)

Ms. DeShazo promised. To that end, I spent several days putting together a complete portfolio on each of the above guests, as well as video of the spectrographs and of the poolhouse picture. Thus, Geraldo had an abundance of credible information and credible guests who agreed to appear. Unbeknownst to me, one of the producers of *Geraldo* notified these guests that they were "uninvited." Monte Nicholson went on record and on radio stating that Geraldo's people told him he was "uninvited" because "he was too credible"! Kelly Burgess told me she was also "uninvited" because of being "too credible."

Had I known that I was being betrayed by Geraldo, I would not have appeared – which I am sure was suspected. As it was, I felt tricked. Geraldo tricked the public as well. It would have been difficult to surprise me with a "psychic entertainer" – a Mr. David Darlok or Darlock – had a voice expert from the police been there or had the spectrographs been shown. L. H. Williams told me he had called the show afterwards to see if the man-claiming-to-be-the-voice would be voice-authenticated. I also tracked down the psychic entertainer, but he has refused to talk to me or be voice-authenticated by the police.

Geraldo and his staff did with intent malign the contents of *Is Elvis Alive?*, and did report false information to the viewing public, and did with intent prohibit credible witnesses from presenting their evidence – not on the grounds that the evidence was full of holes but that they (and their evidence) were "too credible."

I felt and still feel that I was invited for one reason: to be the victim of a "bully."

The broadcast was taped in Philadelphia's historic, restored Bourse. Geraldo introduced Joe Esposito as "one of the king's oldest and closest friends, the guy who was at his side when Elvis passed away" and described the show's focus as: "Wanted: Elvis Dead or Alive." After introductions of Dee Presley and Major Bill Smith, I was described as "the next woman over. . . [who] has collected what she thinks are facts that raise questions about the mystery surrounding Elvis Presley." Later, he again referred to me – again indirectly – as "the author of the very controversial book *Is Elvis Alive?* [who] says now that she doesn't claim that Elvis is alive, but her book certainly raises a lot of questions that have led to a lot of speculation about the mystery surrounding his death. And it's also led to Elvis being sighted at the Burger King in Kalamazoo and other places. . ."

Luckily, I had some witnesses of the press with me, and they can attest that I was definitely "set up" and given little opportunity to present my side of it and allow the viewers to make an intelligent judgment.

I have since learned that that particular show received much mail complaining about the treatment extended by "Geraldo Revolver," and, as some letters I received called him: "Morton Downey's twin."

I witnessed Geraldo coddling Joe Esposito and Dee Presley; professional nepotism was apparent. Had Geraldo Rivera been listening, he would have heard Joe Esposito make some interesting comments, such as saying – upon hearing that Elvis had "died"– he was concerned about Lisa and Priscilla back at the house (Priscilla was supposed to be in California) or wondered why Joe said, "Elvis *is* [my italics] a very gentle man . . ." There was much more, but each time I tried to talk I was told to "Hurry, hurry. . . Be quick. . . quick. . ." The end result was, I had less time than the other guests and *I* was supposed to be the featured guest, not the featured victim.

It was an outrageous example of "Let's kill the messenger who brings the news."

After Geraldo's show, many letters of complaint were written, one at least to Bill Burk, editor of *Elvis World*, a fan magazine, regarding his own interview with the psychic entertainer. An extract from a June 1989 letter of Lynn G., of Mansfield, Ohio, to Mr. Burk follows:

> If Mr. Darlok is the voice on "the tape," why did it take him eight years to come forward? Is he really a psychic? It appeared that he was holding something in his hand (taken from his pocket) when he "stopped" Geraldo's watch. A magnet, perhaps? Also, when Ms. Brewer-Giorgio was accused of possible fraud by Geraldo, she offered right then and there to have a voice print done on Mr. Darlok. Has this been done? If it hasn't, why not? What would he have to hide? Has *Elvis World* seen the contract Mr. Darlok signed?

Neither Mr. Burk nor Geraldo has had the psychic entertainer voice-authenticated. Both voice expert L. H. Williams and this writer have tried to make contact with the psychic entertainer. Although I have not been officially allowed to see the contract referred to, the contract seen by Geraldo, I have unofficially viewed it and it appears (if the contract is valid) that Darlok/Darlock is indeed connected in some way with Chanzes and Crown (the two Floridians who released the "Sivle Nora" album, the materials of the Mystery Tape, and – more on this later – the

Eternally Elvis Newsletter). *How,* and *why?* I do not know. However, if this psychic entertainer is Sivle (he says he is not), then he was part of a planned fraud. And always keep in mind that if he is the voice on the tape (sometimes referred to as the "monologue"), then he had to know what was going on long before I had it voice-authenticated—as far back as 1981.

Geraldo in effect accused me of perpetrating a fraud.

How? By asking the same questions that fans and fan clubs have been asking? Had Maria Columbus been present, she would have confirmed that the points I brought out had been asked by her and her club since August 16, 1977. She could also have testified to the fact that I have done everything possible to "get to the truth," and that despite the Mystery Tape's being around since 1981 (she had a copy) I was the only one to go to officials and have it authenticated. Is that fraud?

- Did I change Elvis' name on his grave?
- War it I who persuaded the "not collecting" of insurance, as Monte Nicholson would have verified?
- Was I responsible for the poolhouse picture and its presentation on KCOP as early as 1986?
- Did I voice-authenticate the Mystery Tape?
- Is it I who claim to have seen Elvis Presley since 1977, or am I simply reporting what very credible people (such as Kelly Burgess) have reported?
- Was it I who filled out the medical examiner's report listing the body that was found as 170 pounds?
- Was it I who reported seeing beads of sweat on the body in the coffin?
- Was it I who gave the body in the coffin a pug nose?
- Or did mouth-to-mouth on a rigor-mortised body?
- Was it I who, via ABC's *20/20* show (January 1979) about the death of Elvis Presley, said the following:

> Item #1: No real police investigation was ever made and at nine in the evening of the death, before it was medically or scientifically possible to determine why and how Elvis Presley died, the Memphis Police considered this case closed.
>
> Item #2: Dr. Jerry Francisco said a search was made at Graceland for drugs and there were not any. However, a man who worked for Francisco stated no search was made of the resident nurse's trailor, where all drugs were kept.
>
> Item #3: Stomach contents were destroyed without ever having been analyzed.

Item #4: There was never – ever – a Coroner's Inquest.

Item #5: The Shelby County District Attorney was never officially notified to determine if there were any violations of criminal law.

Item #6: No attempts were ever made – even after the toxicology reports – to find out where Elvis had been getting all the drugs listed.

Item #7: All the photographs taken at the death scene, all notes of the Medical Examiner's investigation, all of the toxicology reports "allegedly" prepared by the Medical Examiner are missing from the official files.

Item #8: Officials of the county government believe there has been a cover-up.

For the record, it was Geraldo Rivera who asked the *20/20* questions – the answers to eight of which are given above – back in 1979, also alleging that Elvis died of a drug overdose. In the book *Unnatural Death,* by Michael M. Baden (with Judith Adler Hennesse; New York: Random House, 1989), Chief Medical Examiner for New York City from 1978 to 1979, stated that Geraldo Rivera consulted him prior to doing the *20/20* exposé. When Dr. Baden said there was room for doubt about Geraldo's claim of a drug overdose concerning Elvis Presley, Geraldo found another doctor who would agree with his claim.

Again, had Maria Columbus been present on *Geraldo* with me, she would have confirmed that Dee Presley had indeed said she received a call from someone sounding like Elvis, saying things only Elvis knew. Instead, on *Geraldo,* Dee denied saying this, despite its being on a taped TV show. Maria had brought up this point on the *Sally Jessy Raphael* show entitled *Is Elvis Alive?* in September 1988.

Along with Maria Columbus, Rick Stanley – stepbrother of Elvis and the son of Dee Presley – was a guest on the show. Maria asked him, "Can I say something? Your mother called me in 1979 and told me that she had received a phone call from a man that she believed to be Elvis Presley." Rick replied: "Mmmmmm. My mother was not around Elvis Presley very much, that very much." Maria continued: "She said that he told her things that only Elvis would have known. And she was extremely upset, and she just called and talked to me. She talked to me about two hours."

Maria also told about the call she, herself, received:

M.C.: I received a phone call in 1981 while I was at work, and it was very brief. He just – He didn't say that he was Elvis Presley, but he said, "You do know who this is, don't you?" And he pronounced my name like Elvis did when I had talked to him in 1969.

S.J.R.:   You had talked to Elvis in '69. How had he pronounced your name?

M.C.:   He pronounced it "Mareer."

S.J.R.:   Mareer?

M.C.:   Yes. Put an "r" on it, on the end of it.

S.J.R.:   And this person who called you in '81—

M.C.:   Did the same thing, yes.

S.J.R.:   What did he want, why did he call you?

M.C.:   He knew about our fan club and that we had been making comments in the newsletters about Elvis' death, and that he appreciated our comments and he wanted to call and say hello, and that he would be keeping in touch and to keep on going.

S.J.R.:   Now, do you believe Elizabeth's [a guest on the show] story?

M.C.:   I think it's very plausible.

S.J.R.:   You do? All right. We said we had some proof that people have given us. Let's take a look first at a picture of Elvis. And who would like to explain what this is. Maria, you?

M.C.:   Yes. This was taken, I believe it was late December of '77.

S.J.R.:   And what are we lookng at?

M.C.:   That's the door that overlooks the swimming area on the back of Graceland. And—

S.J.R.:   There is a close-up of that. What are we supposed to be seeing?

M.C.:   It was taken by a fan who had gone to Graceland to pay his respects and go by the gravesite. And he had taken about twelve or thirteen pictures, and—

S.J.R.:   That was the outline of the shadow of Elvis' face in the bottom of the screen door that leads to the pool, correct?

M.C.:   Right. Overlooking the pool area.

S.J.R.:   All right, now, here is a voice tape supposedly that Elvis made in what year?

M.C.:   Nineteen eighty-one.

S.J.R.:   Nineteen eighty-one. If we could ask our director, Kit Carson, to put that up.

At this point, the Mystery Tape was put on, and listeners heard: "After about a year I started missing people and entertaining. And I been entertaining people the better part of my life, and it's very hard to stop from doing something that you've been doing that long. It's been a constant battle of growing beards and this and that, to keep from being recognized."

S.J.R.:   All right. And the last piece of proof is from the newspaper, is it? This is a picture supposedly— Do you have it with you?

M.C.:   Yeah.

S.J.R.:   Could I ask that you hold it up? All right. There is a picture of the *National Enquirer.* What date is it, do you know?

M.C.:   The date of the *Enquirer* is September 6, 1977.

S.J.R.:   All right. Now, that's supposedly his picture. And what does that

tell us, the last picture? Maria?
M.C.:   I don't think it looks like Elvis.
S.J.R.:   You say it was not him.
M.C.:   The nose is different.
S.J.R.:   That's not his face.
M.C.:   Yeah. Oops.
S.J.R.:   All right there. Closeup.
M.C.:   This was taken by a family member, Billy Mann.

I would be remiss in not relating why I was not on the *Sally Jessy Raphael* show. I was invited to appear and said I would try to be there, but that my brother was critically ill and dying. They said they understood, and they sent flowers. I later telegrammed them that I definitely could not appear. Their return telegram to me read: "Dear Gail, Our prayers are with you. . . ."

However, fully aware of my family crisis, on the September airing, Ms. Raphael announced: "Now, there is a woman who has written a book that is a bestseller. We did ask her to come on; she would not." Rick Stanley spoke up: "We know why. . . . Because I'm sitting here. . .Charlie [Hodge, a friend of Elvis'] is sitting here, and we were there, and we buried the man. But let me tell you something: We wish he was alive, okay? We wish he was, but he's not."

Although the above interchanges would appear to indicate that I was afraid to be on the show, my family responsibilities prevented it; and I have since been on the air twice – with Joe Esposito, Dee Presley, and others.

CHANZES AND CROWN WERE NAMES MENTIONED EARLIER IN THE contract connected with Darlok/Darlock, the psychic entertainer. I have never met either man, nor did I receive any tapes from them; and in fact never knew of their existence until some years ago via Maria Columbus, who, although not knowing the entire story, had more insight than I. The story is intriguing, confusing, and – in the final analysis dead-end. But here goes:

• Around 1981, two men from Florida, Steven Chanzes and Steve Crown, put out a newsletter/magazine called *Eternally Elvis,* several issues translating the text of the Mystery Tape, which they titled: "Sivle's Monologue."
• Also described via *Eternally Elvis* (not to be confused with the Eternally Elvis TCB Fan Club in Florida) is an interview of Bill Payne, Station KTFX in Tulsa, Oklahoma, with Sivle Nora (Elvis Aron spelled backwards).

- There is no doubt that Mr. Chanzes was saying Sivle Nora was Elvis Presley.
- In 1981, the book *Elvis: Where Are You?* was published by Steven Chanzes by Direct Products, Inc., and in conjunction with Eternally Elvis, Inc. (521 N.E. 26th St., Wilton Manors, FL 33305). *Elvis: Where Are You?* asks the question: Is Elvis Alive? and is presented in two parts: the first being Mr. Chanzes' analysis; the second part, a fictitious scenario. The book was advertised for sale by Eternally Elvis, Inc., at an address of 781 W. Oakland Park Blvd., Ft. Lauderdale, FL 33311, for $8.95. (As we see, the company kept moving!)
- Chanzes and Crown also put out the album "Sivle Sings Again – Do You Know Who I Am?", with ten songs. Sivle sounds like Elvis. The "voice" is only accompanied by a guitar; most of the songs were songs Elvis Presley recorded; thus, one could reason: If it's Elvis, the songs could have been recorded pre-1977 and are bootleg or something of that nature. However, "I Love a Rainy Night" – the Eddie Rabbit hit – reportedly was not written until *after* 1977. In addition, during the singing of "Loving You," Sivle pauses and says, "Wait a minute, man, wait a minute – hold it, hold it. Somebody – somebody just told me that, ah, that President Reagan and some other people have been shot. I'd just like to say that I hope they're not hurt badly." President Reagan was not shot until March 1981.

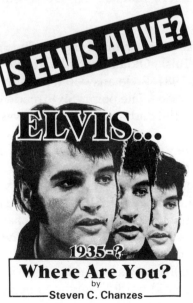

(The songs included on the album "Sivle Sings Again" were: "Do You Know Who I Am?", "Reconsider, Baby," "Are You Lonesome Tonight?", "Blue Christmas," "If That Isn't Love," "Hawaiian Wedding Song," "I'm So Lonesome I Could Cry," "That's All Right, Mama," "Loving You," and "I Love a Rainy Night.")

Chanzes and Crown's issue No. 2 of their *Eternally Elvis* fan newsletter discusses when Steve Crown first met the mysterious Sivle Nora. He says this meeting occurred on Friday, May 29, 1981. There is little doubt expressed in the *Eternally Elvis* newsletter that Crown suggests Sivle Nora is and/or was Elvis Presley. Among the points made:

• It was a shock to see him.
• He asked what he Sivle had been doing the last four years (alluding to 1977, the year Elvis "died").
• He tells how they put Sivle in touch with Lynn Seman of WBAL Radio, Baltimore, Seman being interested in doing an "Is Elvis Alive?" interview–this long before my book came into existence.
• Sivle told Seman how he would like to do a medley of songs, some old ones; then he sings "Are You Lonesome Tonight?"–which sends Seman into shock.
• Crown and Chanzes then took Sivle to a restaurant, where on a jukebox they played Elvis' "Guitar Man," Sivle giving one of his "famous sneers" and asking, "Do you think that guy can make it?"

Prior to all this, Steve Chanzes had put Sivle in touch with Bill Payne, of KTFX, Tulsa, Oklahoma, a live radio interview taking place on May 16, 1981. Sivle answered questions posed by both Payne and the audience. The points Sivle made were a deliberate attempt at making the audience believe he was Elvis:

• He said he would like to record again, in order to give something back to the people who had given so much to him.
• He neither confirmed nor denied that he was Elvis Presley.
• He said that he enjoyed singing gospel music best.
• He admitted that there had been a lot of changes in "my looks."
• He answered a listener's question that Elvis' first Las Vegas suit had been colored black.
• He told where Elvis was born.
• He said that he did not know who is buried in the tomb at Graceland.

"ELVIS" ALIVE OR DEAD ???

YOU BE THE JUDGE
COULD THIS BE THE RE-BIRTH OF THE KING

FOR HIS LOYAL FANS ONLY, WHO HAVE TRULY CARED OVER THE YEARS ....
TO THEM HE DEDICATES THIS **"ALBUM"** WHICH WAS RECORDED BY **HIM SEPTEMBER 25, 1982**

YOU BE THE JUDGE ....IS IT TRUE ....CAN IT BE????
IF YOU READ BOOKS ELUDING TO THE FACT THAT
ELVIS IS INDEED ALIVE
IF YOU HAVE BEEN FOLLOWING ARTICLES PRINTED
IN THE **GLOBE** MAGAZINE
STATED BY HUNDREDS THAT THEY
HAVE SEEN HIM

YOU WONT WANT TO PASS UP HEARING
"DO YOU KNOW WHO I AM"
IS IT THE **KINGS OWN VOICE**
SINGING & TALKING ABOUT EVENTS
THAT HAPPENED OVER THE
PAST 5 YEARS ....CAN IT BE
........IS THIS THE RE-BIRTH OF THE KING.

FOR YOUR COPY OF THIS LIMITED EDITION,
NEVER BEFORE HEARD RECORDING OF.......

"DO YOU KNOW WHO I AM"
AVAILABLE IN ALBUM ONLY...SEND $7.95 PLUS $1.75
POSTAGE AND HANDLING TO

CREOLE ENTERPRISES
P.O. BOX 24074
NEW ORLEANS, LA, 70184

SATISFACTION GUARANTEED OR YOUR MONEY BACK
WE KNOW YOU WILL BE AS PLEASED
AS WE WERE WHEN WE HEARD
"DO YOU KNOW WHO I AM"

DELIVERY IN 2 WEEKS
GUARANTEED OR MONEY BACK

- He said that fans would see him (Sivle) in the near future.
- He said that the drug stories about him were blown up.
- He said that he may never move to Graceland, but that he had visited Graceland since "past experiences" and found it "the same" – except that he could "look at it from a different angle now."
- He told that he was in Florida because "it's kinda hidden from everybody."
- He said that he absolutely believed in "life after death."
- He hedged about coming out public.
- He said that Elvis' mother's middle name was "Love."

During 1981, Maria Columbus, of The Elvis Special, had contact with Steve Chanzes via telephone and letters, reported in the club's newsletter. I did not know Maria at this time because I was busy with my novel, *Orion,* a novel that in no way resembles the Chanzes book *Elvis: Where Are You?* (*Orion* was copyrighted in 1978, whereas the Chanzes book was copyrighted in 1981.) I then knew neither of the existence of these men nor of Sivle Nora. That came many years after the fact. Maria can attest to this truth.

I stress this in order to set the record straight regarding a notice written to *DISCoveries* magazine in June 1989 by the Eternally Elvis TCB Fan Club in Florida – not to be confused with the Chanzes/Crown Eternally Elvis club, also in Florida. Quoting from that article: "On the recent Geraldo Rivera show Gail Brewer-Giorgio mentioned the name Eternally Elvis, Inc. in Florida as the ones who had given her the cassette tape, which meant she had received it from Steve C. Chanzes, who took our original club name." In fact, I never mentioned the name Eternally Elvis, Inc.: It was Geraldo and the psychic entertainer who did so. I never received the tape from Steve Chanzes and never stated I had. Nor have I ever talked to either a Steve Chanzes or a Steve Crown in person or on the telephone, and I've never received any correspondence from anyone identifying themselves as such.

No one from the Eternally Elvis TCB Fan Club ever called me to ascertain the validity of what they wrote in *DISCoveries* magazine.

THE QUESTION REMAINS: WHO IS SIVLE NORA? SINCE THE PSYCHIC entertainer displayed to Geraldo and to the segment producer of Miami's WSVN-TV program *Inside Story* a copy of a contract whereby Chanzes and Crown hired him to be the voice on the Mystery Tape and since that tape is listed as "Sivle's Monologue" in their newsletter *Eternally Elvis,* then logic follows that this is Sivle Nora, right? And if so, then he may be the same Sivle on the album "Sivle Sings Again." Except that. . . the segment producer for *Inside Story,* Justine Schmidt, told me that when she interviewed the psychic entertainer in April 1989, he swore he was *not* Sivle Nora!

First you see me, then you don't?

The psychic entertainer has said he signed the contract with Chanzes and Crown in April 1981, but he did not make it clear to me on the show whether he was talking about the "Sivle Monologue" (the Mystery Tape) or the Sivle album, because we are talking about two *different* tapes. The tape I had voice-authenticated is not the same tape with the songs and with Sivle pausing to say, "Wait a minute, man, wait a minute. . ." I did not discover the existence of the albums/cassettes of the Sivle songs until Maria Columbus provided me copies. Upon talking to voice experts, I discovered we could not get accurate voice-authentication on the singing, but the part where Sivle stops to say "Wait a minute" has been sent to a voice expert, and although there are only a few words and thus not enough to give a full report, evidence suggests that the voice on the Mystery Tape and the voice of Sivle saying "Wait a minute" are not the same!

Confusing? Keep reading.

Since the Mystery Tape and Elvis' voice via spectrographs read the same via voice-authentication, and since the psychic entertainer claims to be that same voice he is either: (1) good enough to fool legal spectrographs or (2) another tape was made or (3) this is simply another smokescreen or (4) *two* voices are involved — one being the psychic entertainer and the other. . . ?

Remember, the psychic entertainer swore to *Inside Story* he was not Sivle Nora, yet that was how the tapes were released! Again, who is Sivle?

(The *Is Elvis Alive?* reader may recall that we discovered there were two Orions — more of which will be discussed here, in a later file.)

Assuming that the psychic entertainer was telling the truth and that he did not use trickery in stopping Geraldo's watch (regardless of what we viewed), and that the psychic did indeed go into a trance and bring Elvis' voice from the Great Beyond, why are certain remarks made by the "voice," such as:

- "a good place to hide. . . Hawaii"
- slowly "getting myself into shape"

- "traveling all over the world"
- "getting very nervous" by being recognized by a waitress in Germany
- going "to football games and to the movies"
- talking to "people that have been sick"
- "concerned . . . about people finding out"
- "working out and playing racquetball and karate"
- not having "taken a sleeping pill in three years"
- "trying to write music"
- "I'm seen by people all the time"
- "looking forward to possibly seeing some people that are going to be shocked"
- realizing "that sooner or later it's [the hiding] going to end"
- "working on an album"

These are only a sampling of statements made on the Mystery Tape. Granted, I do not know much about the spiritual world, but if the psychic entertainer was calling Elvis from the Beyond and allowing his body to be a vehicle for that spirit, why would the spirit be hiding out in Hawaii or growing beards to keep from being recognized? Why would *a spirit* be talking about *any of the above*? (Do spirits need to grow beards to keep from being recognized?!)

The psychic entertainer said a disclaimer was on the original "Sivle Monologue," and I suppose on the Sivle album as well, intimating that perhaps the present author and/or publishers deliberately removed such disclaimers in order to perpetuate a fraud.

Wrong again.

The truth is, I have examined all the early copies released by Chanzes and Crown — as has Maria Columbus — and there is absolutely no disclaimer whatsoever. In fact, they deliberately do everything possible to make people believe it is Elvis on the "Sivle Monologue" and on the album "Sivle Sings Again."

Since Chanzes and Crown advertised the sale of the book/newsletter and album publicly in both 1981 and later in 1982, how can this psychic entertainer state he never knew this tape was made public until *my* book (dated 1988)! After all, he admitted he was contractually connected with Chanzes and Crown, even showing such contract to Geraldo Rivera and Justine Schmidt of *Inside Edition*.

Anyone who purchased the mass-market edition of *Is Elvis Alive?* knows we were not making money from the tape because the entire package was only $5.95, the tape a part of a copyrighted interview with me. Combine the cost of producing the interview tape as evidence of what I was talking about together with the cost of shrink-wrapping and the production costs of the book itself, one doesn't have to be a mathematical genius to see I was not making money from the sale of a tape. As you'll note by samples of ads concerning the book *Elvis . . .Where Are You?* and the Sivle album, it was those connected with the production of said book and album who were making the sales! (Chanzes, Crown . . . Darlok/ Darlock?)

According to Bill Burk's *Elvis World* newsletter interview, this "spiritual entertainer" did do the Sivle album under the name of "Sivle Nora" — yet, again, he swore he was not Sivle Nora to Justine Schmidt of *Inside Edition*.

If fraud was being committed, it was not done by this writer. All I have done is present the evidence, not create it! (In all fairness, it really wasn't Geraldo's fault that Capone's vault was empty. And if Elvis' tomb is empty, it is not my fault either.)

I would like to ask this psychic entertainer: If you are Sivle, then was it *you* who was interviewed by Bill Payne of Station KTFX in May 1981? If so, what were you trying to pull? Surely you can't chalk this off as P.R. for a fan club, as you stated on *Geraldo!*

It is my suggestion that the readers go back and reread my extracts of this May 1981 interview with Bill Payne and Sivle and decide for himself: If David-Darlock-the-psychic-entertainer is Sivle, then was he not deliberately and with intent of fraud trying to deceive the listening public via radio that he was Elvis Presley and that Elvis Presley was alive?

If you are the voice on the tape, if you are the singing and talking voice on "Sivle Sings Again," will you come forward and be voice-authenticated by the police?

SINCE WE HAVE TWO OPPOSITE STORIES FROM THE SAME PSYCHIC entertainer's mouth, how about another teaspoon of confusion to muddy the waters? Recall the following segment of the Mystery Tape included with *Is Elvis Alive?*:

> I've spent most of my time getting myself back into shape. It's not easy to get everything done at the same time. There's been, uh, there's been a lot of things that have happened. I've got to be, I've got to be very careful. I mean, uh, I met a young lady in a supermarket once and she kept following me. Finally she said, "I almost can't believe, but, uh, I think I know who you are," and I said, "Uh, honey, if you don't tell anybody, I said I won't," and right then and there in

the supermarket she started crying and I said, "Honey, don't you cry," and the tears just started falling down her face and she put her arms around me and she said, "I feel I know what you been through," she said, "I'll always love you," and you know things like that are, are experiences that you just can't, uh, you can't buy.

It's very hard. It's very hard to forget anything like that, but, uh, things like that have, uh, have been happening to me a lot.

Then consider this letter I received in August 1988:

Aug 9, 1988

Dear Gail,

I thought my meeting with HIM would go with me as a secret to my grave. I never told anyone. I didn't want to be thought of as crazy. I have never followed Elvis News from day one so I was unaware of all the Hubbub, and until a friend "not knowing I had ever seen him since Aug. 16, 1988" played the tape for me I did not know of you — or your Books. It touched me to know he treasured our moment that day as it has ment so much to me. I can't get my message to him personally but if you ever write a sequal maybe you would put my letter to him in it so he knows I remember too with fondness!

Thank you.

The Young Lady in the Supermarket

He lives.

The "Young Lady in the Supermarket" enclosed, for me, an open letter to Elvis, dated August 8, 1988. Here is something of what she said:

You told me not to cry, but I couldn't help myself. . . . I left that day and went on with my life. I kept our meeting secret. . . . I saw you again some time later at the mall. . . .

Now I feel I know how you must have felt when I wanted to

reveal you. I just want to say I'm sorry!...If you see me again, just smile...and wink. I'll do the same and we can both go our way, having touched each other's lives again without a word...but we'll know, and that's what truly matters.

If Elvis is alive, I hope he will have the opportunity to read the above, or the entire letter, that was written to him.

Although I have no way of ever ascertaining whether people truly saw or experienced what they have related, I have found that most people are sincere and trustworthy. The full scope of the above many-paged letter to Elvis is very sincere; it even discusses religion with him. My point in presenting some of it is that how could it have been the psychic entertainer from *Geraldo* whom the Young Lady in the Supermarket saw? Darlok/Darlock does not resemble Elvis in any way. Yet the voice on the tape relates the same story: that Elvis (?) met a young lady in a supermarket.

One of them is not telling the truth. Is it the psychic entertainer—who said he could mentally stop Geraldo's watch (yet reached into his pocket for a magnet)—or is it the Young Lady in the Supermarket? Or the voice-authentication experts who reported on the tape? Or me, for reporting it all?

THERE IS MUCH MYSTERY SURROUNDING CHANZES AND CROWN. SO many addresses, none active. There was Eternally Elvis in Wilton Manors, Florida; another address in Ft. Lauderdale. Direct Products, which produced the book *Elvis: Where Are You?* in 1981 apparently was involuntarily dissolved in December 1980 according to Susan Payne, Florida Secretary of State in Tallahassee. Direct Products was a company located in Coral Springs, Florida. Maria Columbus of *The Elvis Special* had been trying to locate Steve Chanzes in order that he make good on a bad check he issued. She had been informed that his account had been closed with no forwarding address. From the desk of Ms. Payne, she received the following information:

Our records do not reflect that Steve Chanzes is now or was ever an officer, director or incorporator of Eternally Elvis, Inc. We have no address for this individual.

Attached is a printout for Direct Products, Inc., which reflects that this corporation was involuntarily dissolved 12/8/80. Steve Chanzes was listed as the registered agent. All corporations, companies, etc., incorporate file charters with our office. We have no authority to require someone not to use the suffix Inc. if they are not registered with our office.

Meanwhile, in Eternally Elvis' attempt to keep Sivle Nora in the public eye as "Elvis," Ms. Columbus received a communication (April 10, 1981) from Chanzes (at the foot of the letter was the imprint "MAY THE KING LIVE FOREVER"):

> Enclosed is a tape of excerpts from Sivle's first album, entitled "DO YOU KNOW WHO I AM?" Please excuse the poor quality as we were not able to make the transfer from the original with professional equipment due to the expedience of this matter.
>
> I will be home all day and night this Saturday awaiting with anxiety your call. I spoke to Sivle earlier today and I of course relayed to him the gist of the conversation that I had with Jeannie* last night and he told me to send his personal regards to both you and Jeannie.
>
> With warmest regards...

Note that although Eternally Elvis, Inc., was influencing the public to believe that Sivle and Elvis might be one and the same, from various stories told by the psychic entertainer he wasn't hired until after the date of the above letter.

Seven years later, in 1988, I received the following letters from a so-called Future Productions in Florida. At the time I received them, I had no idea that the writer of the letters could possibly be Steve Chanzes; I'm still not sure they came from him, but... "Dear Gail," the first letter began:

> I have in my possession the most amazing tapes the world has ever heard. Having this information is not only a privilege but also a great responsibility. I have been given instructions to market the tapes any way possible and to use a portion of the proceeds to help a designated group of people.
>
> Please understand that this matter must be kept under the utmost security, therefore I am unable to respond by phone.
>
> Please contact me through Future Prod.
>
> The marketing of the tapes will be a monetary and personal benefit to all involved. ...

(Had not Future Productions run a public advertisement about the tape or given me a name, I would have honored the "utmost security" request.)

*Jeannie Tessum, then co-president of The Elvis Special.

The second letter was in reply to my asking for further information:

A little while ago, I received a request from you for a story regarding a tape that you have in your possession.

After seeing and hearing your sincerity on the *Larry King* show, I am convinced you should know of a tape that has *never* been heard by *anyone* at *anytime*. It is not only the "time proof" you are looking for, but a *world shocker* as well!

If you have any suggestions on how to present this material to the public, please contact me through, Future Productions

1639 S. University Dr.

Plantation, FL 33324

Shortly after, I received a copy of the aforementioned ad — again listing Future Productions. The ad sounded like the same old Sivle tapes. With a picture of a youthful, smiling Elvis, in bold print the advertisement asked, "ELVIS ALIVE???" And then there came: "Finally know the truth!" . . . "Hear newsmen all over the country proclaim Elvis is alive!" . . . "Listen in wonder to music never before released!" . . . "Be amazed at the interview that amazed the experts!" . . . "DESTINED TO BE A CLASSIC!" One-hundred-percent satisfaction was guaranteed if the purchaser sent $8.95 to Future Productions at the Plantation, Florida, address.

The mystery widened when I received the following "un-signed" letter in August 1988. By the envelope and by the type on the letter itself, I have ascertained that it came from the same "hand" which wrote the two letters from Future Productions, and thus I have suspicions that the tape referred to was Sivle Nora, not the tape included with *Is Elvis Alive?*, since the Future Productions advertisement says "music."

The contents of the August 1988 letter infer that the writer knows Elvis Presley and that something went wrong. Note that it mentions the year 1981 as "first acknowledgment," which is the year both the "Monologue" and "Sivle Sings Again" went public. I have no idea if Sivle-on-the-album/cassette is Elvis Presley. However, my instincts, together with the material presented say: ". . . something afoul."

Still, I would be remiss in not zeroing in on what was presented to the public in 1981. I also do not know if those presenting Sivle are involved with the Sivle Enterprises connected with Graceland Express, despite both being in Florida. (From what I understand, Graceland denies any relationship with Chanzes/Crown and Sivle.)

The existence and then nonexistence of "Sivle" has caused controversy and speculation in some of the fan clubs, and I suspect more information will emerge.

The unsigned August 1988 letter – of numerological bent – pointed out that

- I was truly gifted.
- Higher sources were at work; I should be discreet and not push the "time scale."
- Elvis himself has forgotten certain things from his past, things that he has told no one.
- Things are not always as they appear.
- I was just an "experiment" (with Elvis?) – one that he has chosen to put behind him, to dismiss – and that I feel hurt and discarded.

The letter ended with: "There is always more to things than meets the eye."

In April 1989, while researching *The Elvis Files*, I wrote to Future Productions to see why they had written me and whether they knew a Chanzes and Crown or the psychic entertainer from the Geraldo audience. Privately, I wondered if Future Productions might itself not be Chanzes and Crown. I suspect they might be, but I have no concrete proof as my letter came back marked "ADDRESS UNKNOWN."

The contents of my letter made it clear that I wanted correct background information, if they *had* any, on Chanzes/Crown/ Sivle Nora. I also made it clear that I authenticate, wherever possible, via experts – preferably law-enforcement experts.

If Future Productions is Chanzes and Crown, they have once again disappeared. Apparently, these people "have wheels, will travel. . ." Any information will be welcomed.

A proof that the Mystery Tape (included with *Is Elvis Alive?*) had long been around can be found in an excerpt from a letter to me by Lora M., of Tickfaw, Louisiana, dated August 7, 1987:

> The tape you said you received was another area of intrigue. I have that exact tape. It was sent to me by Steve Crown and Steve Chanzes of Florida. I have literature they sent me also. During this time frame, we found out my mother had cancer. I asked Mr. Crown and Mr. Chanzes if Sivle Nora – that's the name he went by – could call her. Well, he did. He called three times, and each time Mom was at the doctor's. He would tell my brother to tell her that a friend called. My brother swore the voice he heard was indeed Elvis Presley's.

Shortly afterward, these men vanished. I wrote letters to them and they were returned. Their telephone number was disconnected and I could not find a listing for them anywhere in Florida. In one of our earlier conversations, they told me they were planning on moving their Eternally Elvis headquarters because of all the people hanging around making Sivle nervous. . . .

If Sivle is an imposter, he certainly went to a lot of trouble calling people who were sick and/or dying. Why? What would his purpose be? And if Darlok/Darlock *is* that man – that "voice" – then why was he doing so? After all, on *Geraldo* he stated he had only made a tape for what he thought was a fan club.

On the surface of these murky waters it appears that Chanzes and Crown were not connected with Elvis at all, and either had bootleg tapes or tapes done by an imposter who knowingly was trying to create a hoax – the psychic entertainer included.

Except that:

- Sivle is a name that was used by Elvis when booking studio time, according to Chet Atkins (in Peter Haining's *Elvis in Private*).
- In the Jimmy Velvet Museum in Florida, on display, is Elvis' wristband, engraved "Sivle."
- On the "Sivle Sings Again" album, etched secretly in the black portion of the record are the words "Elvis, Inc." – which is a registered trademark of the estate of Elvis Presley. (For those who have a copy of this album, ordered via Chanzes, hold the album up to the light. You will see "Elvis, Inc." etched – hard to see, but it's there.)
- And in the July/September 1987 issue of *The Graceland Express*, the official news publication of Graceland and a division of Elvis Presley Enterprises, Inc., on page 12 was the following ad: SIVLE ENTERPRISES, INC. (and where is it located? Florida.)

In 1987, a so-called SIVLE Enterprises, located in Hollywood, Florida, advertised a "Tribute in Blue" as a ten-year commemoration of Elvis' death. It included a blue suede ribbon, T-shirt, poster, and bumper sticker at a "closeout special" of $14.95 (reduced from $24.95). Below is part of an earlier customer invoice for the package (which, for the Florida customer, totaled, with sales tax, $27.95):

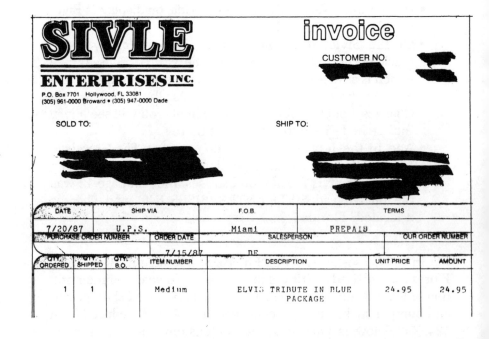

(Many letters regarding Chanzes and Crown wonder if there ever was a real Crown, or whether Crown was symbolic for "king." Elvis had also worked for Crown Electric, in Memphis.)

Although my admiration for Elvis Presley runs deep, I am not the best judge of his voice. Maria Columbus, president of The Elvis Special fan club has long stated, publicly and via her newsletter, that she is 99-percent certain Elvis Presley is alive. The majority of the fans know Maria is above reproach.

Maria also knows that in this chapter I am not trying to fool anyone but to present what is a very confusing series of events, particularly in regard to the Sivle Nora mystery. In September 1981, Maria received a letter from Steve Chanzes bearing the Eternally Elvis letterhead. The letter was printed in *The Elvis Special;* in it it was clear that Steve Chanzes was trying to get the idea across that Sivle and Elvis were one and the same. Steve writes:

> When I first met Sivle, some eight months ago, I was the happiest person on the face of this earth. I was prepared to fight the entire world. But his stubbornness has finally worn me down. I can appreciate that he wants a life of his own, but for the life of me I cannot comprehend why he will not at least make one public appearance. Quite possibly he has some hidden fears or maybe there are some legal complications that I don't know about. I do know that he hasn't told me everything. I can't say that I fault him, because it was not his idea to go public in the first place. It was mine and mine alone. . . .
>
> He is my friend. Make no mistake about that. There isn't anything he wouldn't do for me and there is nothing that I wouldn't do for him. For that I am very grateful. . . .
>
> He lovès to lavish people with gifts, but the best gift that he could give to me, the gift that has the most value, is his friendship. I'll cherish it forever.

Chanzes also says that it is now "time to bid adieu to Sivle as a business"; and from what I gather, it was not long after that that Chanzes and Crown disappeared and Sivle went underground. Could it be that Steve Chanzes was, truly, somehow in contact with Elvis Presley, that something was happening or about to happen, and Chanzes did something to betray Elvis? Did the mystery tape (Sivle's Monologue) actually come from Ellen Foster, whom Elvis knew and who, according to some, Elvis called after August 1977. Can we prove a connection between Steve Chanzes and Ellen Foster—remember, we already know there was a connection between Ms. Foster and Elvis Presley.

The Elvis Special, after printing Chanzes' letter, responded: "We still feel that Sivle could be Elvis. Elvis picked real turkeys for friends – could be he's still doing it. We've given you every chance to follow thru for Sivle & you blew it. If you can't handle the pressure NOW, how in HELL do you expect to handle the pressure of working for ELVIS?! Elvis expects perfection and you seem to fall short of it. If this is Elvis we'll be 110 percent behind him. Sivle wants to continue his music for the fans – fine. Tell Sivle to contact US again and we'll TAKE CARE OF BUSINESS."

THE SAME MR. THOMAS SANOCKI WHOM THE READER MET EARLIER IN HIS responses to Bob Greene's *Chicago Tribune* column and I have spoken several times on the telephone. He has said that many of the statements made by the "voice" on the Mystery Tape were statements made by Elvis to his mother-figure friend, Ellen Foster (this, according to Sanocki's conversations with Ms. Foster). Since Ms. Foster is now dead, I'll extract from a letter Sanocki sent me on April 27, 1988:

> . . .it all started in 1981, when I received a phone call from Ellen Foster, who lived in St. Charles, Illinois. She was a friend of Elvis Presley. She told me that Elvis was still alive and a few chosen people were calling him Sivle Nora, which is Elvis Aron backwards. Well, after a few phone calls I started taping my conversations with Ellen Foster and she, too. . .started taping these conversations [with Elvis?]. Many weeks later, I told Ellen Foster I needed some proof, so a week later I received a tape in the.mail that, in fact, is the interview [the Monologue tape] you got in 1987. I got mine in 1981 and along with it I received a tape of Sivle Nora singing about eight songs. . .
>
> I still have the tape, and I have let many people hear it (some with mixed feelings). But I have believed since 1977 that Elvis was alive. Then, after I received this tape, I received a phone call from Steve Crown and Steve Chanzes, who wrote the book *Elvis . . . Where Are You?* in 1981. I talked to both of these men a few times and taped their calls. After many conversations I told Steve Crown that I would like more proof, so about two weeks later I received another tape in the mail, and this time I was awestruck. For it was Elvis thanking me and a friend personally for all our help with the Muscular Dystrophy Association from our [Elvis] fan club. . . .

Ellen Foster interviewed with Steve Chanzes and became a chapter in his book *Elvis: Where Are You?* In Chapter 5, "It's Now or Never," Chanzes asks: "What is the creditability of Ellen Foster? Ellen Foster. . .bore a striking resemblance to Elvis' later mother,

Gladys. . . . Elvis couldn't do enough for her. He called Ellen Foster
by his mother's middle name. That name, 'Love' – she reminded
him so much of his mother. And he confided in her many, many
things."

In Chapter 5, Chanzes, by means of Ellen's good memory,
reconstructs a telephone conversation Elvis had with her two days
before his death. (They had spoken at least once a week, says
Chanzes, during the preceding three or four months.) The date,
August 14, 1977 – two days before Elvis' "death" – is the anniversary of Gladys' death.

Ellen: Hello.
Elvis: Love, is that you?
Ellen: Why, Elvis. How are you? How've you been?
Elvis: I feel fine, Love. You know, I was thinking of you today.
Ellen: I think of you every day, Elvis. Are you taking care of yourself?
Elvis: Yes. But that's not why I'm calling.
Ellen: What's the matter, Elvis?
Elvis: Nothing. You know, do you know how happy you've made me,
Love?
Ellen: Oh, Elvis.
Elvis: No. No. You know today, today my Mama has been dead for
nineteen years. Nineteen long years. (Elvis starts to weep.)
Ellen: Calm down, Elvis. Calm down. Your mother's probably watch-
ing you now. She wouldn't want you to cry.
Elvis: I can't help it. I sometimes wonder if I caused her death.
Ellen: No you didn't Elvis. Your mother had a bad heart. She was
overweight.
Elvis: Yeah, she was. . .she was drinking a lot because of me.
Ellen: Don't blame yourself for that Elvis. Don't carry that cross.
Elvis: I can't help it. I started making so much money. I started shower-
ing her with gifts, diamond rings. You know, I gave you one that belonged to her. The one that I gave to my mother back in 1955. Cars,
Cadillacs. I bought her this big beautiful home. I thought I was doing
right for her, but she couldn't handle it. She still hung the wash outside,
fed the chickens outside. We're living on thirteen acres and my Mom is
chasing chickens around the backyard. I never should have taken her
away from her roots. I never should have. It wasn't fair to her. She felt
compelled to impress me. . .trying to lose weight. And then when she
had a tough time with that, she started to drink. She became depressed
and it was all my fault. It was all my fault, so Mama, please forgive me.
Ellen: Elvis, don't go blaming yourself. Don't go blaming yourself. You
didn't do anything wrong. Every boy wishes that he could rise to fame
and riches and then provide for his parents. There's nothing wrong in
that, Elvis. What was meant to be, was, and that's all. So, Elvis, are you

getting excited about your next tour? It's just two days away. Aw, I'd love to see ya.

Elvis: (Still sniffling.) Yeah, that's why I called ya, Love, I...Can you...We're talking in confidence. We always do. You're just like my mother to me. I shouldn't even say that...I trust you so much.

Ellen: Aw, Elvis. I love you like you were my son. You know that. What is it, Elvis?

Elvis: I...I'm not going on that tour, Ellen. I'm not going on that tour.

Ellen: You canceled it, Elvis? What's the matter? Don't you feel good?

Elvis: I think I never felt better, Love. And...I'm just not going on that tour.

Ellen: Well, why'd ya cancel it, Elvis?

Elvis: I didn't cancel it, Love.

Ellen: Elvis, maybe I didn't understand you. You're not going on the tour but you didn't cancel the tour. Is that what you just said?

Elvis: That's right, Love. I'm not going on the tour, and I haven't canceled it.

Ellen: Well, when are you canceling it?

Elvis: I'm not.

Ellen: I don't understand.

Elvis: Listen to me, Love. Listen to me real close. You're not to tell a soul.

Ellen: I won't tell anybody anything.

Elvis: I'm not going on the last tour and I'm not going to cancel it. Don't ask me any more questions, just remember one thing.

Ellen: What's that, Elvis?

Elvis: I'll...I'll always...I'll always be here. I'll always be here. Don't believe what you read. Do you understand, Love?

Ellen: Elvis, this sounds scary.

Elvis: Naw...it's not.

Ellen: Are you in trouble, Elvis?

Elvis: No. Nothing. Nothing I can explain. No, nothing, really. No. No, I'm not in any trouble. As a matter of fact my troubles are all ending. Just remember, I love you very much, and I'll always be here. And I'll talk to you again.

Ellen: When, Elvis?

Elvis: Oh, I don't know. But one day I'll give you a call and let you know. I've got your number. I'll always have it with me. I love you, Love.

Ellen: I love you, Elvis.

Elvis: Goodbye.

Ellen: Goodbye, Elvis.

Ellen's reported conversation of August 14, 1977, with Elvis came, said Chanzes, from a woman who appeared to be totally honest. He asked her if she would be willing to take a Polygraph exam, and she said yes.

Chanzes went on to describe the *Eternally Elvis* newsletter that he, with Steve Crown, would shortly be turning out, in which, he said, "All of us, together, will play detective and will set about to find out where Elvis is. . . . Hopefully, one day, Elvis will emerge." To one of the early issues of *Eternally Elvis,* Ellen Foster contributed the following letter, entitled "My First Meeting with Elvis":

> I first met Elvis in Memphis through a mutual friend. Her brother-in-law was connected with RCA and Steve Sholes, who was mainly responsible for having Colonel Parker sign Elvis to RCA.
>
> I don't remember if it was in 1955 or 1956.* Elvis was giving a party at one of the restaurants. I had been an Elvis fan to the extent that I purchased all his records and cut out the articles that I saw in the papers. Two of my friends, Barbara and Jerry Johnson, had seen Elvis the very first time that he came to Chicago, to the Stadium in his gold lamé suit.
>
> I must admit that all the crazy articles I had read certainly helped me to get the wrong impression. I actually don't remember too much of when I shook his hand, as I was shaking so. My knees were like jelly. The strangest thing happened. Five minutes after I met him, it was as if I had known him all my life. He put me completely at ease. We were talking about his mother and what he thought about different things. His laugh was so infectious that I started to laugh myself. But then he started looking at me as if he were puzzled and trying to figure me out. He kept saying, "I don't believe it, but I feel as if I were talking to my blessed mother." There were beautiful girls there and he would look at them and shake his head. He had an amused look on his face. I can never forget his eyes. It was as if he were searching my very soul. There was something that was different about him.
>
> The evening flew so fast that it was time to go before I knew it. He said, would I like to come down to Memphis real soon? I thought that he was kidding. I thought that if I would call, that would be the day. I just said, "Thank you." A week later I got a call. He said, "Ah bet you all thought I was joking." I could not believe it. I knew how Cinderella felt. I was walking on Cloud Nine as I was getting ready. It still seems like a dream. That concludes my first meeting with Elvis Presley. The first of many.
>
> Let me say that the bad things that people write about Elvis Presley are false. I just wish that people could have known the wonderful man that I grew to know, the kind, gentle, affectionate, generous person that I learned to know.
>
> My love to all those who loved him.
>
>   Ellen Foster

---

*We believe that Ms. Foster has either mistyped or forgotten the year in which she met Elvis; it surely could not have been so early in his career.

Another friend of Ellen Foster contacted me, Patricia Elliott. She had had a long correspondence with Ellen, and now shared her letters with me. On February 25, 1990, Patricia wrote to Ellen, unaware that the latter had died several years previously:

> Dear Ellen,
> Someone told me you passed away. I won't believe this. My heart tells me you are still here.
> Do you remember all the letters we shared? All the plans we made? I've moved. [Here she gives her new address, which I do not feel free to include.]
> Please, Ellen, contact me.
> Love, Patricia Elliott
> P.S.: You and our friend still owe me an all-expenses-paid trip, plus a limo ride.

The letters that Ellen Foster wrote to Patricia Elliott were difficult to follow, and I am not certain of the date sequence, since envelopes may have been mixed up. I'll give only some extracts, with, hopefully, the correct dates:

> *March 16, 1981:*
> I met him [Elvis] through a mutual friend. Her name was Pauline Alexander. Her brother-in-law was one of the people who was responsible for signing the RCA contract. . . .
>
> *May 1981:*
> I appreciate what you are doing on the tapes. I will get the scarf to you soon. With this new situation developing, the phone never stops ringing. The correspondence is staggering.
> You see, on January 8, 1981, I got a phone call. My friend, the lady I am staying with, a very dear friend, answered the phone. She was so shaken that all she could do was point to the phone and say, "Elvis." She was white as a sheet. I went to the phone and said, "Hello," speaking uncontrollably. The voice on the other end said, "Hello, Love." I went completely blank. He said, "Don't go through the ceiling. Don't you recognize my voice?" Well, the rest is history. My all-paid trips to Memphis and Florida. Steve Crown and Steve Chanzes have been our dearest friends. If you do not have the tape of introduction, I will send it to you, also some of the songs that are going to be on the record that he is making.
> There is also another magazine coming out that I am writing for, called *Eternally Elvis.* You can have a complimentary copy by writing: Eternally Elvis, 521 N.E. 26th Street, Wilton Manors, FL 33305. I do not think it strange that you love Elvis so much. I told Sivle. He said you sounded like such a wonderful person. . . . Sivle

is now gray; he also has a short beard. . . ."
I will tell you about a big ripoff next time I write. I am suing the two men. Charlie Hodge is also suing. A man wrote a book about us. He said he found Elvis. He called him Sivle Nora (Elvis Aron). I did not know he was writing it. That is not all he did. His name is Steve Chanzes. . . ." [We do not know the date of this letter, but it doesn't fit in with the statement, "Steve Crown and Steve Chanzes have been our dearest friends."]

August 20, 1981:
Well, I can tell you that Steve has ripped off so many people. The Sivle Nora character is really an impersonator from England named Deke Rivers. That was also the name of a person in "Loving You," that Elvis played*. . . .

Pat, I have been so busy with my dealings in the FBI and [with] Elvis' attorney, who is working for me, with me. We are going to put this Steven Chanzes behind bars. Or as Beecher says, in the slammer. This Steve, as you know, said he found Elvis or Sivle Nora. The voice you hear on the tapes that he sold for $85 is Elvis' voice. The tapes were stolen from Graceland. . . ."

About January 1982:
About Sivle Nora — Elvis Aron — it is the biggest ripoff I have ever seen. Beecher Smith† [may have] put it in the hands of the FBI.

August 12, 1982:
No, Elvis is not alive, I am sorry to say. That man is Steve Chanzes. He is using a different approach, that is all. Pat, Elvis would never do anything like that. He would not let his father suffer. Pat, I am telling only you these things. Elvis had cancer, I know how he suffered.§ He did not take hard drugs. He had to take so much medication just to keep going. He would walk along and collapse. . . . I talked to him two nights before he died. He knew he would die soon. . . . He said, "I am not going on the tour. I can't go on. Please do not worry. You may not be able to see the sun at night, but it shines twenty-four hours a day. I will always be with you." Then he wrote a verse that was so beautiful. I remember the bottom line. It said, "If you close your eyes and remember me. . . I will always be there."

---

*Being unable to find a Deke Rivers, I cannot ascertain that this, yet another "voice on the tape" is Deke Rivers. Since *Is Elvis Alive?* has been a bestseller, logic says that if Mr. Rivers exists, he would have made himself known if he is "Sivle."

†Lawyer to Vernon Presley and to the Elvis Presley estate.

§All reports state that Elvis was extremely active that last night, playing racquetball, staying up all night. Cancer rumors have not been substantiated.

September 1982:
Yes, I had the book *Elvis...Where Are You?* I gave mine to the FBI.
They still have not caught up with him. He is now going by the
name of Al Jeffries.*

MANY OF THE LETTERS FROM ELLEN TO PATRICIA INDICATED THERE WERE
many things that she (Ellen) could not talk about because of
"danger." Due to the fact that so many of the people mentioned are
unreachable, we have to play guessing games:

- Sivle is Elvis. He did call Ellen. Chanzes and Crown were
  involved. A betrayal took place.
- Sivle was not Elvis, and fooled Ellen. She later found out and
  turned them in, worked with the FBI.
- The tapes† (Sivle singing) are Elvis and they were stolen from
  Graceland and the FBI stepped in. Chanzes and Crown disappeared. But even if the tapes were stolen, what about Elvis
  saying, "Wait a minute, wait a minute..." and the song "I Love
  a Rainy Night"? That means Elvis was alive...?
- Ellen was wrong and the tapes were not stolen, and it was/is an
  impersonator from England. Why would the FBI step in? There
  are lots of impersonators out there.
- Ellen knew Elvis was alive, but down the road, sometime
  around August 1981, had to change her story in order to protect
  Elvis. That could explain her very visible contradictions, explain
  why she told Tom Sanocki a different story. (Mr. Sanocki and
  Ms. Elliott do not know each other; thus, there was no col-
  laboration on *their* part.) Recall, Ellen mentions the FBI around
  the time she changed her story.
- If something had gotten out of hand, would Ellen – would any
  of Elvis' friends – lie/have lied to protect him? (On the *Larry King
  Show* I asked Joe Esposito if he would lie to protect and cover
  up for Elvis, and he said, "Yes.")
- None of the above. These folks are all telling tales, Sivle never
  existed, none of the above exist, it's all just hokus-pokus
  flimflam.

---

*A book titled *Elvis: Where Are You?* came out of Wilton Manors, Florida, around
August 1982 under the name of Al Jeffries. An article appeared in *Globe* in
August 1982 concerning the book and its premise that Elvis hoaxed his death.
"Al Jeffries" has also disappeared.

† Remember, we are discussing the "Sivle Sings Again," not the tape with *Is Elvis
Alive?*

Phew!

Or, as Paul Harvey does *not* have to say, "This is not the rest of the story."

No. 9

Credible Evidences of Elvis' Being Alive

Seeing is believing.

— OLD SAYING

Question: If Elvis is alive, have pictures of him been taken, or has there been *other* physical evidence?
Answer: Pictures have appeared from time to time. However, since there are so many impersonators, most of these become objects of doubt. I found two pictures of Elvis that, in my mind, erase most doubt: one taken at Graceland, the other in a crowd scene with Muhammad Ali. Another piece of physical evidence involves a monetary gift. All of these date from *after* August 1977.

B esides a voice-authenticated tape and the mystery recordings by Sivle, there have been credible sightings, conversations, and even pictures taken of what appears to be Elvis after August 16, 1977.

I originally saw Mike Joseph's celebrated poolhouse picture of Elvis shown on a news segment of KCOP television (Los Angeles) on January 8, 1986. Tim Malloy, co-anchor of the program, introduced the voice of Bob Walsh, a KCOP reporter, who told how Joseph got the picture:

Mike Joseph took his family to Graceland for a vacation on January 1st of 1978, more than four months after the death of Elvis Presley—

148

perhaps we should say "reported death." At the time the grounds of
Graceland were the only part of the estate open to the public, but
Joseph took some snapshots and put them away for safe-keeping.
Four years later while reading about Presley, Joseph took out his
mementos of the Graceland visit, and he noticed something unusual
in a shot of the bathhouse behind the mansion. It was a shadow in
the lower half of the door. Joseph says he had the pictures enlarged
and the results were nothing short of startling. Someone or something bearing a remarkable resemblance to Elvis Presley was indeed
sitting behind the door. . . . The sequence of pictures including
shots of Elvis' grave confirms that the pictures were indeed taken
after Presley's death. Joseph says he's not trying to convince anyone
that Elvis still lives or that the snapshot is an image of some supernatural phenomenon but there is something there. How it got there
and what it is will no doubt remain as much a mystery as the entire
Presley mystique.

The picture surely appears to be one of Elvis, since his face
is full – which makes sense, since it was taken only four months
after his "death" and he may not yet have lost a lot of weight. The
fact that someone is looking out of the door is quite clear. (The *black-
and-white* poolhouse-door photo, below, cannot clearly show Elvis;
the *color* photo, the original, on the back of the book's jacket does;
and it may be ordered from the Arctic Corp. [see Bibliography].)
Two years later, in February 1988, on *Breakthrough* (an inde-

pendent telemarketing program shown on various channels), Mike
Joseph was interviewed by Leonard Grant. Joseph told how,

> One day, after reading a book I decided to look at my pictures again.
> I pulled them out and this time I saw something in one of the
> pictures that I hadn't seen in over the years, course, I wasn't really
> studying them. But the sun had just hit on this picture in such a way
> that it picked up this image sitting in the doorway, a shadow in the
> doorway. For curiosity sake, not that I would know who was there
> I wanted to see what it was. I took my son's magnifying glass, put
> it on the picture and started pulling it away from the picture to get
> a good visible view of it and I was just shocked. I couldn't believe
> what I saw. My, God! I had Elvis Presley sitting in the doorway,
> looking out at the fans walking past his grave. Why? I asked myself
> a million times. Why? I don't know. Did he fake his death? Did he
> have to fake his death? Why couldn't he go off to an island some-
> place. Lock himself up in Graceland. I mean, I understand he stayed
> inside his house for months at a time. I remember the night of the
> vigil there were something like 80,000 people outside the gates of
> Graceland. All of a sudden a car with teenagers in it – they were
> intoxicated – ran into the crowd, hit three women, two died. Maybe
> he was gonna come back, fake his death, come back for the ultimate
> comeback. He was a practical joker. Maybe now he can't come back
> because of this accident.

Grant next asked Joseph how we could be sure the photographs had not been tampered with. Joseph replied that they were
"the only negatives I've had" and that he had had the negatives
examined by Kodak. "They were taken in sequence, uncut. By the
negatives being original they can tell. The emulsion number of the
film was manufactured in '77. . . . A roll of film . . . has a manufac-
turing date in the emulsion number. You couldn't pay Kodak to say
something like that if it weren't true."

Grant then wondered how Joseph knew it was Elvis in the
chair and not simply a photograph. Joseph replied: "Because
we. . .have a photograph here [too] that shows the chair, empty,
that he was sitting in. In photograph number four it shows I was
taking the shot of the people with the background of the house,
the bathhouse there. And we happened to close in on that and
there's just an empty chair." It is said to have been one of Elvis'
favorite chairs, one in which he sometimes got his hair cut.

Elaborating somewhat on the series of shots, Joseph
explained:

> We couldn't go near the house. . . . This is a security guard's car.
> [Things were] sorta makeshift. It was too early; it wasn't opened up

as a museum yet. So the house was closed to the public. Uh, this is Elvis' headstone, and right here in the corner is his mother's. So this shows that this was taken after August 16, 1977, and before '79, when his father died, because his father would be right over here, and in '80 his grandmother, Minnie Mae. This is the shot that I took of people walking and the bathhouse in the distance. We zero in here, and this is the same shot with just the chair, no one sitting in the chair. . . . [Elvis] would be seeing us, sitting there, and the people walking past his headstone.

Having said the above, then why – on *Larry King Live* on Channel CNN, on August 13, 1988 – did Joseph claim *not* to have said he thought the picture was of Elvis? I was taped, with King and Joseph and Joe Esposito, on that same show. (By then, I was hard at work on *Is Elvis Alive?*)

"Now, who is that in that picture?" asked King.

Joseph answered: "As Gail very well knows, when I had met Gail for the first time in February, it is not Elvis Presley."

A moment later, I remarked, "We have you on tape saying when you took the magnifying glass and pulled it back, you said, 'My God! It is Elvis Presley.'"

Joseph said he "swore it was Elvis Presley up until last year."

King asked, "What changed your mind?"

M.J.: What changed my mind, I had met with a couple of Elvis' friends, one of them George Klein, who was also a friend along with Joe Esposito. And as soon as George looked at the picture he knew it wasn't Elvis. I thought I would catch Joe by surprise and say, "Joe, can you tell me who this is?" And I expected him to say, "It's Elvis." And then I was gonna hit him with the date when it was taken.

G.G.: Why haven't you notified us of that when you presented us the pictures?

M.K.: When I had met Gail, Gail had said to me, they offered, they wanted to use the pictures.

G.G.: Right.

M.J.: And I said, "Well, you know it's not Elvis Presley." They said it's O.K. The picture is for this book (*Is Elvis Alive?*] and this book is really based on hypothetical ideas of putting it out. Of what would happen if Elvis was alive.

G.G.: We never said that.

M.J.: So I said to them, that, well, as long as I'm telling you this, that's it, and they said okay. So I went down to L.A. and made a deal with them to use it. At that time Gail said, "Would you like to appear with me on television shows?"

G.G.: To tell your story. We have you on tape telling your story.

M.J.: Larry King, Phil Donahue . . . I said, "Yea, great." I didn't know

what they were going to do with this. So about three days later I did this
film that she was talking about, saying what had happened with the picture. I never said it was Elvis Presley. I just said the picture was taken
there.

G.G.:   Yes you did.

M.J.:   I had then left L.A. Three days later, I got a call from one of her
associates saying they would like to buy the rights to the picture. They
knew I was just going to dispense with it anyway, from that time on.

L.K.:   The only way you know that it's not him is that a friend of his said
it wasn't him.

M.J.:   No.

L.K.:   They don't know who it is. Right?

M.J.:   Basically, my wife had brought it to my attention. She was on the
trip with me. As she remembers, not too long ago, "You know there was
a guy standing at the pool area. And with glasses on and everything."
George Klein had told me – and he didn't say Al Strada, [because] Al
Strada can look a little bit like Elvis. But George Klein told me it was his
cousin, Jimmy, who Elvis never liked, and [after] Elvis supposedly died,
Jimmy would then come around and then hang around Graceland.

G.G.:   And it's not Al Strada, it's Jimmy.

L.K.:   One guy says it's Jimmy. Joe, you say it's Al Strada.

J.E.:   Yes, I do.

L.K.:   Well, we have three different opinions. But you're the photographer, and you're now saying that you never said it's Elvis.

M.J.:   I never told them it was Elvis. In fact, the contract I have with her
associates says "the likeness of Elvis Presley." It says it right here in front
of me.

L.K.:   Okay. I understand we have a tape here where you're saying it is
Elvis. I'm not. I'm not verifying that. Is there a tape where you're saying
it *is* Elvis? Are you aware of a tape that you're on saying [that].

M.J.:   No. Well, you know, I wish they'd play it.

G.G.:   We have it. Play it.

Keep in mind, in the above dialogue, that Mike Joseph says he
changed his mind *after meeting with two of Elvis' friends, George
Klein and Joe Esposito.* But Esposito, who thought it must have been
Al Strada, had admitted earlier in the show that Strada does not
look like Elvis – except in this picture.

Most important, *who changed Joseph's mind?*

Although Mr. King had the *Breakthrough* video in his possession, and could have then and there publicly displayed to the
viewers the "change of story," this was not done. As for Elvis'
"cousin, Jimmy": Elvis has a cousin Jimmy Gambill, son of Elvis'
first double cousin, Patsy Presley Gambill. Indeed, Jimmy
resembles his cousin Elvis. However, Jimmy is only in his twen-

ties at this writing, and would only have been in his early to mid-teens at the time the poolhouse picture was taken! Anyone who has viewed the poolhouse picture knows that it is *not* a young teenage boy sitting there.

As for Al Strada, an extract from a letter from Todd H., of Merrillville, Indiana, is revealing: ". . .about this picture taken at the back of Graceland [showing] what looks like Elvis. I heard that this is Al Strada, but when I was in Memphis this year I was at the Days Inn and they had Strada there as a guest, and he told the crowd of people that it was not him in the picture!"

More: In the January 18, 1983, issue of *Globe*, an interview of Mike Joseph by John Blackburn was printed concerning the poolhouse photo. The article was headlined: "CAN THIS BE PROOF THAT ELVIS IS ALIVE?" Joseph is quoted as saying:

> On New Year's Day, 1978, my family and I decided to visit Graceland. I brought along my 35-millimeter camera.
>
> Some movement inside the back of the house caught my attention Through the glass door, I could see a man wearing dark glasses sitting in a chair staring out at the crowds. It was definitely Elvis – not a ghost, but Presley in the flesh. I almost dropped the camera as I turned to my wife and said: "Oh, my God, it's him. I just saw Elvis Presley, I really did. . ."
>
> But when I looked again, he was gone. Only the chair remained. My wife, of course, said I was imagining things. I felt embarrassed and agreed. So I wiped the incident out of my mind.
>
> [Later] I decided to dig out my old pictures of our trip to Graceland. This time I really scrutinized them and was shocked to discover that in one photo you could distinctly see a seated figure behind the glass door. "It can't be," I thought. "It just can't be." But after I viewed the figure through my son's magnifying glass, I realized I hadn't imagined my glimpse of Presley nearly five months after his reported death. Because my camera had also captured his image.

After the poolhouse photo became known to Graceland, the poolhouse door was built solid – no glass – so that no one could see in.

Once again I stress how obviously changed was Mike Joseph's story after his encounters with Joe Esposito and George Klein. Note also that in the Larry King interview, Joseph said his wife brought it to his attention that there "was a guy standing at the pool area. And with glasses and everything," yet in his *Globe* interview he says he noted a man sitting behind the glass door?

Maria Columbus and many others, including this author, met

personally with Joseph in California and he told the same story he gave to KCOP and to *Breakthrough*; we have many witnesses to this. Again, why did Joseph tell a different story on the *Larry King* show in August 1988, when only a year earlier, in an interview with Jane Van Der Voort of the *Toronto Sun* (August 1987), he talked about pulling out the pictures taken at Graceland: ". . . got out my son's magnifying glass, and I couldn't believe what I saw. It's strange because he's not in any other pictures." The article states that the photo left Mr. Joseph breathless. "A lot of people think he faked his death," said Joseph. "If he did die, his father was still alive and why would he allow an impersonator inside the house?" he said at the suggestion of a Presley lookalike.

Obviously Mr. Joseph believed it was Elvis enough to sell the temporary rights to *Playboy* magazine, according to his interview with Los Angeles' KCOP TV in January 1986, again repeating this sale in the *Toronto Sun* interview. Joseph also repeated this belief when selling the rights to the pictures to the man allowing us their use. When Joseph sent the negatives to Kodak, he must have believed it was Elvis, for he took pride in stating that Kodak said the film showed no sign in being altered in any way.

An added note: Some have suggested that the man sitting behind the poolhouse door could be Elvis lookalike Johnny Harra, who was used in the docudrama *This Is Elvis*, filmed in part at Graceland. However, *This Is Elvis* was not filmed until more than two years later. (See File Case No. 14.)

Although the following short section does not describe a "credible sighting" of Elvis, it will establish for the reader the mutual connection – for Muhammad Ali as well as for Elvis – to Michigan. A question I've frequently been asked goes something like this: "I have read and heard Mrs. Louise Welling talk about seeing Elvis Presley in Kalamazoo, Michigan, in 1988. *Is* there a Kalamazoo Connection?" I can only answer that there appears to be one. In 1977, a Kalamazoo newspaper ran this headline: "ELVIS SAW KALAMAZOO INCOGNITO." The writer of the article stated that Elvis came to do an April 26, 1977, concert (part of the final tour) and saw the city from the window of a nondescript Buick.

No one knows exactly what Elvis was looking for, but it would be well to note that Elvis had performed in Kalamazoo previously, and later at Wings Stadium in Kalamazoo. Kalamazoo is not a big place, so it was a bonus to have such a big star. The 1977 article says that "Elvis had been impressed with his treatment here."

Others have reported seeing a man by the name of Jon or John Burrows going into an old hotel that stood dormant for some time before being renovated into private offices. The management of that complex denies that either Mr. Burrows or Mr. Presley have anything to do with the complex. However, one radio interviewer did call prior to all the fuss of the sightings and asked to speak to Mr. John or Jon Burrows. Messages for this man – who wasn't there – were taken. Eventually Mr. T. (the radio man) was called back and told there was no Jon Burrows; then he was asked: "But what did you want with Mr. Burrows, anyway?"

This is not the first time this happened.

Kelly Burgess, a former assistant editor and feature writer with the *Detroit News*, contacted me twice in 1988–89 both for an interview and later with some shocking news. (In spring 1989, out of Las Vegas, she was interviewed on the *Billy Goodman* show, and now she told me the same story.)

At first, like many, Ms. Burgess was skeptical about the many rumors of Elvis sightings in Michigan – Kalamazoo in particular. Nevertheless, she decided to drive there from Detroit. Kelly told me that on the outside the hotel was rather nondescript, while on the inside the five-story building was attractive and hosted an atrium elevator. She encountered three security guards, who asked her to leave. But she remained unintimidated, going into several offices asking either for Elvis Presley or Jon Burrows. (Kelly was with her son at the time.)

The last office she went to was on the main floor, off the lobby. She asked a secretary the same question: "Is Jon Burrows or Elvis Presley here?" This time, Kelly was told to wait a minute, that the woman would get her manager. When the manager came out, he seemed very interested in her reasons for being there. Kelly's back was to the office door. Finally, the manager said, as he looked beyond Kelly to the office door, "There's the man you want to see."

Kelly turned around. She says it was like being hit by lightning. "It was Elvis Presley," she exclaimed. "His presence was overwhelming!" She was stunned, shocked. He motioned her to the lobby and she followed him. He shook his finger at her angrily and asked, "What are you doing in this building, bothering the tenants. I will not *have* this!" Kelly said she was doing a story on him, explaining that there were so many unanswered questions about his unclaimed insurance, etc.

"He stood and listened, without saying one word," Kelly continued. According to her, he said very little. Then his mood suddenly changed: He became very kind and somehow no longer felt threatened by her.

She was standing at an angle, and when Elvis turned she says she was looking at the "Elvis expression." He wore gold-rimmed glasses, slightly modified from what he had formerly worn. "His eyes sparkled, the same color, that expression. . ." she said. Kelly explained that it was his soul shining through, that his eyes seemed to say, "This is me."

For some reason, Kelly said she could not tell him that she knew he was Elvis Presley, so she said, "You look like Elvis Presley. Are you a relative?"

"Nope," he said.

He continued to listen quietly to the facts she outlined (why the life insurance was never collected, why the gravestone misspelled his middle name, etc.). His expression was now pleasant, and he was half smiling.

She said he was around six feet tall, weighed around 195, had a small pot belly, a full head of white hair, no sideburns, but with the same mouth, same eyes, same cheekbones. "It was Elvis."

Although he spoke little, before she left he said, "You know, it's against the law to hoax your death. . .?"

She left, but then decided to return to take a picture. She followed him into a construction office, where he sat behind his desk and put his head down, still saying very little. She wanted to give him her telephone number, but couldn't find a pen. He, too, searched for a pen. Neither finding one, she ripped out a deposit slip from her checkbook and handed it to him.

"It was Elvis. And his presence was electrifying!" she concluded, and our interview ended.

In a later telephone conversation with me, Kelly Burgess related that she had discovered evidence that was mind-boggling. I can understand why she does not want to reveal whether she managed to get pictures, or what other evidence she uncovered, because she has stated on the *Billy Goodman* show and to me earlier that she was doing her *own* book about Elvis, the years 1977 to 1988. Leter, she said she decided *not* to do the book, the evidence uncovered being "too frightening."

Kelly Burgess was a credible lady (she died last year). She was not the new kid on the block career-wise, but a mature woman with grown children. She had agreed to go on *Geraldo* with me, but, like all the other credible guests I was promised he would have besides me, Kelly was also "uninvited." Too credible?

(The entire *Billy Goodman* interview with Kelly is worth hearing. For those who wish a copy of the complete show, with other guests who had like stories, please contact me via Arctic and I'll give you that information. Stamped envelope please.)

Postscriptum: On Monday, August 22, 1988, an item in the *Detroit News* told that Harold Schuitmaker, a well-known Michigan politician and resident of Paw Paw (15 miles outside of Kalamazoo), said, "Elvis is alive and living in Kalamazoo. That is what I understand. I have not seem him personally, but I know people who have and I trust those people. Why Kalamazoo? It's a good place to hide."

IN AN INTERVIEW WITH MUHAMMAD ALI BY *MODERN PEOPLE* MAGAZINE in 1979, Ali called Elvis

> my close personal friend. Elvis came to my Deer Lake training camp about two years before he died. He told us he didn't want nobody to bother us. He wanted peace and quiet . . . and I gave him a cabin in my camp and nobody even knew it. When the cameras started watching me train, he was up on the hill sleeping in the cabin. Elvis had a robe made for me when I fought Joe Buckner in Las Vegas. I don't admire nobody, but Elvis Presley was the sweetest, most humble and nicest man you'd ever meet.

The robe Elvis gave Ali was embossed: "PEOPLE'S CHOICE."

At the museum at Graceland are boxing gloves Ali gave Elvis, as well as a picture of him and a personal letter. Elvis saw Ali box often in Las Vegas, Ali meeting with Elvis and vice versa when the singer performed there. There is one well-known Vegas picture entitled "The King Hanging Out with The Greatest," and stating that

the two had a mutual fascination with each other. Whenever they met, Muhammad Ali would playfully cuff Elvis, saying, "Gawd, we got to be two of the best-looking sumbitches in the world!"

In an article entitled "GREAT MEN DIE TWICE" in the June 1989 issue of *Esquire* magazine, Mark Kram held an interview with Ali, reminding Ali of a statement made by him concerning Elvis: "Elvis, you have to keep singin' or die to stay big."

Recall, now, File Case No. 2, about Elvis, the DEA, and President Carter. During his administration, not only had President Carter wanted to appoint Elvis to a special post, but the President sent Muhammad Ali on a fact-finding mission to Africa to meet with African leaders. Remember that Elvis spoke with Carter a few weeks prior to August 16, 1977. We also know Elvis spoke with Ali shortly before August 16, perhaps just a few days.

Some years ago, I received a telephone call stating the following: "I work at a hospital in New York where Muhammad Ali was for tests. While Ali was here I am certain Elvis quietly visited him. I know Elvis and Ali were close friends, thus a visit would be natural. However, this visit occurred in September 1984, seven years after Elvis Presley died!"

Because I have often received calls of this nature and since I had yet not planned to do *Is Elvis Alive?*, I mentally catalogued the information as "good but unsubstantiated."

In July 1989, I received a letter from Mary Panko, which I would like to give here almost *in toto*:

> Enclosed you will find a photocopy of the sports page from the *Cincinnati Post*. This copy isn't as clear as I had wanted. For that reason I have also enclosed a number of pictures of the page that I took on February 22, 1989. As you can see, I did not take the original picture.
>
> Note the date on the paper, also the picture in the lower right-hand corner [the Ali/Jackson/Elvis? photo]. All of these are copies of the paper I have here at home.
>
> After reading your book *Is Elvis Alive?* I checked the date on the paper. It seems that it falls close to the dates you wrote about. After thinking about it for months, I decided that you have the knowledge and connections to find out if it *is* important, considering everything that has been going on and all the talk.
>
> I realize it could very well be a very good lookalike and mean nothing. Although I have seen enough pictures of Elvis imitators to know I have never seen one that comes close, as far as I'm concerned.
>
> My head tells me Elvis Presley is dead, but my heart hopes he just found a way to get out and start over again.

I'm sure that between you and Maria Columbus you'll find the answers to all the questions. Whatever they may be.

When you have the time, I would appreciate knowing any information you find concerning the picture.

I hope the photocopies of the newspaper picture were what you wanted. If you need to use my name, feel free. I just didn't want anyone to think I took the picture. I've just given you some information I have had for almost five years. I'll take credit for giving the information, but not for taking the picture.

The news story was from the sports page ("*Sports Weekend*") of the *Cincinnati Post* of September 21, 1984, and was captioned "DISEASE MAY HAVE HURT ALI'S CAREER." The story was that Ali had checked into Columbia-Presbyterian Hospital in conjunction with Parkinson's Syndrome. Ali had checked out of the hospital on Thursday evening (September 23, 1984). With him were some people, among them the Reverend Jesse Jackson.

A surprised Ali found the press waiting. A UPI photographer was waiting and caught the following picture. Remember, the focus was on Ali and only Reverend Jackson and Ali were identified out of the photo. However, it is the man in the back—the only white man in the picture—who caught the attention of Mary Panko, a man who looks identical with Elvis Presley.

The same picture appeared in the *National Examiner,* in *Women's World,* and in *The Elvis Special*—all questioning who the man was in the background? Comments have ranged from "Well, yes, it does look like Elvis, but could it be air-brushed in?" to "An impersonator." (Why would Ali be with an impersonator?)

The questions make no sense: The focus of the UPI picture was on Ali, not the man in the background; it was in the sports section; *Is Elvis Alive?* had not been published; and why would UPI air-brush in anything that was not focused upon in the first place?

Furthermore, what about the woman who called me? Was she seeing a ghost? A physical man air-brushed in?

Fully realizing there are many who take what the tabloids report with a tongue-in-cheek attitude, the *National Examiner* reported on October 24, 1989, that the photo [Ali?] was sent to British experts involved with image analysis using the most advanced techniques in the world—a company that did work for the British Defense Ministry and Scotland Yard. The Photo was enlarged and enhanced by experts, who issued this statement: "We used every computer device to prove the photo was a fake, or that the man simply bore a resemblance to Mr. Presley. But there is no way we can be certain it isn't him. The likeness to Mr. Presley is incredible. It certainly could be Mr. Presley. In fact, the odds are overwhelming that it is Mr. Presley."

(Both the *Examiner* and this writer were unable to locate scientists in this country willing to undertake the task of photo analysis. Perhaps because Elvis Presley was/is a Federal Agent?)

The article continued:

> Another scientist who worked on the photo analysis said: "We have developed our own sophisticated methods of enhancing photographs, using computers to either make features stand out or fade into a background. Taking an image on the screen from a photo, we can change shades, play around with angles, measure noses, chins, and parts of the face to minute fractions.
>
> We compared this photo with dozens of known images of Mr. Presley and the similarities in the face are stunning.

A radio interviewer in Brockton, Massachusetts, said he had tracked down some TV footage taken of Ali leaving the hospital that evening, and that indeed a man resembling Elvis is seen. He reported: "There are several physical traits the man uses that are very Elvis; however, the man in question appears younger than Elvis could have been. . . . At times it looks like Elvis – at times, no. Of course he's only seen a few seconds and his eyes are closed."*

Observations came from others:

• Elvis had glaucoma; camera lights would affect him.
• He looked as though he wanted to get out of the frame in a hurry.
• He could look younger because of a facelift; or, as is outlined in one of Elvis' favorite books, *The Initiate,* rejuvenation occurs via meditation.
• He had lost weight; look at how young Elizabeth Taylor has appeared after her weight loss(es).

And so the analysis goes. Although the TV footage is not available anymore, I did see a private copy and I was as confused as anyone. Even in slow motion I seesawed. At first, when the mystery man comes into the frame, he smiles – a smile very much like Elvis! He squeezes his nose and looks down – a gesture Elvis

---

*In the TV footage, Ali said something to this effect: "I'll give a press conference so people will know I'm alright, because there are some people in this world who think some people are dead who are not dead."

used. On the other hand, as I viewed the seconds' worth, the man did appear too young to be Elvis (who would have been around 48), and at times did not look quite like Elvis. Then I looked back at the still and it looked just like Elvis!

When Muhammad Ali was in Fort Worth, Texas, toward the end of 1989, promoting his cologne, "Muhammad Ali,"* two people showed him the picture again and, as reported in the *Fort Worth Star-Telegram,* Ali identified the man in the picture with him as "my friend Elvis."

Once the picture was made known, many people began writing to Ali, who did not answer the questions posed concerning the picture but instead sent their letters back, sometimes with messages. (But enter more intrigue: The postmark on at least one of Ali's envelopes was Kalamazoo, Michigan!)

Sheila C., of Monson, Massachusetts, asked Ali: "Have you seen Elvis in the last five years?. . .Is he alive?. . .Is he in the picture with you leaving Columbia-Presbyterian Hospital in 1984?" Ali returned her letter with suggestions of books to read (*Is Jesus Really God?* and *Islam Explained*) and the following notation at the bottom of her letter: "Thank you, Love. Muhammad Ali, 9/5/89. Serve God. He's the goal." And he'd drawn a big heart below all this.

Dated October 4, 1989, an interesting letter reached me from Carol B., of Clinton, Tennessee. She told me she had written to Ali, asking him about the picture, and also asking if he would comment on the picture and Elvis' being in it. The night before she wrote me, she had been sitting talking with her visiting mother, father, and brother, and had been telling them about her letter to Ali, when

> the phone rang (about 7:00), and my husband answered. I heard him say, "Carl?" and "You must have the wrong number"; and he hung up. The phone rang again, and my son answered and told me it was for me. I said, "Hello," and this man said, "Carol, this is Muhammad Ali. I got your letter and I am sending you a picture right out." I asked, "What about the first part of my letter?" and he said, "I can't hear you." So I repeated it, and he said, again, "I will send your picture right out. Good-bye, Carol."

In a second note to me, dated February 1, 1990, Carol wrote, "Do you remember. I told you that I wrote to Muhammad Ali

---

*Incidentally, according to the November 1989 *Ms.* magazine, Frances Denney Corp. plans the global launch of a men's fragrance entitled "Elvis" in January 1991 (enough time for "the King" to get back to present it?).

again? This time I asked him twelve big questions – and I didn't expect to hear from him! Well, yesterday, I received a packet from
him with four Islam pamphlets. . ." But Ali still did not answer her
basic question, about Elvis' being in the photo.

Soon after this, I received a letter from Tina G., of Defiance,
Ohio. In response to her writing him, she, too, had had a call from
Muhammad Ali. She describes herself as "speechless" while he
spoke, but reveals that "basically, what he told me was that Elvis
Presley is dead. He said that Elvis' face was superimposed onto
that picture. He made it clear that it wasn't Elvis. He also said that
Jesse Jackson called him up when he first saw the picture and that
they kind of thought it was funny. He said that was because it's all
a joke that someone was playing. He said we have to accept that
Elvis is 'no longer with us.'"

Others who have written to, and received notes back from, Ali
have reported the same kind of response. Some have had
telephone calls, likewise, in which the thread of Ali's comment
about Elvis was that he was "gone," "dead," and that "I only met him
a couple of times," "I saw Elvis put in the ground," and "It's Elvis in
the picture, but it's superimposed."

Those who have called Graceland about the Ali/Elvis picture
have been told:

- We haven't seen the picture.
- It's superimposed.
- It's Joe Namath.
- Even if it were Elvis – which it isn't – why would he be with
  Ali, knowing there might be cameras around?

I recall reading an article, eons ago, that when Muhammad Ali
was asked about Cassius Clay, he replied that "Cassius Clay is
dead." (Many religions say that, in order to become spiritual, one
must bury the old and be born anew – which is why Muhammad
Ali is *not* Cassius Clay.) Could it be possible, then, that the old Elvis
Presley is dead – Elvis Aron Presley no longer living but Elvis
Aaron Presley very much alive? And what about "I saw Elvis put
in the ground"? To the best of my knowledge, Ali did not attend
the funeral – and even if he did, Elvis was not put "in the ground";
he was placed in a mausoleum. Also, what about "I only met him
a couple of times"? That is not true. And "superimposed"? That is
not true, either; this was verified not to have been the case.

Two final items on the Ali/Elvis photograph:

Jo Ann M., of Carrollton, Texas, went to Dillard's department store in Dallas in late 1989 because she knew that Ali would be there, promoting his cologne. She wrote, sending me a picture of herself taken with the ex-boxer, commenting: "I still say there's no reason for him not to say, 'Nope—it's not Elvis.' Why the reluctance to comment?. . . [This is] my hug after I gave him the photo of him and E.P. He put it in his suit pocket and just smiled."

Also in late 1989, a letter arrived from Edith B., of Franklin, Tennessee, who in October had gone to Elvis' stepbrother Billy Stanley's book-signing in Tennessee. (The book he wrote, with George Erickson, was entitled *Elvis, My Brother.*) Said Edith:

> I showed Billy the Ali picture and asked who was in it. Billy pointed out Ali, Jesse Jackson, and the other as 'Elvis Presley.' He then asked me where I'd got it and I said in an old newspaper. Several times more, he said it was Elvis Aron Presley—that *he* should know. He wanted a copy to hang on his office wall, saying it proved that Elvis was not a racist. He was definite about it being his brother, Elvis. However, I did not tell him the date of the picture: September 1984. All of this is on video, which my husband took and Billy said was O.K. if it turned up on TV. . . .

This author has seen a copy of the above video, and indeed Billy Stanley says without hesitation that the man in the picture is Elvis Presley, adding, "It's the same man as is on my book."

If it is not Elvis in the picture with Ali, who is it? I wasn't there when the picture was taken. You will have to be the judge, until more information surfaces. But. . . Kalamazoo?

FOLLOWING IS A SOMEWHAT "RENEGADE" SIGHTING—AND AN INTERESTING bit of Elvis numerology that develops nicely out of it. At the end of 1989 I received a letter from Alexander Longrifle who runs the Alexander Longrifle Youth Reservation for young people who are seeking help for drug or alcohol problems, runaways, throwaways. The reservation is a temporary home, a privately funded education and counseling project that has helped hundreds of teenagers. The reservation sits on ten acres of the Mojave Desert, near Edwards Air Force Base. It was founded in 1983 by Longrifle, actors Iron Eyes Cody, Rudolph Mantooth, Paul Wolfe, and Ben Lee, and "four others."

The letter said that a man who could have been Elvis Presley visited the reservation in November 1989 and presented Longrifle with an envelope in which there was a $15,000 cash donation. I called Mr. Longrifle and he agreed to an interview. Among the points he made were that the man came twice: once, just before dawn; a few days later, when it was very dark. He drove a very shiny, black Mercedes. He said very little. The first time, the man gave him a video and asked that he send a copy to me. (It shows a seated bearded man, whose features are difficult to make out and whose voice is "cloudy"-sounding – a heavy-set man – watching Elvis' last concert on a television set. Some of his words suggest he might be Elvis.) The second time, he handed Longrifle the large cash donation, which Longrifle said he reported, tax-wise. The man wore a hat, had a beard and mustache, and was graying. He was not fat, but a bit overweight. He was at least six feet tall, and wore boots, black leather jacket with some sort of Indian fringe, dark pants, a reddish shirt, no glasses.

"I think it could have been Elvis Presley," Longrifle said, "but it is so dark out here in the desert that I can't be sure. The first time I thought it *couldn't* be. But when he came back and gave me $15,000 cash . . . ?"

Longrifle explained that he taught music, karate, and kung-fu to the reservation residents and that he often raised money for the reservation by singing at various clubs. "I'm not an Elvis imper-sonator – I'm only five-foot-six – but I do a lot of Elvis material," he said. "I do other people's too. I know Ed Parker* well and have seen Elvis, but didn't know him." This explained to me how Elvis may have known about the Indian reservation. "Ed is pretty hushed up about Elvis," Longrifle explained.

Some thoughts come to mind:

- Elvis was part Indian.
- Elvis was interested in fighting drug abuse, especially when it came to youth.
- Elvis was known to give charitable gifts without taking tax deductions; thus, the cash?
- Elvis was into karate.
- Elvis knew Ed Parker.

In the video given to Alexander Longrifle, which he sent to me, a man is sitting alone in what appears to be a theater. He is bearded. But whoever may have taken the video was at a distance, and a positive identification is not possible. By the profile, it could be Elvis. The man is holding a tape recorder and watching a large

---

* A bodyguard and personal karate instructor for Elvis, Parker came originally from Hawaii.

screen on which may be seen Elvis in his final concert. The man with the recorder says these words: "I don't know how to start this message, but I feel terrible about the way I left. I was feeling real depressed and gaining a lot of weight, as you see. The doctor told me I had throat cancer and it was getting hard for me to sing. When I look at my videos and see myself, I know I let my fans down. There was just a handful of people I trusted, and to this day they stood by me. I'm getting a lot older, and, uh, I'm sorry for what I did. I really like keeping it this way." The sound is echoey, distant, and at times it does not sound like Elvis at all – especially when he pronounces the word "did" (too "country").

THE SUBJECT OF ELVIS' INDIAN HERITAGE HAS COME UP, ONCE AGAIN, since I received the Alexander Longrifle letter: many Elvis fans have written me, wondering why the new half-hour Elvis TV series on ABC is a "Navarone Production." Produced in part by Priscilla Presley, it appears curious to them that "Navarone" – meaning "long life" – is the name of her new three-year-old son. A common comment has been: "I would think [the show] would be by 'Lisa Productions.' Does little Navarone have some Indian blood?. . . And, did you note that 'Aron' is part of 'Navarone'?"

Since the name Ed Parker, too, is brought up in connection with my Alexander Longrifle correspondence, I want to reveal a letter received in October 1988 – shortly after a telephone call I'd had from a man identifying himself as Elvis (more about this call in a later File Case!). The letter, postmarked Nashville, reads as if it might have been written by Elvis, but the writer indicates he cannot identify himself. He does give some interesting information:

On your [Mystery] tape, Elvis states that he is playing a lot of raquet-ball, and doing a little karate.

In 1978, I was one of the top martial artists in the United States, and had the pleasure of being involved in a seminar with Ed Parker (Elvis' very good friend, and a karate instructor) . . .

Ed at that time was bodyguarding Elvis, and would often be found backstage assisting Elvis on and off. Ed lives in California, where he runs a chain of top martial arts schools. But are you aware of the fact that Ed is Hawaiian and also maintains a home in Hawaii? If you check a 1977 or '78 issue of *Inside Kung-Fu* magazine, you will find several pictures of Ed and Elvis training. You will also notice that Elvis has the karate school emblem on his guitar. Around Ed's neck is a T.C.B. bolt of lightning that Elvis gave to those who worked for him . . .

There was an incident that took place at one of the Elvis concerts where a man jumped on the stage and Elvis took him out with several karate moves. At the time, I was informed that this was a setup by Ed ("The Big Kahuna," as he was called by Elvis). As far as the pranks that Elvis would pull and his ability to slow down his heart rate, etc., these are things that Ed was very capable of teaching to Elvis. . . . Believe me, karate was Elvis' main thing in keeping fit. If you were a person that lived like Elvis, believe me, martial arts can become a savior. . .

Instead of a signature, the writer of the typescripted letter added some Chinese characters at the bottom. Recently, a master certified graphoanalyst and certified court document examiner, Paul Weast, of Anaheim, California (more from Weast in File Case 16), had the Chinese anlyzed. The top-left group of two figures translated as the number 18; beneath them, four others translated as 36. Numerologically speaking, either figure adds up to 9, Elvis' spiritual number. Interestingly, a Chinese grouping of characters at upper left *could* be translated as a sound we would spell as "sive" (Sivle?).

A Potpourri of Alleged Contacts with Elvis

Though a good deal is too strange to be believed,
nothing is too strange to have happened.
—THOMAS HARDY

Question: If Elvis is alive, has he been sighted?
Answer: Much has been written about a man looking like Elvis Presley and/or sounding like Elvis Presley being sighted or having called into radio stations—enough so that many stations, such as WEBE in Bridgeport, Connecticut, still offer as much as $1 million to anyone who can bring in the king of rock 'n' roll. Another station gave out "Elvis for President" buttons during the Bush/Dukakis campaign.

E ven before my book *Is Elvis Alive?* was released, I received letters of Elvis sightings—this because of my novel *Orion.* After *Is Elvis Alive?* was released, an abundance of letters arrived, some of them obvious put-ons. Most, however, were written with integrity. Whether printed here *in toto,* excerpted from, or paraphrased, the letters mentioned in this file case are in my offices. Because of the ridicule Louise Welling of Kalamazoo, Michigan, suffered in 1988 for publicly stating she has seen Elvis Presley in the Kalamazoo area, I have left off the last name and addresses of those writing.

"I've been telling the truth," Mrs. Welling swears. "I saw Elvis
Presley. Others have too. I am not making this up – I know what
I saw. It was Elvis; he got very nervous when I talked to him. I
know of another woman who saw him at a pet store. There was
a big blue van outside with a beautiful dog sitting in the front seat.
Going into the store, she asked who the dog belonged to and this
man with grayish hair and beard answered politely, 'It belongs to
me.' She swears it was Elvis Presley." Mrs. Welling was heard, via
telephone remote, on the *Oprah Winfrey* show (May 1988) and her
comments have been published in many newspapers and tabloids.

I interviewed the woman named by Louise Welling, but
because of the possibility of ridicule, she did not want to go public.

A media Catch-22? Yes, indeed. "If Elvis is out there, why
aren't they talking?" ask the media. Yet when "they" do talk, those
same media infer that they are "wackos."

THE FOLLOWING ARE A POTPOURRI OF LETTERS, PUBLICATIONS, PRINTED
versions of telephone conversations, all of which nurture the
belief that Elvis may still be alive. Several of them date from the
months and years immediately following his "death" on August 16,
1977. A majority are from the late 1980s, and some cited date from
this first year of the millennium's last decade.

As early as its September/December 1979 issue, *The Elvis
Special* published the following "letter" from a dictation by "J.B."
("Jon Burrows," Elvis' chosen alias). The fan letter entitled it
"Message from a Friend..."

Before I left, my thoughts were of all of you. I wanted to leave
behind beautiful memories for all of you to share. You see, I knew

you loved me and you would grieve deeply for me. I wanted you to remember me with smiles and love. . .of a favorite song, concert or dreams. Also of my belief in my fellow men. . .always wanting the best for my family, friends and fans. Wanting to share my dreams, goals and ideas with people I love.

Now when I should be at peace and you should be going onward and growing, I feel so much hate, envy and jealousy. . .instead of leaving beautiful thoughts behind me. I find only rubbish going down as guidelines from *friends* wanting the public to know the total truth of the legend known as Elvis Presley.

Just what is truth my friends— Is *truth* calculated as *money*?? Is truth known in *friendship*?? Is truth known in *love*?? Is truth known in *caring*?? Just what is it? I need to know!

I want you to know I gave all of these in loving moments in time. I shared myself and found out that I shared it with Judas.

Friends that would turn against me after death who did not have the *courage* to face me in life. This is a reason for dying!!

Thank you Dee, Rick, David, Red, Sonny, David, Lamar and all the others to follow. Thank you for letting the *Truth* come out since I am not allowed to contribute to the great array of intelligent blood-letting. But, may I ask one question? If this is the truth, what must your lies be??

I've always been hungry for love and affection. I thought *my* friends could help, but I found out that *my friends* and certain (ex) relatives only wanted two things. . .money and fame. Well, folks, you got it.

I wish you many, many years of love and enjoyment from life. But I have to say that you will have these *truths* on your conscience. Perhaps in a later life you can work off the Karma for putting the fans who love me through Hell. I'll pay for any Karma I have performed. You are lucky—you have time.

I send love and healing to all the people that love me.

Thank you for believing in me.

J.B.

Although Bill A., of Orange, California, wrote me late in the 1980s, his tale is of that same year, 1979. He retells what a friend of his related to him:

...a mutual friend of ours was trying to sell a limited-edition Harley-Davidson motorcycle (a 1976 Bicentennial model). After placing an ad in most of the papers in the Southern California area, he got a call from a man identifying himself as a representative of the famous car builder George Barris. (Barris is the man responsible for the "Monkees Car," the "Bat-Mobile," the "Munsters Car," and a host of other custom Hollywood-type automobiles.) He said Mr.

Barris was starting a museum, and was looking for one-of-a-kind vehicles, and specialty items. The representative *and* Mr. Barris showed up, bought the bike, and over coffee the subject of music arose (the bike owner plays a little guitar, and likes Elvis). Mr. Barris told our friend that Elvis was a close personal friend of his, and he had done some special favors for Elvis on some of his cars, and that in fact Elvis was not dead. . . .

Although it occurred nine years later, a similar, automobile-related sighting of Elvis deserves to be told at this point. The tale comes from Alton R., who lives outside Nashville. He relates that he was

working a second job at a gas station. At approximately 9:30 P.M. I was talking on the telephone to my mother when a man stopped in for gas. As he approached the store to pay for his purchase, I told my mother, "I think this man is Elvis Presley."

Then the man came in and paid for his gas with a credit card. I said, "Hello." He didn't speak. While processing his change, I said, "You look just like Elvis." No response. I then took notice of his jewelry and the twenty-dollar gold-piece belt buckle, and made a remark about them. And still no response.

As he was leaving the store, I inquired once more, and then I got a response. He turned to me, smiled with the same crooked smile, and winked and left without a word. I am convinced that Elvis was in my presence that night.

SIGHTINGS OF ELVIS AT GRACELAND—NOT TO MENTION MIKE JOSEPH'S poolhouse photo-sighting—began not long after the entertainer's "death," and have continued.

A letter recently received from Dorothy W., of Romilus, Michigan, describes an early sighting: "My sister and her husband went to Graceland not long after Elvis was supposed to have died. One night, they could not sleep. They went [from their hotel or motel?] down to Graceland and were sitting on a bench out in front. It was about 2:30 A.M. They said they saw this big black car come down the drive. In the passenger seat they swear Elvis was sitting. He was wearing sunglasses. . . ." If he were an impostor, they asked themselves, "why would he be there so late—and why?"

In an *Elvis Special Quarterly* in 1986 was printed some startling comment from a British visitor to this country, Jeanette K.: "I've heard something about that January 1978 mystery photo [she means Joseph's], or is this another incident. A Scottish fan took some pictures outside Graceland in February 1985, and from a downstairs window it looks like Elvis watching. I saw these pix at a convention and had to sit down, I got so *shook up!"*

E. Jacob F., of Berkeley, Missouri, tells that he and his wife arrived in Memphis on May 4, 1987, in the early afternoon:

> Upon arrival we immediately got our tickets to tour Graceland. . . . When we got off the bus in front of the mansion, the tour guide told us that after the tour we would be able to come back in front of the mansion and take pictures. The guide then took us inside the mansion. The staircase in the entry hall leads to Elvis' private quarters. The guide said the family didn't want anyone touring the upstairs rooms. She said the employees are not even permitted to see those rooms.
>
> As the tour ended, my wife and I walked out to the bus; we were the only ones at the bus at this time. My wife stayed there while I walked up to the mansion to take a better look. When I got even with the mansion, I looked up to the second floor, and in the corner window I saw Elvis Aron Presley, looking toward the front gate. He turned and in seeing me raised his arms to close the window. . . .
>
> About twenty seconds later, a security guard came up behind me and told me that I couldn't be in front of the mansion and that I would have to get on the bus, which I did. When I got inside the bus, the driver said that Priscilla was down in the yard just up from the gate and that some people were taking pictures of her for a documentary. Then I knew what Elvis was looking at. I also knew why they didn't want anyone touring the upstairs rooms. . . .

When I was a late-spring 1988 guest on the *Bear O'Brian* radio show, in Columbus, Georgia, a woman who would identify herself only as Martha called in, stating that she and her husband had visited Graceland in June the year before, at about 2:30 one morning. As they got out of their car, "a black car with a driver and a passenger pulled up to the gates. . . The windows were down. I was looking at the passenger – looking full into the face of Elvis Presley!" she told me.

An August 9, 1989, missive to me from Dawn M., of Buffalo, New York, describes an Elvis sighting at Graceland that same year. She must have been in the Memphis area for a few days. She tells how,

> the last night I went, there was a lot more security than usual and we were ushered off the grounds very fast. All the previous times I was there, we had all the time in the world.
>
> I decided to watch the house after the tour was over, and I noted

that all the workers seemed also to leave Graceland as soon as the tours were finished. I continued to stay, and at nearly 9:00 P.M., while it was still light outside, the gates of Graceland suddenly opened and two trucks and a big black car with tinted windows came speeding into the driveway up to the mansion.

I was standing on a garbage can, so I could see quite a bit. Out of the trucks came a few men, who started to unload them, and they unloaded what looked like trunks and suitcases. Then, as this was going on, a door opened from the black car and out came a woman [Priscilla?]—who was short, with what looked like brown hair and with a small child. Then a woman with blond hair [Lisa?] holding a baby came out, followed by a man with brown hair. Out of the driver's seat came what I thought was a rather shorter, heavier-set man with a small amount of gray hair. Then out of the passenger's seat came a tall, rather heavy-set man with black or dark brown hair [Elvis?]. It was hard to make out details.

I didn't know what to make of it. Could it have been Lisa, Priscilla, Elvis, and other companions? Maybe it was just a crazy coincidence, though, or a hunch. But it was strange.

"Direct contacts," if that is indeed what they are, with Elvis have been frequently made on CB radio. In a letter received not long ago from Evelyn M., of New Sarpy, Louisiana, the writer tells of one such contact in 1982 or 1983: ". . .on my CB radio one evening about 8:00 P.M., he asked me if I would like to hear a song." Evelyn asked her interlocutor to sing "Blue Suede Shoes," and he complied, "and thanked me for talking with him. . . . I'll swear on my life it was Elvis," she told me.

Along the same lines, the following recent letter—from Debra H., of Jacksonville, Texas, a lady of thirty-five who had had an earlier feeling/experience of Elvis in a friend's house but who said she worked for the U.S. Post Office and had no "loose screws" — relates another experience, this time more real, on a trip with a friend, from Texas to Missouri in (probably) 1983:

We were driving in the Ozark Mountains in Arkansas during the middle of the night and we were talking to truck drivers on the CB radio. I swear to you that if I hadn't had a witness with me, I never would have repeated what I'm going to tell you. No one would have believed me. But my girlfriend was there, so we know it really happened.

We were talking to a trucker and all of a sudden this voice interrupted and started singing an Elvis song. I got cold chills all over my body. We looked at each other and nearly freaked out. He sang part of an Elvis song, and then the radio went dead. I keyed the mike and said, "Please don't stop." The guy laughed and finished the song.

We started talking to him and asking a lot of questions. He answered every question about Elvis that we asked. He sang every song we asked him to. We kept trying to trip him up. We thought that this guy was good – but that he couldn't know *everything*. We drove for hours through those mountains, and he sang for hours and answered oodles of questions. When he talked to us, it was just an ordinary voice – any old Joe – but when he sang, it was Elvis. . . . He said his CB handle was "Ghost of the King." He said that he had worked for Elvis once as a bodyguard. . . .

Two last personal sightings of Elvis, one more direct than the other, should be mentioned before citing the deluge of sightings that have occurred primarily from 1988 on.

Gladys D., of Seattle, Washington, wrote me:

I, too, have twice in the past five years seen Elvis – once with my eldest grandson at a concert here in Seattle. It was the Rolling Stones' concert one time – a huge crowd, but there we were, and we were *positive* that the man right ahead of us with a young lady [was Elvis]. He had a beard, large cowboy-type hat on. But those eyes and that voice we would never have mistaken. I am sure that others watched him and also knew who he was. Many turned around and looked as Elvis kept talking. And they, too, *heard that voice*. It surely was a shock to both of us. I had never gone to an Elvis concert. However, my grandson had.

Again, I saw him in the hospital I was employed in for over thirty years. This time, he visited an elderly gentleman on the floor I worked on. He had on the same hat, only better-looking clothes. But the same beard. I stayed as close as possible, to better hear his voice. "It was Elvis?" I asked the patient later, about his visitor that day. He said, "Oh yes. He is an old friend of mine, John Anderson."

A fan, Sunny, in Jonesboro, Georgia, has written me about a meeting with Elvis in Dayton, Ohio, in October 1987. It is interesting in that she saw the singer in the baseball cap he has several times been spotted wearing. Her words:

I prefer to remain anonymous. I spoke briefly to my husband about the whole experience, and we ended up laughing the whole thing off. It seemed too ironic to have seen *him:* ELVIS.

We were at the Air Force Museum in Dayton. I was becoming bored with the airplanes and jets, and decided to venture off on my own. My husband was very involved in the histories, etc. – I

was more interested in how hungry I was. I went off in search of
a snack bar.

It was somewhere around some W.W. II warplanes that it all
began. There was this man – a bit on the heavy side with salt-and-
pepper hair. A green, maybe gray baseball hat on. He was looking
at an airplane and caressing the propeller. I noticed him and figured
he must work there – cleaning the props or something. I went over
and asked where the snack bar was.

He said, "Beats me. I brought my own." And he held up a paper
sack and a canned orange drink. He grinned a bit and he looked a
bit familiar, but I didn't try to figure out who he looked like. He had
on a brown nylon jacket with the collar turned up and a white T-
shirt with blue jeans.

I remember smiling at him. He just looked familiar – not like
someone I personally knew – but he just had one of those faces that
looks like someone you *may* know. I must have been staring at him
for a while. He was completely clean-shaven, but had razor stubble
and no sideburns. His glasses were tucked onto the neck of his
T-shirt.

He turned around pretty fast and said that the snack bar was
probably upstairs. Then suddenly, the voice sounded familiar – a
sort of Southern drawl, but very deep. I said, "You're from the South
aren't you?"

He answered that he was, but I don't remember exactly how he
said it – something like "Yes. . . but not for long enough." Or something to that effect. I remember laughing and saying that I was from
Georgia and my husband was from Tennessee.

He turned back around and said, "Tennessee." Nothing else, just
that – and he sort of shook his head and grinned. "What part?" I told
him, "Maryville." He said, "Umhm. . . the Smokies. . . pretty country. A man could live happy in the Smokies."

I couldn't stand it any longer. Cat and Mouse was not ever my
favorite game. "Do I know you??" I asked him. He smiled and said,
"Maybe. Maybe not." Then he paused and said, "Probably." I couldn't
place him at all – but God, he looked familiar. "Don't worry 'bout it,
darlin," he said. "It will come to ya. But don't let it get to ya, deal?"
I nodded and said, "Yeah, deal."

He walked away from me and I headed towards the upstairs. It
hit me halfway up the steps, and I felt almost dizzy. I ran back down
the steps to find him. He was getting on a bus to go out to an
outbuilding to view some other planes. I stood in the doorway and
watched as he sat down on the front seat. He glanced out the
window and waved to me. Then he held up one finger and made an
O.K. sign and gave me a friendly look of question as if to say: "Figure
it out??" I nodded, and gave him a peace sign back. He held up one
finger again and, in a second, a young black boy got off the bus and
gave me a paper sack with a balogna sandwich inside and a bag of

Cheetos. The bus drove off – and I couldn't move. I knew I had seen Elvis Presley. It was amazing.

The excitement faded when I told my husband – and, like I said, we had a good laugh and eventually threw away the bag and ate the Cheetos. I had completely forgotten the whole thing until I read your book. I was stunned. Is it possible I really saw him? I don't want to tell anyone but you, because I know he really wants to be left alone. Besides, no one would believe me anyway. I wouldn't believe it either, if someone told me. . . .

THE SIGHTINGS OF, AND TELEPHONE CONTACTS WITH, ELVIS BECOME more voluminous in the last two years of the 1980s decade. Three of the earliest are – remember File Case No. 9 and "Kalamazoo Connection"? – in Michigan.

On May 25, 1988, *Kelly & Company*, on Detroit's WXYZ-TV, reported a call from a man sounding very much like Elvis. On June 5, a postcard sent me from Coldwater/Kalamazoo/Battle Creek's WNWN/WHEZ radio told that that day "Elvis Presley was seen in Battlecreek Mich. . .driving a dark blue or black van wearing a white jump suit, [and] was seen on Mich Ave by the Kellogg Community College Campus. Time seen was 11:55 A.M." And a man from Sterling Heights, Michigan, wrote me: "I have had the most shocking and incredible experience in my life. I'm telling you because you're the only one who would even think of taking me serious. What I am about to tell you is true, although I cannot force you to believe it. On Wednesday, September 7, 1988, around one or two P.M. at the Lakeside Mall in Sterling Heights. . .I saw and talked to Elvis Aron Presley."

The writer then explained that he followed Elvis into Record Town, pretending to look at some sale cassettes. Elvis went to where the Monkees albums were and asked the salesman about a current recording. Elvis then apparently spotted one of his own albums; it was an album of "Elvis in Concert," and he laughed. At this point, my correspondent mustered the courage to walk up to him and ask, "Haven't I seen you before?" Elvis laughed, and they began a conversation, talking mainly about music. Finally, they walked from the music store to a bookstore. No one appeared to recognize Elvis, I was told – his hair was different, he had no sideburns. At one point, the two spoke about dogs, Elvis saying that he had an old English sheepdog and an airedale but that he wanted a "wolf hybrid." Before leaving the man, and the mall, Elvis said that if he did come back, he would make a "public announcement" and that everything would be "different."

Elvis was, reportedly seen and heard from, elsewhere than in

Michigan, however. In its October 25, 1988, issue, the *National Examiner*, a tabloid, told how two sisters, Noreen and Janet Bell, saw Elvis enter the Church of Scientology in Hollywood, unaware themselves that a wedding was to take place there between Lisa Marie Presley and musician Danny Keough. "Janet and I were trying to hail a cab," Noreen told the *Examiner*, "when suddenly we spotted Elvis. He was wearing a blue baseball hat and sunglasses." Before entering a side door, according to Noreen, "he looked around as if to see if he was being followed. He took off his hat and our suspicions were confirmed 100 percent. He was paunchier than we remembered and his lustrous black hair was graying. But it was definitely him."

The sisters waited outside the church for about forty minutes. When Elvis came out, they told, he was in a hurry and they lost him in the crowd. "We didn't know it at the time," Noreen related, "but Elvis must have been attending Lisa Marie's wedding unobtrusively. Since he didn't arrive or leave with anyone, we believe he must have stood quietly in the shadows watching his only child get married."

It is indeed true that Lisa Marie Presley married Daniel Keough in 1988. The date was Monday, October 3. Why would they marry on a Monday–a somewhat curious day of the week? It has been surmised that, numerologically speaking, the date totals 2001. (October is the tenth month; the day was the third day of the month; the year was 1988.)

Also in October 1988, syndicated columnist Ann Landers reported–following a column in which she had affirmed that there was convincing evidence Elvis Presley had indeed died in August 1977–being swamped by a deluge of irate letters. A Stamford, Connecticut, letter writer stated that he had gone to the funeral and tried to linger at the casket but was "hurried on" by guards. He asserted that it was not Elvis in the casket, that it was a wax dummy, and would bet "my life on it." A letter to Ms. Landers from Nashville spoke about a woman who was president of an Elvis fan club and who received a phone call from Vernon Presley asking her not to attend the funeral. The woman, who lived some one hundred miles from Nashville thought something was "fishy." She was convinced the funeral was staged and that Elvis was alive. A Bay City, Michigan, resident wrote Landers about having seen Elvis in a supermarket, and that the singer gave a wink as if requesting the man not to say anything or tell anyone.

Landers concluded her column: "What you have just read is a small sampling of the mail that continues to pour in."

AND NOW, LET US CONSIDER THE POSSIBILITY OF A SWISS CONNECTION with the "dead" Elvis Presley.

A most interesting call reached me toward the end of 1988 from a Mr. Dougherty, a producer of documentary and other films. He told me he had just returned from Switzerland, and that both while he was there and since his return he had been asked to call me, he said, about my novel *Orion* (first published in 1979). I extract, below, from what he said to me:

> Are you familiar with a place called Gstaad? There is a private school there called "The School" – a high-security school where the "sons of shakers" send their children. . .strong bonds are formed . . .a network, an octypus in the world of finance and power – highly secret. I was asked to front an organization to produce a film about the school. In conversation the name Elvis Presley came up; I was told Elvis Presley was one of the money men involved. . . sounded like a fairy tale to me. Somehow the school and other organizations are interconnected; I can't separate them. . .Swiss bank involved. . .Most of the group I was talking to was made up of Italians; they brought up your book *Orion*. . .interested in making a major motion picture but not in Italy. . . .

Mr. Dougherty said that he would get back to me. He has not done so. He said he had offices in Florida and Los Angeles. When I questioned further, about the specifics of what he wanted, he grew hesitant, secretive. I still don't know what to make of him, or of his calls.

But it is curious, about Switzerland. I have heard that, since her father's "death," Lisa attended school in Switzerland on occasion. And a well-known celebrity (who fears being identified) tells me that Elvis spent time in Switzerland after 1977 at a famous eye clinic, where his glaucoma was treated, and that he also spent time at a top-security health spa and clinic that the wealthy frequent.

Then, in April 1989, a Swiss bank based in Lausanne sponsored a series of Elvis "Reunion" concerts, for which many of Elvis' friends, as well as former musicians and backup groups, were flown over. In the April 1989 *Around the World with Elvis News* (as well as in other media) the following news item was announced:

> A crowd of some 1,600 attended the Beaulieu Theatre in Lausanne for the first of five "Reunion" concerts across the country by Elvis' original backup band on April 8, 1989.* Joining original members

---

*This reunion date also equals, numerologically, 2001.

James Burton (lead guitar), Jerry Scheff (bass), Ronnie Tutt, Glenn
Hardin (piano), and John Wilkinson (guitar) was an orchestra of ten
strings, sixteen horns and six Swiss backup singers for a total of
forty-eight musicians and vocalists. Original backup singers Sherril
Nielsen, Charlie Hodge, and Kathy Westmoreland completed the
unit. In addition, J. D. Sumner & The Stamps were also on hand to
add to the excitement. After a nationwide search, twenty-nine-year-
old guitarist-singer Steve Payntor was chosen to perform the Elvis
songbook. Opinions varied on how well Payntor did with his Elvis
impersonation. All agreed, however, that he looked the part! These
were the first public appearances by the backup unit since 1977.
Speaking for the group, J. D. Sumner said performing together again
"felt real good."

The funding of this "Reunion" trip must have totaled an astronom-
ical amount of money. And, another curiosity: Note that the
performance was held in a theater called Beaulieu. Beaulieu is
Priscilla Presley's maiden name.

The above *Around the World* item was sent to me by Carol R.,
of Erie, Pennsylvania. In a phone call to me, she suggested:

Is it possible that Elvis Presley owns the Beaulieu Theatre in
Switzerland? It would take a great deal of money to bring so many
people over – plane, hotels, meals, expenses, etc. Could such an
expense be profitable [to the bank or theater]? Or were these "Elvis
people" brought over for another reason? Was the "Reunion" just
that? Perhaps Elvis was there; perhaps these folks – or the majority
of them – found out for the first time that Elvis was alive. And
where do it but in a neutral country such as Switzerland? Would
they keep the "secret" until Elvis came forward? I'm sure they
would, and I'm not even a close friend! . . . Find out if Elvis has had
any other connections in Switzerland. . . .

"Elvis" would also appear to have a Hawaii Connection. A
woman who identified herself only as S.B., from Palm Springs,
California, wrote that she lived in Hawaii for a year and a half, on
the island of Oahu. "Anyway, on the north shore," she said, "there
is a secluded house, with iron gates, and on them a musical sign."
(Shades of Memphis?) She told me that she managed to peer over
the wall, believing that some famous singer might live there, and
saw Elvis lounging in the grounds. She passed off the sighting as
signs that she might be going mad, since it had been many years
since he died!

Last year, I received another Oahu-connected Elvis item in a
letter from Marjorie H., of Centerville, Indiana. She wrote: "Our

cable TV station from Earlham College in Richmond, Indiana (a religious college), had a DJ who said he talked to Elvis Presley. I asked him, 'How did you know when to call?' and he said that he, the DJ, was from Oahu and had seen Elvis on the street and stopped and talked to him. . . . I asked the DJ for a copy of the show [on which he'd spoken to Elvis]; he said he would send it; he didn't. I went to the radio station, but he said he couldn't talk to me, and that there were no copies of the show. The DJ has returned to Oahu," she added.

Several letters reached me a few months ago, all of them about the Aloha Bowl game held in Honolulu on Christmas Day, 1989, and all writers professing to have seen Elvis. Most of them stated that "at half-time Crystal Gayle sang a couple of Christmas songs . . . the camera moved on, but when it came back to Crystal there was a tall man with black hair and sideburns standing beside her. . . high cheekbones, long slender legs, singing 'The Battle Hymn of the Republic.' " And: "I *felt* more than *thought* that the man was Elvis" was a common statement.

Kay H. of Cheyenne, Wyoming, an Aloha Bowl spectator, wrote a letter to a record promoter in Texas, who says he has heard from Elvis. He replied to Kay that it probably was Elvis in Hawaii: "That's his beloved homeland," the record producer stated. Marjorie H., of Centerville, Indiana, another Bowl spectator, wrote me that she thought she recognized Elvis, but was even more surprised at the song he joined in singing. She thought the choice of "Battle Hymn of the Republic" was "odd" [given Elvis' Southern origins?].

Because there are so many Elvis lookalikes, the man singing that day could, logically, have been an impersonator. However, it is worth remembering that Elvis was made an Honorary Hawaiian because of his love of Hawaii, his Hawaii movies, the fact that he performed at a benefit concert for the U.S.S. Arizona Memorial Fund (helping to raise thousands and thousands of dollars, March 25, 1961), and his 1973 "Aloha Concert" that was widely televised. On August 17, 1977, the day after Elvis' "death," the Navy laid a wreath at the Arizona Memorial in his honor.

"If I could not live at Graceland, I would live in Hawaii," Elvis often stated. I have been told that Elvis did/does have a home in Hawaii, and several Hawaiian radio stations told me that many locals have long rumored Elvis to be alive and living there. While I was in Memphis in 1988 with a film crew, we were told by our van driver, who was from Hawaii, "Elvis is alive and living there, from time to time . . . "

"ELVIS EVENTS" OF THE VERY EARLY PART OF THIS YEAR TAKE US TO Florida, where *newspapers* got into the "sightings" act. The *Palm Beach News* had some interesting reportage in early January. Donna H., of Palm Beach, sent me the article "LEGENDS HAVE GHOST OF A CHANCE LURING ELVIS," by Pedro Abigantus. It appeared that Elvis was coming to town (again, for a sporting event). The paper reported:

> Officials of the Senior Professional Baseball Association's St. Lucie Legends say they have received telephone calls from an Elvis Presley. "Elvis has called five or six times," Legends General Manager Ray Negron said. "We have him on tape. It sounds very much like him."
>
> The caller has identified himself as the real Elvis Presley and says he lives near Lake Michigan. He did not leave his phone number. The first call came three weeks ago, Negron said. Looking for proof, Negron took the tapes to a Port St. Lucie radio station. A station official, Negron said, made voiceprints and has concluded the voice on the tape is a perfect match. . . .
>
> Why would Elvis rise from the grave and return a decade later in Port St. Lucie?
>
> Elvis told Legends office manager Sue Schaming, "I consider myself a legend and want to be with the Legends. I also love the senior-league concept." Schaming believes it was the real Elvis. "I heard him sing . . . it couldn't be anybody but him," she said. "My heart and soul know him that well. My parents were crazy about him, and my boyfriend is an Elvis freak. All my life I have been around his music. I know it was him."
>
> Negron isn't as sure that Elvis is Elvis. But the Legends are willing to accommodate him. Elvis, Negron said, made two requests: He wants the Legends to open the center field wall for him to drive onto the field, and he wants extra security. When Elvis drives in, his automobile will circle the bases. He will be escorted by private guards and perhaps a K-9 unit. The rock legend then will "explain a few things and sing a few songs," Negron said.
>
> And what has Elvis been doing since death?
>
> "He said he watches a lot of sporting events and enjoys a regular life. The reason he has stayed away from the public eye is he wanted to rest from everyone [because he was] harassed constantly. He wanted to be a plain citizen."
>
> Is this a publicity stunt by a team averaging 723 fans per home game?
>
> "I am curious, too," Legends publicity director Estelle Krieger said. "We are not saying it is him. We are not saying it is not him. All we are saying is someone claiming to be him called and said he would be here that night. Maybe he is alive and wants to make a comeback."

Donna H. also wrote me that radio station Z-93, of Port St. Lucie, told her an "Elvis" person started calling in early December, saying he would be in town the week of January 8, loves baseball, and wanted added security!

A letter dated January 5, 1990, reached me from another fan, Regina H., of Pelham, Georgia, telling that:

> I heard that Elvis might show up at a Legends ball game in Port St. Lucie, Florida, Thursday night, January 11. Friday night I still had not heard anything on the news about it, but a friend called me to say that a man dressed like Elvis driving a white limo, who had a policeman with him, did show up at this game. So I called the Port St. Luce Police Dept. I asked the lady who answered if she knew anything about a Legends ball game there Thursday night. She said she did. I told her what I had been told about Elvis being there. She said, "Yes, maam, he was there."

A letter to me from a young North Carolinian named Linda S. is a bit more informative. Linda called the Legends' main office on Friday, January 12, and talked with a young woman there who had been at the game and who confirmed that "Elvis," in a white limo, had sung three songs – "Teddy Bear," "American Trilogy," and "I Can't Stop Loving You" – then talked awhile, and left. He had stayed fifteen to twenty minutes. Then Linda tossed in some numerological data: "First of all, when calculating January 11 using Elvis' new spelling of Aaron, it comes out to be a day that would certainly have suited his coming out. If you have *Cheiro's Book of Numbers*, check out the compound number 17, which is what this date adds up to for Elvis. Second, the caller mentioned a farm on Lake Michigan." Ali's farm is indeed in Michigan.

As it turns out, Linda also called the Port St. Lucie newspaper "and learned that they did not even bother to cover the event – no report or photos. I just felt if he ever did do something like this, the media would be too skeptical to cover it."

In a Sunday, July 1, 1990, article in the *New York Times* entitled "Nostalgia Can Choke the Ongoing Stream of Your Life," writer James Gorman protested that "the continuing cults of Marilyn Monroe and Elvis Presley speak of the acute sense of personal loss that underlies the dream of American progress and success." He rather snidely suggested that, "as in several recent films featuring angelic emissaries, a sighting of Elvis in a supermarket ennobles the everyday, transforming failure into redemption."

A FITTING ENDING TO THIS CHAPTER OF ALLEGED COMMUNICATIONS with, and sightings of, Elvis should rightly include a roster of his

compères in the world of entertainment. The Jordanaires' "experience" – they had been an Elvis backup group – seems, to me,
a good beginning.

In August 1988, the Jordanaires did a charity show for crip-
pled children in Reno, Nevada. Gordon Stoker, a member of the
ensemble, in an interview with Gary James of the *City Edition–
Downtown,* Syracuse, New York, on April 1, 1990, told James that
the group had received a letter in Reno, supposedly written by
Elvis, concerning their show. The letter was really written to the
people who had booked the Jordanaires, and read: "Dear Sirs: I
was very excited to here [an "Elvis"-type misspelling] you were
bringing my longtime friends, the Jordanaires, to Tucson [an
earlier show]. I miss them very much. Tell them I still blame the
Colonel for what happened. (They will know what I mean.) I've
seen Elvis Wade. He's great. I think it was destiny that he rise out
of all those impersonators. The Jordanaires have chosen well. I
understand you are giving part of the money to children. They
were always my weakness. Bless you. I will be there!" The letter
was signed, "Elvis."

What tickled Gordon Stoker was the misspelling of the word
"hear." "Elvis did misspell common words," Mr. Stoker admitted to
reporter James.

Not long after, Aaron Y., of McEwen, Tennessee, wrote to me
to say that when the Jordanaires were on a late 1989 *Crook &
Chase* show, out of Nashville, "Ray Walker. . .said that in 1966,
when they were recording some songs with Elvis, and they had
taken time out to relax, Elvis said, 'Know what, Ray? The only way
I'll ever get out of this business is to die. Think I can pull it off?'
Ray returned with, 'If anyone can, you can. Go for it!' Ray went on
to say that with all this about Elvis' being alive coming out, it
makes that statement look funny." (Larry Geller, in *If I Can Dream,*
mentions that Elvis made "very strange" remarks about never
wanting to become a "pathetic fifty-year-old singer," saying he
would never allow that to happen to him. Did Elvis, indeed, "go
for it"?)

A panorama of other entertainers' thoughts follows:

- Country singer Waylon Jennings, is cited in Steve Tamerius
  and Fred Worth's book *Elvis: His Life from A to Z* as "one of the
  many people who suggested that Elvis probably faked his own
  death in order to return to a quiet, secluded life."
- "One year after Elvis Presley's death, [singer] Ronnie

McDowell,"* the Associated Press' Joe Edwards reported on August 13, 1978, "still has trouble believing the King is gone. 'Sometimes I wonder if he really is dead. I wonder if maybe he just wanted to be free to walk around. What gets me is they moved him [his body] so fast. It makes me wonder if he's out there watchin' what I'm doing.' "

- Singer Merle Haggard, quoted in *People* magazine in June 1979, said: "Elvis may have faked his death. It would be the first chance for freedom in his entire life – it could have been a scheme Colonel Parker dreamed up."

- In a December 1989 tabloid interview of Jerry Lee Lewis, the singer said: "What people don't realize is how smart Elvis was – he knew when to pull out. I didn't."

- Entertainer Joan Rivers, on the WXRK *Howard Stern* radio show on March 16, 1990, said she truly believed that Elvis was alive.

- The Bon Jovi rock group lead singer says – according to *Circus* magazine (February 1990) – that there is one idol of his whom he has yet to meet: "Elvis. He's around, man!"

And early this year, singer Gloria Estefan was interviewed by William Norwich of the *Daily News* in her hospital bed in New York, where she was recovering from a bus accident. She related how, recently, in Las Vegas she had had an extraordinary experience. In the middle of the night the phone had rung, and she heard the words "Hello, Gloria, this is Elvis." She'd grown more and more stunned as the voice on the other end continued, convincing her that it was Presley. She admitted that, afterwards, friends had assured her that the voice had been that of an impersonator.

Many Elvis fans have written me to ask if I noted that singer Wayne Newton, in his autobiography *Once Before I Go* (William Morrow, 1989), says he recalls that on August 10, 1977, he was at his ranch when he received an emergency telephone call telling him, "Elvis just died . . ." Of course, Elvis did not "die" until six days later. (Newton was another friend of Elvis' who attended neither the singer's viewing nor funeral.) At a March 18, 1990, live concert in Kalamazoo, Michigan, Newton addressed the audience, asking if any of them had seen him out walking that day. No one

---

*McDowell is the "voice" for the ABC half-hour TV series *Elvis* (Michael St. Gerard is the actor); McDowell recorded the hit "The King Is Gone" and was the singing voice in the movie *Elvis and Me* by Priscilla Presley.

in the audience could say yes. Again he asked them the question, and again there was no response. Then he asked, "Do you mean *no one* saw me out walking today? See, that's how Elvis does it. In fact, Elvis was walking with me! He loves this brisk weather!"

ELVIS/JON BURROWS SHOULD RIGHTLY CONCLUDE THIS CHAPTER, AS HE began it.

Tony Thomas, of radio station KQWC, Webster City, Iowa, received a revealing letter, dated February 5, 1989, from Burrows. It read:

On a recent drive through Iowa, I happened to come across your radio station and heard the name Tony Thomas as the announcer! Normally, the name wouldn't ring a bell, but not too long ago I had read an article in an Iowa paper that quoted Tony Thomas like he was some kind of an Elvis headquarters that had the latest news about Elvis and sightings concerning Elvis. I have news for you, sir. . . .

I want to live the rest of my life in peace. I don't have to explain my actions to anybody. I deserve that much. I can now see anyone that I want to see at any time I wish. I can come and go as I please (something that I haven't been able to do most of my life). If I want to drive cross country, I can. I'm watching my little girl grow without being watched.

I'm asking you to please let me do that. I do not interfere with your life and I ask the same courtesy of you. You are not the only one that I have made this request to, so you needn't feel singled out.

I trust that this letter will be between you and me, and maybe someday we will meet face to face. Please don't get excited about this Hallsville, Mo., address, because I will address anything according to where I am at the time.

T.C.B.

FILE CASE No. 11

Other Mystery Songs/Singers— and Orion

When words leave off, music begins.
— HEINRICH HEINE

Question: Have other mystery songs and singers appeared who sound like Elvis?
Answer: Songs of tribute have appeared, as well as mystery singers and mystery songs—all underlining the premise that Elvis Presley is alive.

B esides Sivle Nora (File Case No. 8), other singers sounding like Elvis have raised speculations about a living Elvis. Tribute songs have also been written, the premise being that Elvis is alive. Many of these songs are not necessarily sung by an "Elvis voice"—but their lyrics do raise questions. Consider the following item, printed in *The Tennessean*, December 3, 1988:

Chillicothe, Ohio—Mystery shrouds NuElvis. What is his real name? How old is he? Where is he from? Promoters of his upcoming appearance in Chillicothe, Ohio, insist they don't know. "NuElvis is NuElvis," said Gene Cash, owner of ANA Records, the Lewisburg, Tenn., label on which NuElvis' first single recording, "You Know Me," was released in early September. "When radio stations started playing the record, the people were all calling the stations and saying, 'Play that new Elvis record.' We heard it so much, that's what

185

we decided to go with. What's scary is, the man looks like Elvis and sings like Elvis." Cash, who said he's been in the music business about 20 years, does not believe Elvis is alive. "Although sometimes I wonder...I see this man who looks and sings and sounds like him."

NuElvis has reportedly been identified as Alan Roe of Nashville, Tennessee, originally from Texas. Even if this is so, it is still intriguing to note, from the lyrics of the song "You Know Me," the premise of Elvis Presley's being alive. Points made in the song indicate that its subject:

• was born in Tupelo, Mississippi
• became king of rock 'n' roll
• died, but is alive and free
• threw it all away
• would never have left, but couldn't stay

And he says, "Though the stage is bare, I'm still standing there..."

In September 1989, I received a letter and record from Paul Richey of Richey Music Group, Inc. Richey is the brother-in-law of singer Tammy Wynette; he cut the tribute 45 recording "Wherever You May Be" — again illustrating that many in the world of music believe Elvis may be alive: "Dear Gail: I hope you enjoy the record. I think it is very tastefully written. One of the writers believes Elvis is definitely alive – one does not believe he is – and due to the facts I am aware of, I believe it is very possible that he is, for whatever all that means. Enjoy."

The lyrics follow:

WHEREVER YOU MAY BE*
(Paul Richey/Barry Paul Jackson/Toni Dae)
Paul Richey

I remember exactly where I was when I first heard the news
Driving to my office down South 16th Avenue,
It was a hot 16th of August but I began to feel the chill
When the word came from Graceland it seemed the world stood still.
To deal with life on life's terms sometimes can be so tough.
All the things fame and fortune brings just never is enough.

---

*"Wherever You May Be," sung by Paul Richey, and written by Richey, Barry Paul Jackson, and Toni Dae; 1222 16th Ave. So., Nashville, TN 37212 (Richey Music).

We can't know what you've gone through until we walk in your shoes.
But we do know you gave us more than we ever gave to you . . .

Wherever you may be,
We still love you.
Wherever you may be
You're still Number One.
If you feel you need forgiveness,
That's already done.
We hope you found your place
In the sun.

Known by millions, loved by all
Can be a tough road to hoe.
And should I ever meet you face-to-face,
I'll just smile and say, "Hello. . ."

Now, some say they've seen you.
As for me I can't say.
But however you've found peace of mind,
We accept it either way.

Wherever you may be,
We still love you.
Wherever you may be,
You're still Number One.

If you feel you need forgiveness,
That's already done.
We hope you found your place
In the sun.

THERE HAS BEEN A GREAT DEAL OF CONTROVERSY OVER THE 1988 release of L&S' recording "Spelling on the Stone." (L&S is Lee Stoller, husband of top gospel singer Christy Lane.) On the album, and via radio interviews, the following was related: "A man around 200 pounds, salt and pepper hair, mustache, about six feet tall, sunglasses, came into L&S (after getting out of a black limousine) and handed the secretary a single, saying for Lee Stoller to play it. (Later a box of other tapes appeared with such titles as: 'Poor Heart,' 'Only Child,' 'Rock and a Hard Place,' 'Everything's Taking Me Back,' 'Father of the Bride,' 'Hit the Bricks,' 'Outside Looking In,' 'Resurrection' – the first single left being 'Spelling on the Stone.')"
Here are the lyrics to "Spelling on the Stone"*:

*"Spelling on the Stone," LS Records, 120 Hickory St., Madison, TN 37115.

> People wonder, people ask
> Am I present, am I past?
> I never left, I haven't gone
> Check the spelling on the stone.
>
> Was my leaving you a sin,
> Did my faith somehow grow thin?
> My secret's out, so many know
> Check the spelling on the stone.
>
> Chorus: The legend lives, he never died
>   It's up to you to decide. . .
>
> Say the word and I'll come home.
> Check the spelling on the stone.
>
> Would you miss me quite the same
> Had I never come to fame?
>
> So the truth may now be known
> Check the spelling on the stone.

More than one news article that noted the "Spelling on the Stone" album cited "a voice expert at the University, who scrupulously tested the record [and] says he's certain it is Elvis." Voice experts whom I have contacted say that voice-authenticating singing is inconclusive. Rob Thompson, the so-called "expert," even called Graceland, talked to Elvis' Uncle Vester, played the record for him. Vester reportedly told him: "Son, don't bet any money that Elvis is in that tomb."

According to my investigation, the writers registered on the songs on the album include Lee Stoller. The song "Spelling on the Stone's" own writers are listed as Lee Strauss, Tony Crow, and Jimmy Young. And, according to the May 1989 issue of *DISCoveries* magazine, the "mystery/unidentified singer" is Danny Willis. Dan Willis is also listed as one of the writers on the cut "Resurrection."

There are some who believe *two* different voices are on the album. Who is Dan Willis, however? And *if* there is another voice, whose is it?

A fan, Ruth H., of Toronto, Canada, went to a Christy Lane concert a few years back, she tells me – before "Spelling on the Stone" was released. When the lights went down, she noted a man dressed oddly, with a scruffy beard, seat himself when the hall was darkened. She found herself staring at him, and he stared back. She had a strong feeling that it was Elvis. (Thus, do we have a Christy Lane–Elvis connection?)

IN 1987, VULCAN RECORDS OF BIRMINGHAM, ALABAMA, RELEASED THE
single "Down in Mississippi," recorded by the mysterious Steven
Silver, who later turned out to be Jimmy Ellis. In 1989, "Down in
Mississippi" appeared as part of Toronto, Canada's, Aron Records'
album "New Beginnings," sung by "Orion" (Jimmy Ellis). The lyrics
of "Down in Mississippi"* follow:

> I remember down in Mississippi
> They picked cotton in the sun
> And I'd sing with the black folks
> When the day was done
> And I'd dream even then
> The world would be my stage
> And someday my shoes would shake
> loose the Mississippi clay.
>
> Then we moved on up to Memphis
> Just trying to survive.
> I cut a record for my mama
> And almost overnight
> The Colonel signed me up.
> I was living out my dream.
> My mama was so proud
> When you called me the king.
>
> Down in Mississippi I play my guitar,
> Sing my rock 'n' roll songs
> And dream I'd be a star.
> I went from down in Mississippi
> To Nashville, Tennessee,
> But my shoes never shook loose
> The Mississippi clay.
>
> And then one day I was no longer
> A kid in a Cadillac.
> Just a rock 'n' roller
> Tired of coming back.
> I was a prisoner of my fame
> And when my mama died,
> The Lord seemed to say to me
> You need to change your life.
> Well I was much too big
> To just turn my back and leave,

*"Down in Mississippi," sung by Steven Silver (AKA Orion), written by Chance
Jones, Mike Lantrip, and Johnny Martin; Vulcan Records, Nationwide Sound
Dist., 1204 Elmwood Ave., Nashville, TN 37212.

So I changed the way I look
Now no one knows me.
Everybody in the world
Believes the king is gone,
But I'm down in Mississippi
And it's good to be back home.

Down in Mississippi
Not far from Tupelo,
Beneath the magnolia tree
And an old dusty road,
Oh, I sing & play my guitar
And sit in the shade
And my blue suede shoes are home at last
In this Mississippi clay.

The singer speaks a last line on the disc: "You know, I sure do miss you folks. Until we meet again, *adios!*. . ."

Again, there are those who wonder if perhaps two voices exist on the album. Or: "Is there an Elvis–Ellis connection?" According to Allen Damron, a writer for *DISCoveries* magazine, Elvis knew of Jimmy Ellis in the early 1970s. "Steve Kelly," wrote Damron, "worked for Jimmy Ellis and was also a friend of Elvis' for about eight years." Damron says that Kelly gave Elvis some of Ellis' recordings. Kelly doesn't know whether Elvis and Ellis ever met.

Luc Dionne, a producer with Gala Productions in Montreal, Canada, told me early this spring that recently, in checking out Aron Records in Toronto—its charter background—he was informed that an American had applied for a corporation application in late 1989. When Mr. Dionne asked the American's name, he was told it was "John Burrows." Later, Mr. Dionne went to Toronto to see the paperwork and was told no such name existed. "I am telling you," Mr. Dionne swore to me, "that I was told this name—John Burrows—several times."

(In *Is Elvis Alive?* I mentioned that there is an Elvis Presley licensing agent in Japan called Orion Press.)

As for Jimmy Ellis/Orion, the question remains: Is there room in this world for both a Leonardo Da Vinci and a Michelangelo? Jimmy Ellis wonders.

Ellis is definitely not Elvis Presley. He is not a Presley impersonator. Nevertheless, this tremendous talent has been penalized for possessing the living voice closest to Elvis', other than Elvis himself. Mickey Gilley sounds like Jerry Lee Lewis. And there are Engelbert Humperdinck and Tom Jones. . . . Yet, somehow—sadly—Ellis is pushed aside by many DJs because he sounds

too much like "the King," and they say, "There is only *one* Elvis."
Would, when Michelangelo came along, such men have rejected
his God-given gift on the grounds that he was too close to
Leonardo, saying, "There is only one Da Vinci?" The indictment
would have allowed us the splendor of the *Mona Lisa* while deny-
ing us a glorious view of the Sistine Chapel.

Although I do not like what happened to my novel *Orion*, via
Sun Records, as touched upon in *Is Elvis Alive?* (in my opinion, Sun
acted unprofessionally when it would never enter into any legal
agreement whereby my novel and all its characters would be used
to sell its Orion albums), I can appreciate the fact that Ellis has
been a victim, too. Rumors and mystique continue to surround – to
plague? – the singer Ellis/Orion:

- Is Jimmy Ellis related to Elvis Presley?
- Is Jimmy Ellis a "front" for Elvis Presley?
- Are there two voices on the Orion albums?
- Are there two Orions – two "masked men"? (One possibly Elvis himself?)

At one point, Ellis did admit to me that there were two Orions,
that he did not know the identity of the other. In a recent interview, he said there was but one Orion: himself.

For a time, Ellis discarded the Orion persona – the mask – and
went back to being simply Jimmy Ellis. In late 1989, he put the
mask back on and became Orion once more. "It works," he has said
on radio shows and in print. "Plus, people know I am not Elvis,
that I am Orion. Elvis did not wear a mask. This separates me,
creates interest and mystery. The mask is my trademark."

There *is* a known picture of Elvis in a mask. It is amazing how
much the two men resemble each other in "masked" pictures.
Several years ago, I received a telephone call. "Turn on the TV," my
neighbor said. "Jimmy Ellis is on *Nashville Now* – with no mask; his
hair is white, light gray. With his hair that color, he is a dead-ringer
for Vernon Presley! He could be his cloned son!" My neighbor was
right. The resemblance *was* amazing. (Remember, Elvis dyed his
hair because he, like his mother and father, was becoming pre-
maturely gray.)

Later, in a conversation with Ellis, he admitted to me, "Yeah,
a lot of people told me that."

"Are you related to Elvis?" I asked.

He laughed shyly. "Not that I know of . . ."

"You sound more like Elvis at times than Elvis."
"Jerry Schilling* told me that too," Jimmy revealed.

A MORE PERSONAL ELLIS-ELVIS CONNECTION IS REINFORCED BY THE FACT
that members of Elvis' family welcome Ellis warmly. He has never
denied this. When I met Elvis' Uncle Vester in 1988, I asked him
if he knew Orion† and he said he did: "Jimmy Ellis has been here
many times," he asserted. Ellis recently told me that it was only
once. Yet, a closer, more frequent association of Ellis with Elvis
seems to follow from the facts that

- Ellis was adopted by the Ellises of Alabama/"Ellis" is the name
  of a Memphis auditorium where Elvis performed in February
  1961.
- Ellis' biological mother's name was Gladys/Elvis' biological
  mother's name was Gladys.
- Ellis' first Sun recordings were "Blue Moon of Kentucky" and
  "That's All Right (Mama)"/Elvis' first Sun recordings were "Blue
  Moon of Kentucky" and "That's All Right (Mama)."
- One of Ellis' California shows was choreographed by Jamie
  Rogers; Earl Brown did his arrangements; and Bill Belew
  designed his costumes/Elvis' NBC-TV "Comeback Special" on
  December 3, 1968, was choreographed by Jamie Rogers; Earl
  Brown did some of his arrangements; and Bill Belew designed
  many of his costumes.
- Both Ellis and Elvis have had business connections with a
  man named Loeb.
- Orion's (Ellis') Sun recordings were "Smith Productions"/
  "Smith" is Elvis' mother's maiden name.
- Ellis owns horse-farm property/Elvis had a horse farm.
- After Sun Records, Ellis' label was Aron Records/"Aron" is the
  correct spelling of Elvis' middle name.

Despite all the above, Ellis denied not only any biological relationship to Elvis, but told me he had never met him. However, it
is the "Duets: Jerry Lee Lewis and Friends" album of 1978 that
raises questions that presuppose an Ellis–Elvis connection.
      I received a letter in 1988 from a TV interviewer who wrote

*Jerry Schilling is a longtime friend of Elvis and Priscilla, now Creative Affairs
Director for the estate.

†Albums by Orion: DixiRaks, P.O. Box 22325, Nashville, TN 37202.

that he had had a call from a Columbus, Georgia, viewer stating: "A man in this area was told by Jimmy [Ellis] that he [again, Ellis] had been invited to Graceland two months prior to August 16, 1977, to meet with Elvis and Jerry Lee Lewis." (This was of course before my novel, *Orion,* had been conceived.) Recall how, in *Is Elvis Alive?,* I outlined the controversy surrounding a 1978 Sun Records release, "Duets: Jerry Lee Lewis and Friends." Well, everyone who heard the "friend" with Jerry Lee said it was Elvis Presley. But please note the following biography, which appeared in the encyclopedic volume *Elvis: His Life From A to Z:*

ELLIS, JIMMY
(1945–   ) Singer who for a time sang under the alter ego Orion (Orion Eckley Darnell). Ellis was born in Washington, D.C., on February 26, 1945. He has an excellent voice and as Orion recorded a number of records that sounded very much like Elvis.

Shelby Singleton of Sun International decided to disguise Ellis's identity on his first Sun single, "That's All Right (Mama)" . . . (Sun 1129), leaving listeners to speculate that the songs might be alternate takes of Elvis's first two songs. Instead of listing Ellis on the label, Singleton printed a question mark. Ellis's first album appearance for Sun was as an unidentified singer singing duet with Jerry Lee Lewis on ten tracks of the 1978 album *Duets* (Sun 1011). Charlie Rich sang along with Lewis on two other songs. Again, the speculation was that Elvis had sung the songs, particularly "Save the Last Dance for Me." In 1979 Jimmy Ellis finally emerged with an identity, but it still wasn't himself. He appeared as Orion Eckley Darnell, the character created on August 16, 1977, by Marietta, Georgia, housewife Gail Brewer-Giorgio. Her 1978 novel *Orion* told the story of a rock 'n' roll singer, very much like Elvis, who faked his own death. On Orion's 1979 debut album, *Reborn* (Sun 1912), Ellis appeared on the album cover wearing a mask over his eyes. The album featured some excellent songs, including "Ebony Eyes," "Honey," and "Washing Machine." They were sung in the style in which Elvis would have sung them. . . .

Listeners of Orion were initially split into two camps: those who knew that Orion was Jimmy Ellis just having some fun sounding like Elvis, and others who sincerely believed – or wanted to believe – that he was truly Elvis coming back on the scene after faking his own death. As Orion, Ellis reached *Billboard's* country chart with nine singles. For those who still insist that Jimmy Ellis is not Orion, Ellis has publicly admitted to being Orion. Ellis left Sun Records in 1983. . . .

A fine talent in his own right, Ellis in 1978 recorded the song "I'm Not Trying to Be Like Elvis" (Boblo 536) and the album *By Request – Ellis Sings Elvis* (Boblo 78-829).

Note that the above discusses the fact Jimmy Ellis is supposed to be a "friend" on "Duets: Jerry Lee Lewis and Friends." But, then, what about the 1978 article that syndicated columnist James Bacon wrote asserting that Elvis had told him personally he had cut "Duets" with Jerry Lee (prior to 1977, of course)? And what about the flip side of this album, where at the end of the song "What'd I Say," you hear Jerry Lee at the back of the studio say, "Man, you're ready tonight, Elvis"?

Okay, perhaps Sun Records put Jimmy Ellis on the "Duets" track and even had Jerry Lee say what he did, as a sort of promotional ploy. Then what about Bacon's nationally read article, which warrants reprinting. It was entitled "ELVIS DEBATE CONTINUES":

> The mail won't stop on that column about Elvis Presley of a few weeks back. You know, the one that said Elvis was the mystery singer on the Jerry Lee Lewis record "Save the Last Dance for Me" (from the "Duets" album).
>
> So far I have the word of Elvis himself and Red West, a member of Elvis' Memphis Mafia, and both said Elvis just went into the Sun Recording Studios in Memphis and did it to help out an old friend. Elvis said he was unbilled on the record for a very good reason – he was under contract to RCA at the time.
>
> This probably happened sometime in the 1960s, and Jerry Lee is not talking because of the contract situation.
>
> One letter from Fresno says the record is a Jerry Lee Lewis hoax – that the singer is trying to get the public to believe it's Elvis. That's hard to believe, because Jerry Lee Lewis is one of the big names in country music and he doesn't need hoaxes to get attention.
>
> Another called it a hoax to promote an Elvis imitator – Jimmy Ellis. This letter says Ellis overdubbed the original Jerry Lee Lewis recording and will make a big announcement soon.
>
> Most of the letters come from Elvis fans, who all say it is the King himself on the record. One writer comments: "There are dozens who can sing like Elvis, but no one pronounces words like him. I have played the record a hundred times and I know it is Elvis."
>
> Of course, there is that group that refuses to believe Elvis is dead – that his death was a hoax. These people all believe it is Elvis on the record, but that it was recorded since Elvis died.
>
> What I don't understand is how anyone could insist that the record is a hoax, or that it proves Elvis is still alive. After all, Elvis himself admitted to me that he did the recording with Jerry Lee Lewis. That eliminates any chance of an imitator. And, since Elvis was still very much alive at the time he told me about the record, it's obvious the record was cut before his death was reported and thus does not prove a thing.

See why I am confused? Sun Records says it was Jimmy Ellis on the "Duets" album, whereas James Bacon says that it's Elvis.

TO END THE CHAPTER, I OFFER A FINAL SELECTION OF LETTER-EXTRACTS, which came to me from fans who had information to contribute about the singer who used the name "Orion."
From Michael D., of Mansfield, Ohio, I heard:

In your book-about-the-book you raised some damn good questions. Around 1981, my parents took me to see Orion in concert. Ellis did sound a lot like Elvis, and after the show some members of his band were invited to our motor home for drinks. Orion's bus was next to ours and he was inside wearing a robe and his mask. Even then, I had the feeling that Elvis was alive. Then I noticed someone else on the bus; he was dressed just like Orion, then he quickly ducked into the back of the bus and I never saw him come out again. Two Orions. Welcome to the Twilight Zone! I didn't think much of it then, but now it explains a lot of things.

From Janice R., of McMinnville, Tennessee, I had:

When the masked Orion appeared in my hometown at the McMinnville Civic Center, I felt Elvis could be alive. Even when Orion performed onstage, I felt it was a different man from the masked man who signed autographs. You see, I was close to both men (even kissed by one onstage). He was sweaty and hair out of place and had a different look in his eyes. The one signing autographs had no sweaty clothes and every hair was in place – a lapse of time of maybe ten minutes, not enough time to shower, get every hair in place, and change into a fresh new identical jumpsuit of blue.

Sarah I., of Law, Kentucky, wrote: "I asked Orion backstage, 'Do you think Elvis is alive?' He looked at me and started smiling. He asked me if *I* thought he was. I said, 'I asked you,' trying to get a comment. He finally said, 'No comment.'"

And from Gil B., of Springfield, Missouri, came these words:

I know both Elvis and Jimmy Ellis. I have been with both on the same day. I know what took place at Sun.
I have spent the last few years waiting for someone to pull the plug. I did not, nor do I want to be the first one to do so. But if I ever write about what I know, you will read a book like you have never read in your life. You think there are two Orions? I say there are

three, and all have been at Graceland at the same time. Someday, if I can ever feel I will not hurt anyone, then maybe I can tell.

On November 22, 1988, came a letter from Robin S., of Bellflower, California, that I would like to repeat in full:

> I have read, with great interest, your book *Is Elvis Alive?*, with the mysterious character Orion and the singer Orion. I have come across something you might find interesting.
>
> I was doing some Christmas shopping a couple of weeks ago, when I ended up in a record store. What led me to this store I don't know, as I hadn't any reason to be there. Anyway, they had their Christmas music displayed and I was drawn to one in particular – "Christmas to Elvis, 1935" – dated 1977, from the Jordannaires. I looked at it to see if there were any songs sung by Elvis, as I have at least twenty Christmas albums in general and really didn't need another one. This album contained 23 songs – eight of which were sung by Orion. The album was dated after the death of Elvis Presley. Why would Orion be on an album from the Jordannaires to Elvis?
>
> I couldn't wait to play this at home! My husband and I listened to it together and went right to the Orion songs. We both agreed that if the person singing wasn't Elvis Presley, we weren't alive and breathing right now. I called several friends, played it, and asked who they thought it was. Without fail, everyone without any hesitation though it to be Elvis Presley. Several said they *had* to have it, but it isn't to be found in the stores in our area. Finally, a friend found it and bought a couple of copies in cassette form. She asked me to listen to it. When we opened what appeared to be the exact same thing, it was – with one exception: The Orion songs *were not on the tape.* The tape contained only the songs by the Jordannaires.
>
> Everyone who has read your book listened to the tape with Orion, and who knows of the tape without Orion, thought that I should write to you. I find it all to be very puzzling – another mystery!

Possibly *some* copies of the cassettes do not contain the Orion songs. My cassette does contain them.

An artist's rendering of a masked Orion and myself was sent to me by a fan:

Postscriptum: For those fans who wrote to me asking whether I had "hired" Orion, the singer, I want to express an emphatic "No!" Sun Records and Jimmy Ellis took the identity of Orion from my novel of the same name, copyright 1978. Letters from my attorneys to Sun Records show that it was a clear case of copyright infringement.

Elvis' Will, Trust, and the Push for a Postage Stamp

*In the last decade, politics has gone from the age of "Camelot,"
when all things were possible, to the age of "Watergate,"
when all things are suspect.*
—WILLIAM HUNGATE

Question: What has happened regarding Elvis' will, his
trust, and the petition presented to the U.S. Government
suggesting he be honored on a postage stamp?
Answer: The terms of the will/trust have been changed
since 1977. The government has turned down Elvis for
a postage stamp because, it says, he does not meet the
dead-for-ten-years requirement.

In order to place everything in perspective for this "legal"
chapter, it will be best to enumerate some important dates
and events in Elvis' life regarding his wife, Priscilla, and his
daughter, Lisa.

Following her move into Graceland in October 1962, Priscilla
Ann Beaulieu and Elvis Presley were married on May 1, 1967,*
in a private ceremony in a suite at the Aladdin Hotel in Las Vegas,
Nevada. Nine months later, on February 1, 1968, Lisa Marie

*For a visual copy of the marriage certificate, see File Case No. 4.

Presley was born. Five years later, on February 23, 1973, Priscilla left Elvis, and on August 18, 1973, Elvis sued for divorce. On October 9, 1973, the divorce was granted. Under the terms of the settlement, Priscilla received a cash payment sum of $720,000, *The Elvis Special* reported in its October 1973 issue, and she received $6,000 installments monthly on a second $720,000.

However, according to an October 12, 1976, article in *The Star,* Arthur Toll, Priscilla's lawyer, was quoted as saying that Elvis and Priscilla were still legally married, despite a judge's granting them a divorce four years earlier. Neither Elvis nor Priscilla had, it appeared, bothered to obtain the final judgment that was essential; thus, they were still man and wife at the time of Elvis' "death." In the article, Toll said, "Priscilla never indicated to me she wanted to file for the final judgment of divorce and obviously Elvis had not instructed his attorneys to do it either." But this same report states that Elvis had arranged things so that Priscilla's alimony would cease on August 15, 1977 – one day prior to the "final" day of his life!

To further substantiate the fact that Elvis and Priscilla were still legally married is the way in which Priscilla identified herself in connection with the short-lived (February-to-June) 1990 ABC-TV *Elvis* series, which she co-produced with longtime Elvis friend and employee Jerry Schilling: A widespread advertisement for the show – which dealt with the teen years of the entertainer – proclaimed, "Elvis Lives!", with, near the bottom, "Produced by Elvis' wife – Priscilla Presley." It did not say "ex-wife" or "former wife." Doesn't all this, therefore, help to explain why she is in fact running the estate of Elvis Presley?

Perhaps even more curious is the fact that in May 1977, Elvis signed a trust deed, giving Priscilla a half-million-dollar lien on Graceland!

Another interesting fact is that, although Priscilla has worked in film and on television – five years on CBS' *Dallas* – and is owner of Navarone Productions, she copyrighted her own Elvis book, *Elvis and Me,* in the name of Graceland Enterprises, owned by the Presley estate, of which she is not an heir. One might argue that she did so because her daughter, Lisa Marie, is sole heir to Elvis' estate. Nevertheless, logically she should have copyrighted it under her own corporate name, because Lisa would surely be heir to profits from it – as would Priscilla's three-and-a-half-year-old son, Navarone. Placing the copyright under the Elvis umbrella effectively denies her son any rights to one of her valuable properties.

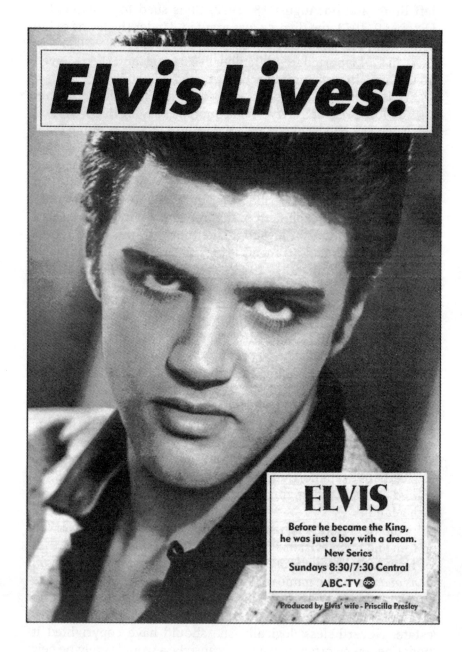

Elvis Lives!

ELVIS

Before he became the King,
he was just a boy with a dream.
New Series
Sundays 8:30/7:30 Central
ABC-TV abc

Produced by Elvis' wife - Priscilla Presley

Newspaper photos showing Priscilla wearing a wedding ring have also raised such questions as whether Priscilla is married? And to whom? Many also write that they find it hard to believe that Priscilla would have a young son and not be married. Priscilla gave birth to Navarone on March 1, 1987, stating the father was Brazilian writer-director Marco Garibaldi, of Italian descent and ten years her junior. Little else is known of Marco other than some news that told that Marco was in charge of security when Lisa gave birth to Elvis' first grandchild, Danielle Riley Keough, on May 29, 1989. Priscilla has never married Marco.

Of course, if Elvis is alive and if Priscilla's public identification as "Elvis' wife" is correct, then she cannot legally marry anyone — which also might explain why she is running Graceland. (In an interview with David Rensin in *US* magazine, October 12, 1988, she was quoted as saying how proud Elvis would be that she had "done very well with his estate, probably better than anyone else."

There is little doubt about Elvis and Priscilla's continual love for each other, even after the so-called "divorce." In fact, Priscilla has stated many times that she will "always love Elvis." Not long prior to his "leaving," they met and talked about their love, how they wanted to grow old together and sit on some front porch in their rocking chairs. They spoke of "another time, another place." Elvis told people that if he ever married again, it would be to the mother of his child.

Very few biographies of Elvis omit how deeply Elvis and Priscilla cared for each other. In any marriage, it takes two people to make it go wrong, two to "right" it. From everyone I have spoken to, Elvis regarded the losing of Priscilla as a major tragedy, and she him. It was primarily his lifestyle that distanced them. Priscilla was only fifteen years old when she fell in love with Elvis. My instincts tell me that it was difficult for Elvis to separate his view of the little girl 'Cilla from the mature woman Priscilla.

WHICH BRINGS US TO ELVIS' LAST WILL AND TESTAMENT, A THIRTEEN-PAGE document dated March 3, 1977, replacing an earlier will and witnessed by Charles Hodge (a close friend), Ginger Alden (a current girlfriend), and Ann Dewey Smith (wife of Vernon Presley's attorney, Beecher Smith III).

Besides the puzzle over *why* Elvis chose to revise his will only a few months prior to his "death," the question has arisen of why he disinherited everyone believed to have been included, earlier, naming his daughter as sole beneficiary, with the stipulation that she would inherit the estate at age twenty-five, on February 1, 1993. Although Elvis left out his stepmother and stepbrothers, close friends, and diverse other members of his family, he made the following provisions, in Item IV, Residuary Trust, Paragraph (b), directing the trustees of the estate to provide for

> . . . the health, education, support, comfortable maintenance and welfare of: (1) my daughter, Lisa Marie Presley, and any other lawful issue I might have, (2) my grandmother, Minnie Mae Presley, (3) my father, Vernon E. Presley,* and (4) such other relatives of mine living at the time of my death who in the absolute discretion of my Trustee are in need of emergency assistance . . . †

People have wondered about the part "other lawful issue I might have." Did he mean another child, somewhere? Also, the question has been raised that if Elvis was planning to marry Ginger Alden in a few months, why didn't he wait until such marriage to make will changes that would include his new wife?

Dee Presley, Elvis' stepmother, lamented in her book *Elvis, We Love You Tender*, that Elvis had promised her he would always "take care of her boys" by her first husband (Bill Stanley) – Rick, Billy, and David Stanley – and was upset to discover they had been left out of the will. Marty Lacker, a friend and best man at Elvis' wedding, in *Elvis: Portrait of a Friend* asked why Elvis had said he was going to leave all his guys something, then just months before his death changed the will? He also said he had other funny feelings about the will, wondering particularly why Elvis had left out his close friend and cousin Billy Smith.

Others have wondered why Elvis would make his elderly, very ill father executor of the will? Logic says that a man forty-two years old who only weeks before passed a physical examination would outlive a sick father by decades – unless, of course, Elvis knew that his "death" was close.

The will entitled Lisa Marie, on her twenty-fifth birthday, to take ownership of all assets in the trust created for her. These consist of: Graceland, record royalties, licensing fees for use of the Presley name and image, and other properties. Lisa Marie would inherit the entire estate in 1993, sixteen years after Elvis' "death."

---

*Vernon Presley died on June 26, 1979.

†For those who wish to peruse a complete copy of the will, I suggest Tamerius and Worth's book *Elvis: His Life from A to Z* (page 111).

(The reader may recall the sixteen missing years of Jesus' life, spoken of in File Case No. 5. Also, he or she should keep in mind the number 16 as in August 16, 1977, and the sixteen white Cadillacs used in the final farewell, the funeral procession.)

However, in 1988 both Priscilla and Lisa Marie appeared in a Memphis court to extend the conditions of the will so that Lisa would not take control of her inheritance until 1998, when she would be thirty years of age, rather than taking control at age twenty-five. The reason given for the extension was so that the estate would be in a better position to negotiate long-term contracts for movies and "other transactions."*

Several attorneys have informed me that long-term contracts entered into *pre*-1993 by the estate would have been valid and held up in a court of law. Thus, the reasons for the extension seem puzzling. Second, why would Lisa at the age of twenty agree to an extension when she still had five years left on the original decree to make such a decision—a decision better made with greater maturity on her side. In other words, the extension had little to do with the legality of "taking care of business."

STATE LAWS VARY IN REGARD TO WILLS AND TRUSTS, THUS THE following letter may not necessarily reflect Tennessee law. However, it does reflect what fans-at-large have noted. It comes from Jo Ann M. of Carrollton, Texas. She entitled it "The EP Estate Trust."

> Now, let's talk about a "trust" and how it works. There is the "revocable" and there is the "irrevocable" trust. When a revocable trust is set up, the "Grantor" may elect to name himself and/or others as Trustees. The Grantor has full control over the trust, estate, and monies while still alive. The trust can be administered and conrolled by the conditions and stipulations set forth in the trust agreement. The trust agreement can be exclusive and separate from a will. If at any time or for any reason the conditions/stipulations are not being met, the Grantor may elect to change or revoke his trust. A LIVING REVOCABLE TRUST. The irrevocable trust does not work this way. Once it is set up, it can not be changed or revoked by the Grantor. At least, not without a court battle.
>
> We know there is a trust, and I bet it was "a living revocable trust." This means EP can and could be controlling his millions and no one would ever know. Priscilla's role as a named Trustee could include

---

*The new inheritance date, February 1, 1998, also equals, numerologically, 2001.

some pretty strange requirements. In most cases, Trustees receive payment for administering the trust: sometime a percentage based on the value of the estate. I would suspect Pris' salary would make us all do a double take.

Remember, the will does not stipulate who the Trustees are or will be, only discussed the will Executor's role – a role which is pretty insignificant given the scope of estate management. An Estate Planning Attorney could give you a whole realm of possibilities! Note in the will: Item IV, Paragraph (b), Number (4)! Compare with Paragraph (c). The Trustee – not Vernon, who is only named as the will Executor – has the power to distribute funds to other relatives. After Vernon dies, the Trustee (whoever it or they are) can no longer make these disbursements. Look at Paragraph (e). This stipulation has a great deal of significance which needs to be checked out! It's been reported that Lisa Marie's inheritance will continue to be handled in trust until she reaches age thirty. A CHANGE IN THE ORIGINAL TRUST. Can one Trustee make such a major provision change? Not hardly. Is Lisa Marie a Co-Trustee? As Trustees, you have EP's old law firm, his old Memphis bank, and an ex-wife. Even though Lisa Marie was a minor child at the time EP "left," this did not automatically give the Executor an active role or power, which is so evident. A lot of thought went into the EP trust and, believe me, there is someone or something controlling [it]! Maybe the Grantor, Mr. EP, himself! Remember, inheritance does not become community property. If the speculations about protecting the estate from an unscrupulous husband (say, Lisa's Danny) were a consideration, putting the inheritance off until you see if the marriage flies wouldn't really apply. There's no tax advantage from the five-year delay. Why? . . .

Believe me, what we have here is a *revocable trust,* which someone established prior to a will. The will is nothing more than an eye-wash document with simple legal mumbo-jumbo wording. The EP trust document would answer every question we ever thought about!

Other points Jo Ann made were (1) that a trust can be set up in any state beyond the one where the Grantor resides (which means that Elvis Presley could have been better off than the public knew, he could have owned properties, islands – half of Tennessee – under a corporation name that falls under the protection and privacy of a "living trust") and (2) that such a trust offers protection against wills being contested by family members (with a living trust, Elvis had the ability to change Trustees and revise the trust status any time he desired; assets could be added or removed; trustees and trust conditions could easily be changed by the Grantor, E.P., prior to death).

Jo Ann agrees that Lisa Marie and the inheritance-age change
has invited more questions. When a Grantor stipulates an age requirement for the Heir's inheritance of a trust, then it cannot be
changed by the Heir or Trustee(s), even if all parties agree. The trust
is established for insuring that the Grantor's wishes are followed
precisely. Take a reverse scenario: If the Trustee and the Heir decided they wanted to acquire the estate earlier than the stipulated
age, do you think this would fly? Hardly. Although we are not privy
to the reasons for the five-year delay, it makes little difference. The
only time that trust conditions are modified is to prevent losses to
the estate, generally related to properties and taxes.

What Jo Ann is speculating about is that if the Grantor were alive,
there would of course have been no problem in Lisa Marie's
changing the inheritance age.

Jo Ann imagines that there may have been two reasons for
Priscilla and Lisa's wish to delay Lisa's inheritance: (1) Someone
might marry her for her money (Lisa was still single). However,
inheritance money does not become community property; only
assets acquired during a marriage do so. Jo Ann notes that "there
could have been a pre-existing condition included in the trust that
stipulated that, should Lisa marry before age twenty-five, then the
trust management would continue for an additional five-year
period. We will never know." And (2) Lisa might not have been
capable of using good judgment in handling her inheritance. Jo
Ann points out that

> this would have been difficult to prove, and would have been a
> messy family and legal situation, drawing too much public atten-
> tion. I can't see Lisa's admitting that she lacked good judgment
> and/or was incapable of seeking financial assistance in handling her
> estate. Besides, she was, at this time, only twenty-one. Why make
> the change four years prior to her becoming twenty-five? Lisa could
> have turned around and established a trust of her own upon receiv-
> ing Elvis Presley's estate. Elvis could have had additional millions,
> other homes, cars, planes, and assets that the public would never
> have known about: assets purchased prior to and after August 16,
> 1977, and protected and maintained in a trust, funds available but
> maybe under a corporation name.

Finally, three unusual monetary moves were made by Elvis
shortly before 1977. The first—revealed to me by Detective Monte
Nicholson, nineteen-year veteran of the Los Angeles Sheriff's
Department and author of *The Presley Arrangement*—was the

cashing in by Elvis of many paid-up life insurance policies. The second was the placing of over $1 million in a private checking account, somewhere, that only Elvis and his father could touch. The third move – reported in several major news articles, as well as on NBC – was the investment of $510,000 in late 1976, which netted Elvis a tax deduction of $2.5 million. What is unusual about this third event is that prior to 1976, Elvis always paid his taxes "off the top," taking no major tax deductions.

THIS CHAPTER WILL END ON A SOMEWHAT "LEGAL" NOTE – SOMETHING OF a governmental puzzle, too. Several years ago, a campaign was initiated by Elvis fans petitioning the U.S. Government to issue a postage stamp honoring the singer. However, in its May 1988 issue of *The Forum*, Suspicious Minds Fan Club, based in Memphis, indicated that neither Lisa nor Priscilla Presley would speak about or support the stamp campaign.*

In late 1989, a *Los Angeles Times* article entitled "STAMP FOR ELVIS?" suggested that the interest in the singer's being alive was also a

> matter of philatelic interest. A U.S. Postal Service rule says that, except for ex-presidents, anyone honored on a postage stamp must have been dead for at least a decade. Some Presley fans say that the time has come to commemorate their idol. An anti-Presley faction argues that it would be absurd to accord Elvis the same honor given such musical giants as George Gershwin, Duke Ellington and Igor Stravinsky.
>
> Caught in this crossfire, the Postmaster General has taken refuge in the strict constructionist position. A stamp honoree, he says, has to be not just dead but "demonstrably dead" for 10 years. With that qualification in mind, foes of a Presley stamp will no doubt now happily join the chorus of those proclaiming that, yes, indeed, the King still lives.

The Elvis Special commented in its October/December 1989 issue: "Anthony M. Frank, the U.S. Postmaster General, has said he likes the idea of an Elvis stamp, but 'the rules for entry to the

---

*The reader should also be told that, reportedly, Vernon Presley refused to accept an American flag at Elvis' "death" – this despite Elvis' being a veteran. Certainly if Elvis was alive after August 16, 1977, he would not have allowed the American flag to be placed on an empty or dummy-filled coffin. What's more, if Elvis was dead, surely Vernon would have accepted the flag with great honor.

philatelic hall of fame require a person to be demonstrably dead
for ten years.'"

New York's *Daily News* reporter Tom Webb (of Knight-Ridder
Newspapers) wrote, on May 6, 1990: "By its resistance to issue an
Elvis Presley stamp, Geiger [Pat Geiger, who heads the Elvis
Postage Stamp Campaign] swears the U.S. Postal Service is missing out on a great financial windfall." Pointing out the Post Office's
deficit, Geiger reasoned that "Presleyphiles, speculators and collectors would snap up millions of Elvis stamps but never stick 'em
on a letter." The Postal Service would be paid for the stamps but
would be asked to deliver relatively few letters bearing them. "I'll
never give up," Webb cited Geiger as saying. "Either I die or Elvis
gets his stamp."

Another Elvis fan, Mitzie H., of Santa Maria, California, wrote
me: "On our local radio station the other day, the disc jockey was
interviewing a postal authority who said there would soon be a
stamp out for Claude Pepper. The DJ jumped back with, 'Claude
Pepper? Why haven't you given us an Elvis stamp? So many people
want it. Why this guy?' The postal man said, 'Because they're sure
Claude Pepper is dead.'" From D'Lores G., of Ogilvie, Minnesota,
came this note: "At our post office there is a sign advertising stamps
depicting: *The Wizard of Oz*/Judy Garland, *Stagecoach*/John Wayne,
and *Gone With the Wind*/Clark Gable and Vivien Leigh. I asked the
Postmaster, 'All right, where's Elvis?' He replied, 'For a person to
be on a postage stamp, he has to be dead. The government is not
sure Elvis is dead.'"

The question, from many fans, remains: If the United States Government is not sure Elvis Presley is dead, then "Is Elvis alive?" is a question with substance.

A Sampling of Contradictions Surrounding Elvis' "Death"

If you can't answer a man's argument, all is not lost;
you can still call him vile names.
— ELBERT HUBBARD

Question: Besides those you have already mentioned, are there other puzzling inconsistencies that have been noted concerning the "death" of Elvis Presley?
Answer: There have been many—from Elvis' many fans, primarily—who have noted that even the contradictions sometimes have contradictions!

In fact, there are so many puzzling contradictions in the stories told by Elvis' family, friends, and biographers regarding his "death" that it would take an encyclopedia to contain them all. Keeping in mind that news sources, as well as biographies, may have in some cases misquoted a family member or friend, it is interesting to note—in brief (omitting the names of those who have written to me)—what has been pointed out. Many of the following points are direct quotes from communications I've received;

others are paraphrasings; a few are taken directly from the book(s) that stated them.

- On page 89 of the paperback version of Mike Edwards' book *Priscilla, Elvis and Me*, Mr. Edwards says that he and Priscilla were in New York on the one-year anniversary of EP's death. Priscilla asked him to go with her into St. Patrick's Cathedral so she could say a prayer and light a candle for Elvis. When Mike asked her what she had prayed for, she replied that she could not tell him, that it was a secret; but she continued, "I hope he's happy and peaceful." A Catholic myself, [I can say that] one lights a candle for the living, the sick, the troubled – asking for spiritual intervention. In that same book, page 218, Mike awakes to discover Priscilla and Lisa sitting on a sofa at the end of the bed, where they were laughing, grinning while involved in a conversation about Elvis, Lisa ending with, "Bless his sick little ol' self." Since Elvis was presumably "dead" for some years, the laughing, kidding, and talking about him in the present tense is strange.
- Why can't the Stanley boys get together and decide how their stepbrother Elvis died? Rick says Elvis suffocated in the shag carpeting, David – according to columnist Liz Smith – says it was definitely suicide. Earlier, they intimated drugs, while stepmother Dee Presley says it was something else. And they wonder why we ask questions?
- I have noted in several pictures featuring Priscilla that she is wearing a wedding ring?* However, she has never married the man she is supposed to be living with – the reported father of Navarone.
- In Mike Edwards' book *Priscilla, Elvis and Me*, Chapter 28, when Edwards asks Priscilla what really happened between her and Elvis, she responds with, "I grew up." She talks about Elvis not being satisfied, that he was tired of singing rock 'n' roll, and that his age was scaring him. Later I saw Priscilla on *Oprah* (ABC), NBC, CBS. In all, when asked about Elvis' being alive, she usually avoids it or says, "Let him rest in peace." Even when she did the 1985 cable TV show "Elvis Presley's Grace-land," she did not say Elvis died. Another mistake she made was to say Elvis' grave was between his mother's and father's – which is totally untrue.

---

*Priscilla's press agent says the ring is a personal one, not a wedding ring.

- Writing to me about this same "Elvis Presley's Graceland" TV program, another fan "found it interesting, if not odd, that [Priscilla] called Elvis a 'living legend.' He's a legend, but not a 'living legend.'"
- Dirk Vellenga's book *Elvis and the Colonel* asks: "How strange it is that Elvis' famous manager, Colonel Tom Parker, was actually an illegal citizen from Holland, who after changing his name, allowed family and friends in Holland to think him 'dead.' Has a familiar ring to it?"
- Why did Colonel Tom Parker display no emotion whatsoever, even showing up for Elvis' funeral in a loud short-sleeved Hawaiian shirt and baseball cap, never once approaching Elvis' coffin or even entering the room where Elvis lay?
- Why, before the lid of the coffin was closed, is it reported that Joe Esposito removed the diamond T.C.B. from Elvis' left hand? Isn't that the one piece of jewelry Elvis *should* have been buried with?
- Why, in the Stanleys' *Elvis, We Love You Tender*, did David Stanley say he recalls seeing no injections or catheters, yet in his second book, *Life with Elvis*, he says he saw tubes running down Elvis' mouth while paramedics started administering electric shock? And why does it say in Jerry Hopkins' *Elvis: The Final Years* that Stanley rode in the ambulance, while in the author's *Elvis, We Love You Tender* he states that those riding in the ambulance were Al Strada, Joe Esposito, Dr. Nick, and Charlie Hodge and in his *Life with Elvis* he reports only Al Strada, Joe Esposito, and Dr. Nick rode? Why didn't Vernon Presley ride in the ambulance with his only son? And, since Vernon did not see fit to go to the hospital at all, how did he sign the request for the autopsy?
- Why is it that Charlie Hodge, Elvis' friend, says Elvis died of cancer of the bone marrow, yet Elvis' nurse says no, not true. First, we hear it was a heart attack, then drug overdose, then suffocation in the carpeting, then suicide, then cancer! If none of these folks know what is what, why the indignation about the rest of us asking questions? Also, the reports vary as to when Elvis was last seen alive, and when his body was discovered. The Medical Examiner's Report says Elvis was last seen alive at 8 A.M., yet according to Paul Lichter, in his book *All My Best*, Elvis signed for a certified letter on the morning of August 16, 1977, around 9:00/9:30 A.M. And why don't those who found the body even know its correct position or what color Elvis' pajamas were?"

- How did they get all those T-shirts printed and ready for sale within hours after Elvis' death?
- Why does the Medical Examiner's Report state that Elvis was found with rigor mortis, while the police report states "unconscious"; and why would Joe Esposito even think of giving mouth-to-mouth to a rigor-mortised body that was blue/purple/black, tongue hanging out, face contorted, eyes red?
- Why did ABC's 1979 show on the cover-up in the death of Elvis state that all stomach contents were destroyed, whereas Bill Burk in his *Elvis World* stated that officials at Baptist Memorial Hospital assured him that the stomach contents were shipped to a California laboratory for examination and then to a lab in Utah, and then destroyed?
- In a fan-newsletter interview with Kathy Westmoreland, Elvis' back-up singer, why did she say he had bone cancer throughout his entire body, yet he played racquetball the night before?
- Since many biographers state Elvis played racquetball in the wee hours of the morning of August 16, 1977, and that he whacked himself so hard in the leg that there was a hard knot and he limped, why is such a contusion not shown on the Medical Examiner's Report?
- An interview with Charlie Hodge appeared in the October 1988 issue of *Elvis Monthly*. Charlie states he was in the kitchen when Vernon and Patsy (Elvis' cousin) came running down saying something was wrong with Elvis, and that he ran upstairs to help Joe. I thought it was Al Strada who was first called in the kitchen by Joe Esposito, yet in another report I heard that Joe Esposito was at the Howard Johnson's, doing paper work.
- The book *Elvis, We Love You Tender* talks about a conversation between Joe Esposito and a doctor at the hospital in which Joe asks how long Elvis was without oxygen and the doctor replies that it was too long, that even if Elvis lives he'd be like a vegetable – which indicates Elvis was alive when brought in. Yet Joe says that Elvis had been in a state of rigor mortis when found?
- Why did it take twenty minutes for paramedics to drive only sixteen blocks to Graceland, if the call was actually received at 2:33 P.M.? And why, if the body was already rigor-mortised, was the announcement of "dead" not made until an hour later?
- Joe Esposito's explaining the pug nose on Elvis in the coffin from Elvis having fallen forward on his face is ludicrous! I've fallen flat on my face and my nose doesn't turn "pug." Plus, the

nose doesn't support the body like a top: Weight disperses. People sleep on their faces all night long, sometimes rearranging their noses, but they don't remain such!

- Perhaps this is insignificant, but Elvis' Uncle Vester, in his book *A Presley Speaks,* says that the last book Elvis was reading was the Bible, while others say it was a book on the Shroud of Turin?

- I've been going over a lot of information acquired lately: newspaper accounts, etc. One of the paramedics was quoted as saying that Dr. Nick was giving Elvis CPR when they arrived, but in Priscilla's book [*Elvis and Me*] she says Dr. Nick arrived just as the paramedics were leaving. Dr. Nick said in one account that he attempted resuscitation efforts because Elvis' pupils were constricted, indicating life. Pupils become *dilated* after death.*

- Every medical person I have talked to says that it is ludicrous to give CPR to a rigor-mortised body.

- Every biography about Elvis states that he knew his drugs, knew which prescribed drug did not mix well with another. Yet one of the drugs listed as being found in Elvis' system was Dexedrine, a drug that is not to be taken if one has glaucoma, which Elvis had. Thus, who would prescribe such to Elvis, and why would he even have taken it?. . . So whose body was autopsied?

- According to the video documentary "Elvis Presley's Graceland," Elvis wanted his elderly aunt to have the gold grand piano, because he no longer needed it. Why? Was he going someplace?

- I called a local funeral home and asked about a seamless copper coffin, similar to the one Elvis was buried in. Normally, funeral homes do not stock these extremely expensive, solid-copper coffins. They weigh around 300 pounds. It usually takes about 60 days to order a complete unit.

- I find it interesting that Elvis is not buried next to his mother. Instead, he is buried between Minnie Mae [his grandmother] and Vernon—odd, since Elvis "died" first. This means that there is an empty place between Elvis and his mother, Gladys. A clue?

- In the book *Elvis, We Love You Tender* the authors commented that Elvis in the coffin was dressed in a white suit, looking

---

*It is interesting to note that Elvis' doctor described a life condition in a body that had been reported to be rigor-mortised.

noble, tranquil, frighteningly different. Then they say that
Elvis was later changed into a pale blue suit. Why would anyone *change* Elvis' clothes? Symbolism? What?
- Elvis was very active in karate and had calluses, scars, and a
  crooked finger. The body in the coffin had hands that were
  smooth, had no scars, no crooked little finger on the right
  hand . . .*
- Why was Lisa Marie laughing and playing and riding around
  on her golf cart right after Elvis "died"? Even at nine, she would
  have been grief-stricken.
- Why was Vernon Presley talking business with the Colonel
  within hours after Elvis' "death." Where was the grief? And
  why, in all reports, was Priscilla described as calm and
  unemotional?
- Why did Vernon state he had opened the gates to the grieving
  fans because it was Elvis' request. Obviously, Elvis knew
  something we didn't: that his very ill father would outlive him
  and would be around to handle it all.

The "all" included a public viewing, a seamless, specially
ordered coffin, sixteen white Cadillacs for the funeral procession,
sealed autopsy reports, the moving of Gladys' coffin to the mausoleum, the telephoning of dozens and dozens of people – asking
them *not* to attend the funeral! As for the sixteen Cadillacs, one
may recall a line in one of Elvis' songs, "Mystery Train": " . . . train
I ride, sixteen coaches long."

Despite Vernon's telephone calls to fan-club presidents and
personal friends, the funeral was probably one of the largest in
American history. Fans swooped down on Graceland in unprece-
dented numbers, and obviously not all of them succeeded in pass-
ing by the open coffin. What is odd is that biographies had and
have reported that Elvis was very upset when his mother's funeral
turned into a pseudo-carnival. Vernon, too, was reported to share
those sentiments. A fan has written me: "Logic says that if Elvis
had died, the family would have had a sedate, private viewing so
that the fans would always remember Elvis onstage rather than
in the coffin."

Billy, Rick, and David Stanley, in their *Elvis: We Love You
Tender,* have asked why false information concerning Elvis' death
was given the public. And ABC, in its specials, has charged that

*In the Graceland section (File Case No. 15) I will speak about an interview with
Gene Smith, Elvis' first cousin, who said that the body did not have Elvis' hands.

Elvis did not die of heart disease but, rather, of a lethal combination of prescribed drugs—the *Geraldo* show in particular upholding this view. Now, if Geraldo Rivera can intimate that documents describing the singer's "death" are fakes, then what prevents one from regarding the "death" itself as a fake, a hoax? Where does one lie end and the other begin?

ABC has even demanded that the body be exhumed, so certain were they that a cover-up had been arranged. And a fan has written me: "Why was it alright for Geraldo to make charges of a cover-up—and not you?" She went on: "I can fully understand why all the evidence was destroyed—stomach contents, internal organs. After all, they're not Elvis'. Also, it's good that the 'body' was moved onto private grounds. This makes exhumation just about impossible!"

THE MEMBERS OF ELVIS FAN CLUBS HAVE CONTRIBUTED MANY OF THE foregoing suspect contradictions. One might add, from members of The Elvis Special, in particular:

- An inventory of Elvis' estate lists three to four pieces of jewelry, no photographs of Lisa or Gladys, fake suede and leather furniture and clothing, as well as mismatched crystal, silverware, etc. What happened to most of Elvis' jewelry and his "real" clothing, etc.?
- Elvis had more property and assets than were listed by the inventory. What happened to them? Were they sold prior to August 16? By whom?
- In 1978, Dee Presley told us that she thought Elvis had called her on the phone. He didn't identify himself but he knew things only Elvis would know.
- Elvis visited the dentist on August 16. Why weren't there traces found of novocaine in Elvis' body?
- If Elvis' heart was so enlarged, was it possible to play racquetball for hours on August 16?
- Why did the estate receive a bill for moving Gladys' body to Graceland but no bill for moving Elvis?
- Why was the date on Elvis' will crossed off and changed by hand?
- Elvis had had a physical exam prior to his August tour. How did he pass, if he had such a bad heart?
- Why hadn't Elvis had any new jumpsuits made for him during 1977?
- Elvis' hair at his "death" was said to have been gray around the

sideburns. He was going on tour the next day. Would Elvis
have left his hair this way just before the tour?
• Why were many of us personally asked by Vernon Presley *not*
to come to Memphis for the funeral, but to come a week
later?*

Perhaps most important of all, why did Elvis make these comments not long before August 16, 1977: "I Am and I Was" . . . "I may
not look good tonight, but I'll look good in my coffin" . . . "I will not
live past the age forty-two" . . . "Goodbye. You're not going to see
me again" . . . "I'm tired of living the life I'm living" . . . "This life I
am leading is going to change" . . . "If I could walk around and see
things without mobs of people, be free, it would be worth a
million dollars, if only for a week. Just being plain little ol' me,
instead of an 'image.' I want to breathe fresh air. I've been a slave
too long."

The contradictions, the puzzles, go on and on, yet no answers
have been forthcoming, and thus the question remains: Is Elvis
alive?

*Both Maria Columbus (president of The Elvis Special) and the late Jeanne
Tessum (once co-president of the club) have said that they believe Vernon knew
that if they came, they would *know* it was not Elvis in the coffin. The pug nose,
the eyebrows, the chin were all *wrong*.

Television and Other Media That Question Elvis' Death

I keep reading between the lies.
—GOODMAN ACE

Question: What other segments of the media, besides the press, radio and books, have questioned Elvis' death? **Answer:** Long before the book *Is Elvis Alive?* was released, the validity of his death had been raised in print, both in nonfiction and fiction. Especially since the release of *Is Elvis Alive?* has the death question moved into television, the movies, cartoons, popular slogans, etc.

Television has been interested in Elvis' "death" since late 1977. Fans have kept me apprised.

One fan wrote me about an episode on the new CBS *Twilight Zone* series. Aired September 27, 1986, it was entitled "The Once and Future King," and was about Elvis, with the cooperation of his estate. In the plot, an Elvis impersonator went back in time, met Elvis, accidentally killed him, then took his place "in history." Another fan informed me that HBO's *Kids in the Hall* did a sketch in 1989 about Elvis as a landlord.

A fan has asked me: "Did you note on *Roseanne* [ABC] that Elvis was spotted in Montana? Elvis is mentioned as being alive a lot on her show, and she has the collectors' dish 'Elvis at the Gates of Graceland' hanging on the wall. . ." Similarly, a fan has asked: "Have you noticed that on *Designing Women* [CBS] Charlene mentions Elvis' being alive quite often?" I was also told that on a *"Coach* episode [ABC] Jerry Van Dyke was convinced that he had found where Elvis was hiding out – and he wears a button that says, 'The King Lives.'" And, it appears, Cannon Television's *D.C. Follies,* which features caricatures of living people, has had Elvis as one of its shows. What's more, NBC's *True Blue* has featured an Elvis fanatic holding a young woman hostage in a music store, threatening to shoot her unless the store produces his idol, Elvis!

An Elvis fan has told me that NBC's *The Hogan Family* had Mrs. Poole walking into the room saying, "Ooooh, it just gives me the creeps." To which Mr. Hogan responds: "You don't really believe that stuff, do you, Mrs. Poole?" Marc and David ask: "What are you talking about?" and Hogan answers: "Mrs. Poole is reading *Is Elvis Alive?*" The book is seen, and Mrs. Poole continues: "Well, I'm not saying I believe or don't believe, but it's verrrrry interesting."

"I found the January 1989 *Alf* show [NBC] interesting," wrote a fan. "It was called 'Suspicious Minds' –Alf believes his mysterious neighbor, Aaron King, is really Elvis Presley." On the show, Kate responds: "Alf, let's assume for a moment – and just a moment – that Aaron King *is* Elvis Presley. What do you think he'd want you to do?" Alf answers: "He'd want me to leave him alone. . ." Another fan "noticed on *Alf* that Aaron King goes around wearing a baseball cap. [I] remember hearing that some of those who spotted Elvis said he was wearing a baseball cap." And another asked: "Did you note that NBC's showing of 'The Wickedest Witch' came from the creators of *Alf?* Upon [her] looking into the Magic Mirror for truth comes this answer: 'I know where Elvis is.'"

It is strange that the January 1989 *Alf* show mentioned above listed the cooperation of the Elvis Presley estate, since the show ends with Elvis' being alive and the estate does not accept this.

I've received countless letters that soap operas, such as NBC's *Days of Our Lives,* are using the hoaxed-death idea and that many see this as a connection with Elvis. From the Johnny Carson, I'm told, to the Arsenio Hall and David Letterman shows, the "Elvis is alive" theme is being mentioned, albeit tongue-in-cheek.

MOST MOVIES THAT HAVE HAD SOME CONNECTION WITH ELVIS – HIS LIFE or his "death" – have been Orion productions. Let's begin, however, by examining some non-Orion films that fans have admired and commented on.

In 1979, the movie *Game of Death* was released by Columbia Pictures as a Golden Harvest Film. An Elvis fan, Linda S., of Maiden, North Carolina, wrote that she was

> totally shocked when I viewed the video of the Bruce Lee movie *Game of Death*. This was Lee's last movie – in fact, he died mysteriously while making the movie and it was completed many years later with a stand-in. The movie is about a world-famous entertainer who is being exploited by the syndicate. He decides to fight the syndicate, gather information, etc. Then his life is threatened; he is shot at. He fakes his death and, with the help of his doctor and a close friend, false death reports are issued. There is a death announcement and the world mourns.
>
> The "body" is put on display in an open coffin. Thousands and thousands of fans pass by, crying, lamenting. Headlines across the world mourn this man. However, the body in the coffin is a dummy.
>
> The entertainer goes underground in order to continue his work on gathering information on the syndicate. He gets into karate. He goes around in various disguises: white hair, beards, sunglasses. Those closest to him do not even know the truth – he fears that if they knew the truth, their lives would be in danger.
>
> But eventually, people who knew him begin to suspect. Finally, the syndicate gets wind of the rumor through a number of circumstances: sightings, the fact that someone unknown is after them . . . Late one night, the syndicate goes to the cemetery and exhumes the body, and they discover it is not the entertainer but a dummy. They go on a search, but in the end the entertainer wins out, emerges, and rejoins his loved ones.
>
> I could not believe what I was seeing! In fact, the open-casket scene, the crowds, etc., looked as though they were lifted from the events at Graceland! But of course this could not have been, since the movie was filmed in 1973, during which time Bruce Lee died.
>
> I have read many times that Elvis Presley and Bruce Lee were friends, owing to their common interest in karate, kung-fu – the martial arts. Elvis admired Lee and they had talked, I believe, of doing a movie together. Could *this* have been the movie? Was it finished in 1977 *because Elvis saw it finished?* Could it be that Elvis got the idea of how to pull off his own death hoax from this movie? . . . It has been rumored that Lee was being exploited by the syndicate and that he intended to fight them, and in doing so was murdered. He was only thirty-two. . . . Could it be that Bruce Lee's movie was a "message" movie?
>
> Chuck Norris and Gig Young were also in the movie, and I've read that Elvis and Priscilla were introduced to Norris by Ed Parker. This

connection is too close to be chalked up as pure coincidence. (Even Gig Young died a strange death.)

In Michael Munn's *The Hollywood Murder Case Book* (New York: St. Martin's Press, 1987) the mysterious death of Bruce Lee is explored. Lee, described as the "king of kung-fu," was considered one of the fittest men in the world who have achieved international superstar status through the star-making machine. One of the hottest properties around, MGM was trying to put him into a picture with Elvis, MGM being Elvis' movie home.

On July 20, 1973, Lee had gone to bed rather early. He was later found in a coma, barely breathing, with almost no pulse. At 11:30 P.M., at the age of thirty-two, one of the finest-honed men in the world was dead. And no one seemed to know why. The autopsy raised questions—but his swollen brain could be attributed to nothing, and brain hemorrhage was ruled out (although traces of cannabis around his lodgings started a tidal wave of stories about drug abuse).

Stories began to be heard that Lee was not dead, but would reappear. Still other reports intimated that he was working undercover for the government as a secret agent or (like the character he had played in *Game of Death*) he had uncovered an international drug ring operating out of Hong Kong. (Some had it that he had been murdered by this ring by lethal injection.)

There is every reason to believe Elvis had seen the unfinished movie sometime in his "final" year, if not for his admiration of Lee, then because of his love for the martial arts. If, indeed, Elvis viewed his situation as similar to Lee's in the movie, then *Game of Death* becomes even more intriguing—especially the part in which the mob exhume the fake body—because Elvis, if he "related to" this movie, *he* made certain that no such exhumation could take place.

In 1980, Columbia Pictures/Rastar Production released *Touched by Love*. Based on the book *To Elvis with Love*, by Lena Canada (New York: Everest House, 1978), it was the true story of a cerebral palsy victim, Karen, who, as the film indicates, was "locked up in a [physical] prison"; she responds to hearing Elvis' music, says, "He is *so* alive" and "He is good, really nice, so God gave him everything." Karen writes to Elvis, and he is not too busy to care. They become pen pals; Elvis sends her many gifts. Finally, God releases Karen from her "prison," takes her home.

Filmed at the Dr. Gordon Townsend School, in Calgary, Canada, it was copyrighted by the Elvis Company ("Elvis" and

"Elvis Presley" are trademarks of Elvis Presley Enterprises). Elvis' music was played throughout the film. Although Karen's relationship with Elvis took place pre-1977, it is interesting that Elvis' (later) company holds the copyright.

"Elvis' love and caring are so apparent throughout *Touched by Love*," wrote one fan. "A message was apparent: Do not become too busy to care. The main theme, however, was the story of someone who turned her back on the whole world but through faith and belief in someone came back. Also, did you notice that the Production Auditor was called Lisa King?" my correspondent asked.

A documentary-type film released by Warner Bros. in 1981 (although it was filmed in 1980), *This Is Elvis* starred Elvis lookalike Johnny Harra; the singing voice was Elvis'. Seen on Cinemax, Showtime, and other channels, it prompted the indefatigable Linda S. to say that she "saw in a photo of the poster for the film the words: 'Intimate memories and reflections *in his own words!*'" This docudrama has been seen, too, in movie houses in this country as well as abroad.

The motion pictures *Eddie and the Cruisers I* (1983; Nelson Entertainment, produced by Joseph Brooks and Robert K. Lifton) and, especially, *Eddie and the Cruisers II* (1989; Scotti Bros. Pictures; produced by Stephane Reichel) build on the Elvis legend and mystery. A fan who lives in Brookings, South Dakota, has written to me about both of them. The first movie is about a rock 'n' roll singer who fakes his death. The second, which opens with an Eddie seen several years after his "death" – "the only thing different about him is a mustache," says the Elvis fan – has several items of interest:

- His new name is Joe West ("a combination of Joe Esposito and Red West?"*).
- The film opens with an Eddie lookalike contest (Eddie is in the audience, but no one knows him).
- A "mystery tape" of songs is found; the tape is analyzed, and a huge reward is offered to anyone who can prove that it was made after Eddie's death; Eddie says he is rebuilding his career incognito.
- There are sightings of Eddie in twelve states, as well as in Paris, France.
- Eddie says that he can't return – because "they like me better dead than alive!"

*Red West was, like Joe Esposito, a close friend of Elvis'.

- Eddie tells that he "left" because he believed he was washed up as a rock 'n' roll singer.
- On several fake segments of *Larry King Live* women swear they have his children.
- Eddie had made his albums on Satin Records ("Satin" was Elvis' nickname for his mother).

Top Secret, a 1984 Paramount/Kingsmere Film, also aired on cable TV as well as by Fox Television, was filmed in England (David and Jerry Zucker, producers), and was seen by at least one fan – again Linda S. – who noted how much the picture "poked fun at the numerous Elvis 1960s movies. . .done in the way EP might have seen it, especially in the later years of his movie career." The lead character, played by Val Kilmer, is a rock 'n' roll singer named Nick Revis, who throughout the movie sings Elvis songs while on tour in East Germany, where he gets involved in a rescue/liberation movement. There are just a few things worth noting:

- At one point (following an underwater fight!), Revis waves goodbye using Elvis' familiar hand gesture.
- Revis finally decides to give up his singing career for the girl he loves.
- The freedom fighters at this point make an interesting comment: "As long as we hear Revis' music, we will never be alone and he will always be with us!"

Linda wrote that in "the last of the credits was a notification that the song recordings performed by 'Nick Revis' were available from a record company (I didn't catch the name) in Canada – recordings by a fictional character! Why not use the actor/recording artist's real name?"

In 1985, an Elvis documentary film, *Elvis Presley's Graceland,* was seen on cable television and soon became available in video stores. One fan pointed out to me that in it, "when Pris is explaining about the long, white sofa in the living room, she says, 'This holds a lot of memories for Elvis and me.' (Present tense?)" The film was made with the endorsement of Elvis Presley Enterprises.

In 1988, a Touchstone/Buena Vista feature film, *Heartbreak Hotel,* starred David Keith as Elvis Presley. Written and directed by Chris Columbus, it was set in 1972 and filmed on location in Austin, Texas. A small-time rock singer brings home, to his broken family, a man who turns out to be his mother's idol (the mother role was played by Tuesday Weld): Presley. Elvis brings to her, and to the family, a new sense of hope, of life. "Yet," according to *News from Touchstone Pictures,* "the Wolfe family is not the only one to benefit from the mythical performer's visit: returned to his roots and removed from the insidious and addictive web of celebrity that usually surrounds him, Elvis finds himself confronted with some revealing truths about his current status in the world of music and the man he has become in recent years."

The film had the support of Elvis Presley Enterprises. In the release of the soundtrack album, Jerry Schilling was thanked, and there was also "a special thanks to J.B." (Jon Burrows?) The title song "Heartbreak Hotel," with lyrics by Mae Axton and Tommy Durden, had, in 1956, been Elvis' first million-dollar recording.

BY FAR THE GREATEST NUMBER OF MOVIE-RELATED LETTERS I RECEIVE from Elvis fans are about films released by California-based Orion Pictures. In 1978, five former film executives left United Artists to create Orion: Arthur Krim, Robert Benjamin, Eric Pleskow, William Bernstein, and Mike Medavoy.* They were men who had had a hand in such work as the James Bond films, the Woody Allen pictures, and *Heaven's Gate.* Orion, financed and distributed, early on, by Warner Bros., bought a dying company, Filmways, Inc., as its base of operations. (Later, Orion would create a largely art- and foreign-oriented division known as Orion Classics.)

Medavoy is cited, according to James Monaco's *American Film Now* (New York: New American Library, 1979), as explaining the choice of the corporate name Orion this way: "Orion is a five-main-star constellation." But astronomers have it that the constellation has seven main stars (not counting the more minor stars in Orion's "sword"), which might lead some observers to conjecture that there may be two *so-far-silent* partners.

Normally, for a production company to raise a huge amount of money, it takes in private investors. The reader may recall, from File Case No. 10, that a Mr. Dougherty telephoned me from Switzerland, saying that "Elvis Presley is one of the money people behind a film investment group." However, there exists no verifiable evidence that Presley and/or his family or estate is one of the two unnamed investors – if two there are.

Elvis a film producer? Could it be possible?

At any rate, one of the earliest Orion productions was *The Life of Brian,* in 1979. The Monty Python group, featured in the film, was one of Elvis' favorites!

*Robert Benjamin has since passed on, and Medavoy has left Orion.

In 1983, an Orion Pictures release, *Breathless,* starring Richard
Gere, engendered a great deal of speculation. With a soundtrack
by Jerry Lee Lewis, the plot concerns a man named Jesse who is
obsessed with Lewis, as well as a comic-book hero called the
"Silver Surfer." In one scene in the movie, Elvis' voice is heard singing "Suspicious Minds." A fan wrote that he believed the movie was

> the transition clue from Orion the performer [who disappeared at
> about this time] to Orion Pictures.* I have a soundtrack album to
> *Breathless* and you'll never guess where I bought it! At the Sun
> Studio in Memphis. Now, get this: The Presley estate now owns the
> Sun Studio.
>   When I was in Memphis in October 1988, we went on the Sun
> Tour from Graceland. At the end of the tour of the recoraing studio,
> I asked a question about the current Sun company. The guide
> seemed to want to hasten on and not get into any kind of a discus-
> sion about this topic. . . . Well, as we were leaving the studio, we
> bought a book and a tote bag. Then one of the guides pointed out
> the *Breathless* soundtrack (as I remember, this was the only record
> they had for sale) and told us that if we bought it there, they would
> put the gold label sticker on it and make it more valuable.
>   At that time, I was missing a lot of information: I did not know
> that Elvis might be connected with Orion Pictures; I did not know
> that *Breathless* was an Orion Picture; I did know that the Presley
> estate owned the Sun Studio. The bottom line is this: The Presley
> estate is selling an Orion Pictures "clue." Now, isn't *that* interesting.
> (Almost like *The Passover Plot's* being put on sale at Graceland.)

The chapter "The Early Years," in author/scholar Lee Cotten's
The Elvis Catalog, states that Sun Records is owned by the Presley
estate, although the estate today denies such ownership. My correspondent (above) says he believes he remembers that "Lee's book
was written with the estate's backing/approval . . . it would stand
to reason that [Cotten] was well informed and knew what he was
writing about. It sure is hard to piece all this together."
    One Elvis fan considered the Orion 1983 release of *Class*

> one of the most significant of all. While watching it and picking up
> the "clues," it was interesting; but the more I think about it, the more
> important the film seems. . . . There are no Elvis clues such as
> songs, etc.—but there are a lot of Jon Burrows clues.
>   The two co-stars play roommates at a prep school. One's first

---

*Orion Pictures, the fan forgets, had been producing films since the late 1970s.

name is Jonathan [Andrew McCarthy] and the other's last name is Burroughs [Rob Lowe]. Jonathan is referred to by his first name all through the film, while his roommate is referred to, many times, by his last. Also, Burroughs is predominantly mentioned throughout. Jonathan fakes his death (a suicide) as a practical joke on his roommate early in the film. A group of students break into the home of an investigator after a rumor is heard that he is checking out their school. They find a Special Agent ID and badge, and jump to the conclusion that he is a "narc." They rush back to the dorm and flush away all their drugs.

Now, Orion Pictures may try to say that it just *inadvertently* has given clues in twenty-six other movies about Elvis. But in 1983 they had no reason to be giving clues about Jon Burrows. P-r-e-t-t-y interesting, huh?

. . . because in 1983 the general public would not yet have known that J.B. was Elvis' alias!

In 1985, Orion Pictures' *Return of the Living Dead* had, I am told, "a theme of drugs destroying the brain, and in one scene there is a baseball cap lying on the floor." The plot has characters Freddie and Frank at a place called Resurrection Funeral Home, neither of them with a pulse or blood pressure, both with temperatures of 70 degrees. "Paramedics are called, who say that rigor mortis has set in with Freddie, that they are both dead—but are still alive. . . . The President is involved, and a helicopter. . ."

Another fan wrote, about a 1985 Orion film, *The Heavenly Kid,* that people in the picture are said to be going "uptown" or "downtown" when they die. One character in the film asks his guardian angel, "What happened to Elvis?" The angel's reply: "He's uptown."

Of all the Orion movies, 1987's *RoboCop* has attracted most Elvis fans' attention. The movie is about a police officer who is thought to have been killed in the line of duty. In reality, he is not dead, and only one person knows his identity when he returns as RoboCop—a superman hero who fights crime, drugs, etc. The film was made in Michigan, and, as one caller pointed out, "During the filming of the movie radio stations received calls from a man sounding like Elvis Presley." Many fans of course reminded me of the previous Michigan Elvis sightings, of how much the entertainer loved Michigan, and that he made Michigan a part of his final concert tour. Many fans saw it as a "message" film.

Later, when it reached television, one fan reminded me that *RoboCop* was going to be aired immediately after TV's *Elvis* series.

She exclaimed, "[Elvis] just keeps putting these Orion Pictures clues right under our noses! I love it."

On March 18, 1990, the *Detroit News* featured an illustrated article on RoboCop, the by now well-known film character. "Walking stiffly and talking in a booming voice," wrote staff writer Denise Crittendon, "RoboCop spoke to about 500 young members of the Boys and Girls Club of Southeastern Michigan." The children, ogling their idol, listened to his twenty-minute anti-drug and stay-in-school lecture. "I hate drugs," RoboCop shouted. "Don't let drugs destroy your mind. Don't use drugs!"

RoboCop was in Detroit as part of a nationwide anti-drug campaign, three months long, organized by the FBI, Orion Home Video of New York, and the Boys Club of America. The article pointed out that

- RoboCop was not the same actor who had played in the movie—and that his true identity could not be revealed.
- He was a special agent helping the FBI fight the war against drugs.
- His suit was bullet-proof.

He led the children in an anti-drug pledge.

Later, Renee R., of the Detroit area, wrote me: "During the picture's filming in the late 1980s, you cannot imagine how many people swear they spotted a man resembling an older Elvis Presley, especially in the Lake Michigan vicinity. Orion's movie *Prancer* [1989; more about it later] was also filmed in Michigan, and, again, there were Elvis sightings. *RoboCop* is right up Elvis' alley—the superman hero who as a secret agent of the government is fighting the wars on crime and drugs."

RoboCop 2 was released in summer 1990. And yes, it's set in Michigan again. "Robo," as he is known on the streets, has become a Detroit celebrity. As Janet Maslin put it in the *New York Times*, in a June 22 review, "RoboCop's archnemesis in the new film [is] a drug dealer and cult leader named Cain," who has been marketing "a virulent new street drug called nuke." A fan, Candy C., of Jacksonville, Florida, wrote me almost immediately after the film's release: "There's a scene in it with a coffin . . . [and] over the coffin is a picture of Mother Theresa, another picture of Christ, and a large picture of Elvis—inside the coffin propped up is *another* picture of Elvis!"

The year 1988 brought a deluge of Orion Pictures in which there appear to be Elvis connections. One of the most popular was

Mac and Me, the story of a young alien lost, a million miles from home, on a strange planet. Elvis fans were most intrigued "automotively." One asked, "Have you seen. . .at the end of the movie [how] the alien family is shown driving away in – now get this – an *old pink Cadillac convertible!*" As the car drives off, a balloon caption at the end says "We'll be back." The writer hoped that this was Elvis' message that he would be back. He adds: "A friend has pointed out to me that the soundtrack to *Mac and Me* is on Curb Records, the same label as "Spelling on the Stone" [see File Case No. 11]. I also found that one of the singing groups on *Heart of Dixie* [another '88 Orion release] appears through the courtesy of Curb Records."

Another fan noted that "lyrics to songs sung during the Cadillac's driving-away scene are very poignant when related to Elvis. Also, a little boy in the movie is dead – but then comes back to life. And the scene at the end, in which the black man is swearing in the aliens as U.S. citizens is meaningful – reminds us of our duties as citizens." A third fan signaled out some of the highly significant song lyrics:

> Tired of being myself,
> Being different from everyone else.
> Somehow you knew I needed your help.
> Be my friend forever.
> I never found my star in the night;
> Living my dream was far from sight.

The same writer singled out the scene in which "Eric" asks "Debbie," "Why didn't you tell him that you saw him [the alien]?" – to which she responds, "Because no one would believe me." Another 1988 Orion release was *Johnny Be Good.* A fan who recently rented the film has commented:

> Wow! This is about a high school football star who is suddenly sought after and swamped by people clambering all over him with bribes, girls, etc. Anyway, to make it short: The movie parallels Elvis' early life in many ways. They show an Elvis decanter – the one with pink jacket and black slacks – in the coach's house early in the movie. The star says to his mother, "I'm going to make enough money so you never have to work again, Mama." Later, he tells her that he wants to buy her a big house. He goes to Hollywood and comes back later in jewelry, fancy clothes, etc.
>
> A scene of a striptease act is filmed to resemble the same scene in Elvis' *Jailhouse Rock,* in which he is sitting at the edge of the stage

looking up at the stripper. The song "Johnny B. Goode" [the song title
was different from the movie title] somewhat describes Elvis' life,
too – not that of a football player!
   You have to see this movie to put it all together, but it is remarkable. One scene in a motel room with three girls and a friend of
Johnny's is classically Elvis: Johnny is sitting at a table talking to this
girl about life, love, and philosophy, and she is bored and about to
go to sleep – while his friend is "enjoying" the other two girls. Finally,
Johnny's girl asks him if they are going to. . .or not. (I have read tales
of how women wanted to get to "know" Elvis and were disappointed
when he only wanted someone to talk to.)

   Another popular 1988 Orion film – in movie houses as well as
on TV–was *Married to the Mob,* starring later Oscar-nominated
Michelle Pfeiffer. It was a spoof about the FBI and the Mob. The
end of the movie showed a scene in a hair salon with an Elvis
lookalike mannequin on the counter. The end-of-film credits were
accompanied by a scene that is almost a re-enactment of the dance
scene in *Jailhouse Rock*; at one point, the undercover FBI agent
said, "You're surrounded by the FBI, the DEA. . ."
   Orion's *Mississippi Burning,* also released in 1988, tells what
might have happened in 1964 when three civil rights activists
turned up missing. A well-received film, it starred Gene Hackman
and Willem Dafoe. In the early part of the movie, Memphis,
Tupelo, and Tennessee are all mentioned. A fan wrote that the
"movie is a very thought-provoking movie about the good work
done by the FBI. The moral behind the movie is something I feel
Elvis would hope it conveyed." Another fan, while reading his copy
of Muhammad Ali's *The Greatest: My Own Story* (New York:
Random House, 1975), "found something very interesting. There
is a recounting of a story told to Ali by a black man who has been
abused and mutilated by some white men back during the civil
rights protests. His story is almost identical to a portion of the plot
of *Mississippi Burning.*"
   A 1989 Orion movie, *Heart of Dixie,* was based on the novel
Heartbreak Hotel by Ann Siddons. The movie dealt, in part,
with the integration movement, and it featured two Elvis songs.
According to the same fan:

   The most dramatic part of the movie takes place during Elvis'
   homecoming performance in Tupelo in 1957. . . . The album cover
   for the soundtrack says that "Blue Suede Shoes" was recorded in
   April 1956; however, I have two 1956 recordings of "Blue Suede
   Shoes" – one of which RCA released as part of an April 1956 per-

formance, and the one on the soundtrack is a different version: Some of the words are different. I wonder what this means. (Do you suppose it is a newer recording?)

Anyway, my point is this: I feel that it is no coincidence that you discovered the picture of Elvis, Ali, and the Reverend Jesse Jackson at about the same time Orion Pictures released two movies [*Mississippi Burning* and *Heart of Dixie*] dealing with racial injustice. Both have very strong messages and are excellent motion pictures.

Do you think that maybe Elvis is trying to tell us something about the work he is trying to do now? In ads for the video of *Mississippi Burning* and ads for the movie *Heart of Dixie* the name of the production company, Orion, has been given a lot of prominence.

Also, *Heart of Dixie* has a character in it named Tuck (short for Tucker?*); there is a horse farm on a plantation named Groveland; and "Heart of Dixie" is the movie's slogan on the auto license plates for the State of Alabama.

Those who were paying attention may also have noted that in the closing of Orion's *Great Balls of Fire* (1989; the story of Jerry Lee Lewis), the name Jack Baron was listed. It caught more than one fan's eye "because Elvis and Priscilla were going to name their baby John Baron (with 'aron,' his own middle name in it), if Lisa had been a boy." *Great Balls of Fire* gave thanks to the Presley estate at the end of its credits.

1989's Orion epic *Farewell to the King* caught many Elvis fans' attention. Starring Nick Nolte, it is the story of a World War II soldier who deserts, following General MacArthur's retreat from Corregidor. He escapes to the jungles of Borneo, unifies the tribes, whom he has grown to love, teaches them to sing, and at length becomes king. Startlingly, at one point in the movie, a fan noted, "the King says, 'I died once. I had to be willing to give up everything—even the will to live.' Finally, it dawned on me, after listening to the song 'The Last Farewell' from Elvis' last recording session at Graceland, that I had missed the most important message from the movie: The title of the film and the title of the song are obvious—but the *lyrics* to the song and the *story plot* of the movie interlock completely!"

Another fan noted that the entrance to the village had "two big columns, out of place in the jungle, that remind one of Graceland." And another mentioned that the film had "one really cute clue. Elvis recorded 'Big Boots' for his 'G.I. Blues' album. In the film

*Could there be a connection here? Tuck, in my novel, *Orion,* is Orion's best friend.

230 The Elvis Files

there is a little boy wearing soldier's boots and clomping around in them, and someone tells him that they are the largest boots in Asia, perhaps in the world. Such a cute clue!"

A brief note from an Elvis fan about Orion Pictures' 1989 film *She Devil* is interesting. The film co-starred Meryl Streep and Roseanne of TV fame. The fan thought the film "very symbolic of Elvis' sending us messages. Besides his singing 'Devil in Disguise' at the end of the film, the 'disguise' name for Roseanne was Vesta Rose – pronounced 'Vester.' The rose is an Elvis symbol used in souvenirs, such as pins, sold in Memphis gift shops; Vesta Rose and her army of women wore rose pins."

Orion's *Prancer,* released in December 1989, is the tale of a young girl who believes she has found Santa's reindeer Prancer. "Love of children and of Christmas," wrote one fan, "were always important to Elvis. This movie is just like him. In a monologue in the film he mentions that Christmas would be the time when he would come out, if he ever did." Filmed in Three Oaks, Michigan, about ten miles from Muhammad Ali's farm, the movie may have indicated that Elvis was again in Kalamazoo (he had been sighted there the year before). "This movie could be his Christmas present to those of us who believe, and are paying attention," the fan concluded.

Orion Classics (a separate division of Orion) released *Mystery Train* in 1990. A three-episode film, in one part a teenaged boy and girl, both Japanese, visit places where Elvis lived and worked; in another, an Italian woman whose husband has just died sees Elvis' ghost; and in another, three misfits – one of them named Elvis – shoot a liquor-store clerk and hide out. A short time earlier, a fan wrote that he read in Memphis' *The Commercial Appeal* that Orion films would be "producing the movie in Memphis with special scenes at Sun Studios, using extras such as Shelby County Mayor Bill Morris, a friend of Elvis'. A spokesman at Orion," he continued, "said that Elvis allusions are involved in each segment. Why does Orion use so much of Elvis in its films? Could he be a silent part-ner/investor?"

Madhouse, another 1990 Orion release, is the story of a young married couple who have relatives staying with them, never giv-ing them any time alone. (This could be based on Elvis' and Priscilla's experience with friends' and family members' constantly being around.) A fan saw "EP signs all through it. A cat dies four times, and each time comes back to life. There is a Jerry Lee Lewis telethon. And there are two seated lions on each side of a wrought-iron gate facing a mansion."

And another Elvis fan found Orion's 1990 release of *Cadillac Man* "chock-full of clues." She says she "knew it would be, just as soon as I saw the title." As she describes the movie:

> Robin Williams is the star. He is a car salesman. The movie starts out with a funeral procession.
> Williams is divorced and is running around with a lot of women. He has a teenage daughter named Lisa. And he still cares about his wife. Williams uses the words "taking care of business" twice, early in the movie. When asked over the phone who he is, he says, "This is Elvis. I'm back from the dead and I'm P. . ." He answers the phone, "Heartbreak Hotel!"
> The daughter is only seen in the very last few minutes of the film; the actress who plays Lisa resembles Elvis' Lisa Marie an awful lot. At the film's end, Lisa and Williams' ex-wife are sitting in the front seat of a car talking to him about getting back together. The scene bears a strong resemblance to the Oldsmobile commercial that Priscilla and the real Lisa did recently. And, of course, *Cadillac Man* is about car sales too!

Oddly, the fan failed to mention Elvis' penchant for Cadillacs.

THE CARTOON WORLD HAS HAD A LOT OF FUN WITH ELVIS. I CAN GIVE only a few samples.

One by cartoonist Ken Alexander/Copley News Service, seen in the Salisbury, Maryland, *Daily Times* on a recent July 4, has a Statue of Liberty, which proclaims: "I guess I *do* look like Elvis Presley. . .and I'm almost as popular." A cartoon of a billboard, by Rodrigues/Tribune Media Services, Inc., gives this advice: "Remember – When Sighting Elvis Presley, Call 911." And Doug Marlette's (Creators Syndicate, Inc.) strip "Kudzu," in July 1988, had drivers pulled up at a gas station in the town of Bypass, asking, "Which way's *Elvis*?" As they drive off, the reader sees a sticker on their car's bumper, "Honk, If You See Elvis!"

On May 24 this year, a fan saw a Dan Piraro/Chronicle Features cartoon in the *Winnipeg Sun,* Canada. Under the cartoon title "Bizarro," it showed a picture of Elvis in Hawaii, stating, "I've decided to come out of hiding just long enough to do a few gigs impersonating myself – then I'll be back."

One of my favorites appeared in *Memphis Star* magazine in February and March 1989. It was a two-part "series," for Jim Palmer's "Li'l E" – a comic strip character who frequently appears in Elvis getup or sings Elvis songs. Palmer had his character watching the *Geraldo* show while the host interviewed a syndicate

type who had written a book, *Why the Mob Killed Elvis*. As Geraldo
continued his in-depth investigation of the crime, the final frame
found "Li'l E" saying, "Gol-Dang. . ."*

During the 1988 presidential race, mentions of Elvis turned
up frequently in cartoons. Soon-to-become Vice President Dan
Quayle was identified as Elvis; and Elvis was said to be more
"alive" than either George Dukakis or George Bush. A Houston-
based Elvis fan letter suggested that Bush should be glad he had
Dukakis as an opponent and not Elvis!

The "Doonesbury" comic strip (Garry Trudeau/Universal Press
Syndicate) has run many Elvis cartoons, their theme being that the
singer is alive.

*Panels (out of sequence) copyright © Jim Palmer, 1989, 1990. All rights
reserved.

I would like to end this chapter with a cartoon drawn by my friend D'Lores Gossen, caption by myself:

What Is Graceland Doing?

Why shouldn't *truth be stranger than fiction?*
Fiction, after all, has to make sense.
— MARK TWAIN

Question: What are Graceland, and those connected with it, doing to promote not only the Elvis legend but, especially, to answer the question "Is Elvis alive?"
Answer: Graceland and the Presley estate, as well as members of Elvis' family, have rather noncommittally taken the question and run with it.

Besides cooperating with a great many television shows, the estate has worked with the nationally advertised Bradford Exchange* in promoting sales of the first-issue, limited-edition wall plate "Elvis at the Gates of Graceland." Along with purchase of the plate goes a promotional package that includes advertisement of my book *Is Elvis Alive?* and encourages tourism to the estate. Other "Elvis" products available from Graceland are: (1) bath towels bearing the words "The King Lives On!" (and, in smaller acknowledgment, "Elvis and Elvis Presley are trademarks of Elvis Presley Enterprises"); (2) the most recent MGM films catalog, in which every page of films is headlined "Recent

---

*The Bradford Exchange is a major vehicle that offers limited-edition merchandise via mass-media advertisement.

Releases," except the pages of Elvis' films, which are highlighted with "Elvis Is Alive!"; and (3) copies of a late-1989 issue of *Elvis International Forum* magazine, licensed by Elvis Presley Enterprises, page 41 of which features a full-page picture of the entertainer lying on a bed reading fan mail (an old picture, a young Elvis).

The Presley-licensed magazine's Contents page lists Elvis' friends Joe Esposito and Eddie Fadal as current columnists, which is true. Therefore, the print beneath the Elvis-on-the-bed image is strange. It says: "Please take the time to drop me a line. I would love to hear your personal thoughts, memories, or maybe how we met at one time. Write to me in care of E.I.F. at . . ." And then an address is given. The magazine says that it ran the page because it meant for people to write to its *editor,* but admits that the mail coming in is addressed to Elvis. (Now, why would I want to write to the editor, sharing memories, how we maybe "met at one time"?)

Graceland, maintaining a "Maybe he is"/"Maybe he isn't" alive posture about Elvis, is the frequent recipient of letters of criticism. *The Elvis Special's* October/December 1989 issue reported that DJ Terry McGovern of radio station K101 in San Francisco talked of a survey that said an average of four people call Graceland each day and ask to talk to Elvis. Terry decided to call Graceland himself and see what its response was. Calling, he spoke to Bonnie Greenwell, in Communications, and she answered him, "We just say Elvis is not here right now." Todd Morgan, Graceland's Manager of Communications, has said in a recent syndicated newspaper review that "the positive side [of the incoming calls for Elvis] is it's really a testament to Elvis Presley's continuing popularity."

Normally, letters from Todd Morgan are signed with the words "Best regards" or "Respectfully." However, a form letter sent out around Christmas, in 1989, ended with a play on Elvis' own words: "As always, thank you very much for your support. You're beautiful subscribers [to *The Graceland Express* news quarterly], ladies and gentlemen. Until we mail to you again, may God bless you. Adios." (Was someone at Graceland trying to tell us something?) And Elvis fan Darlene D., of Tulsa, Oklahoma, asked the following about the March 26, 1990, *Graceland Express,* which said, "Keep up with the latest news about Elvis and Graceland": "If Elvis is dead, what kind of 'latest news' could there be about him?"

Visitors to Graceland have noticed not only that Elvis' name is misspelled on his gravestone (as well as his brother's), but they have questioned the memorial plaque in the poolhouse area, which reads:

In Loving Memory

Elvis Aaron Presley

1935 – NEVER

Of course, the significance of "NEVER" on the plaque – presented by the E.P. Continentals fan club of Kissimmee, Florida – might be "alive in spite of . . ." Nevertheless, it is unusual as a death date.

Finally, although Graceland and the Elvis estate did not initially welcome my book *Is Elvis Alive?*, the book is sold in area souvenir shops. And a fan reported that in a call and talk with Graceland Public Relations Manager Patsy Anderson she was told, asking about the book and the tape, "We are getting a lot of publicity from it!"

Much of the recent mail Graceland has received concerns the now-defunct television series *Elvis*. Most letter writers have asked why all the advertisements were headlined "Elvis Lives!" and why the ads said, "Produced by Elvis' wife – Priscilla Presley." Other fans have questioned why Navarone was one of the production companies of the series. One writer, Annette D., of Ackworth, Georgia, asked: "It seems strange that while producing a show about her ex-husband, she would produce under the name of a child who is supposed to have been fathered by a live-in lover." And another stated: "Why Navarone Productions? Why not Lisa Productions? After all, Lisa is Elvis' child, while Navarone is not."

IN MARCH 1957, ELVIS PURCHASED GRACELAND FOR $102,500. LOCATED today at No. 3764 on what is called Elvis Presley Boulevard, Graceland sits on almost fourteen acres in the Memphis suburb of Whitehaven. In its earlier history, Graceland had been used as a house of worship by the Graceland Christian Church.

The house was constructed in the late 1930s of beige-colored Tennessee limestone and originally contained twenty-three rooms, five of which were bedrooms. When Elvis purchased it, he repainted it and added several rooms, including a trophy room – forty feet long, built over the back patio. Originally begun as a playroom, it now displays Elvis' sixty-three gold singles, as well as his twenty-six platinum and thirty-seven gold albums. Elvis also built a barn and a raquetball court, along with a $200,000 private recording studio.

Because the upkeep of Graceland ran around a half-million dollars annually, Priscilla Presley decided, after Elvis' "death," to open the estate to the public in June 1982, although visitors could tour the grounds as early as late 1977. Graceland visitors may see the living room, dining room, music room, TV room, pool room, and "jungle"-styled den. The upstairs – Elvis' real "headquarters"– is closed to the public.

Not far from the house sits Elvis' airplane, the *Lisa Marie,* which he named after his daughter. It bears the now-familiar letters "TCB" as well as a lightning bolt in gold on the tail section, under an American flag. Elvis had the plane equipped with a $14,000 queen-sized bed, a conference room, four television sets, a bar, leather swivel chairs, and a pair of sofas. Tours of the plane are, of course, offered, as they are of an automobile museum across the street in the gift-shop plaza.

Visitors may tour the grounds, free, as well as the gravesites and the swimming-pool area that is near them.

I have seen reports that name Graceland the second-most-recognizable home in the United States, the first being the White House. Many visitors are surprised to discover that Graceland, which Elvis walled in shortly after its purchase, sits in front of a busy highway, originally Bellevue Road, and not out in the country.

Graceland has certainly prospered. The estate is projected to be worth around $500 million by 1993. Graceland welcomes ap-

proximately 670,000 visitors annually; Graceland Tours grosses about $4.5 million a year. The $750,000 car museum opened in June 1989, and the estate purchased the Graceland Christian Church, on 4.2 acres north of the mansion, in the same year. Currently, Graceland has embarked upon a joint project for the construction of a $40-million Graceland Hotel and Convention Center.

Across from Graceland sit Elvis souvenir shops and other visitor attractions. So popular is Graceland that in 1986 singer Paul Simon recorded the album "Graceland," for Warner Bros., with a theme of heavenly redemption. (The album won the Grammy Award for Album of the Year in 1987 and the song "Graceland" became Grammy Record of the Year in 1988).

Although at this writing *The Passover Plot* is out of print, according to Mitchell Fink in the *Los Angeles Herald Examiner* in November 1988, Hugh Schonfield's bestseller could then be purchased in the Elvis Presley Museum. "Know what it's about?" asked Fink. "It's about Christ faking his own death. Stew on that awhile."

In the assorted Elvis shops – if one doesn't know the facts already – one can discover that:

- Elvis Presley sold more than 1 billion recording albums. Set down side by side, that many LPs would wrap around the Equator more than seven and a half times; stacked, they would form a tower 10,638,298 feet high; they would cover 5.2

percent of the United States' landmass.*
- Between 1956 and 1970, Elvis made thirty-three motion pictures.
- Through 1977, Elvis gave over seven hundred live concerts.
- Elvis Presley bookends, originally priced at $1.29, today sell from between $400 and $500 per set.
- A 1956 Elvis Presley Board Game, originally sold for $3.49, today is priced between $600 and $800.
- Elvis Presley mittens, originally $1.50 a pair, sell for around $250 today. Elvis Presley skimmer leather pumps, which originally sold at $4.99 a pair, now cost around $500. Elvis Presley felt-denim-corduroy shirts, originally costing about $5, today sell for around $500. And Elvis Presley handkerchiefs, once $.39, sell today for about $250.

USA Today revealed in its August 26, 1988, story on Elvis that a stage costume once worn by him recently brought in nearly $50,000. And in a national poll by the newspaper, Elvis the King beat out Bruce Springsteen the Boss by two to one. A 1987 *Guinness Book of World Records* showed Presley as surpassing Bing Crosby as the top-selling solo artist of all time. Recent television surveys, such as Fox network's *Late Night* with Ross Shafer (August 1988), showed that of 30,000 persons polled, approximately 84 percent believe that Elvis is alive. A January 1990 *People* magazine poll asserted that Elvis would be packing them in again at the Las Vegas Hilton for the New Year's Eve 1999 show!

OFFICIALLY, THOSE WHO SPEAK FOR GRACELAND SAY THAT ELVIS PRESLEY died on August 16, 1977 – which is no surprise, since that is what the media announced, around the world.

On Palm Sunday (April 8) this year, I spoke on the telephone with Gene Smith, Elvis' first cousin (Gene's mother, Lavalle, and Elvis' mother were sisters). Born seven weeks before Elvis, Gene grew up with him in Tupelo, Mississippi, where they played together, double-dated, and later worked together at Precision Tools, in Memphis.

"We were closer than brothers," Gene told me. "Aunt Gladys always wanted me to stay around Elvis, especially when he slept. I'd go out on the road with him, and sleep in the same room because Elvis walked in his sleep – we were always afraid he'd

*The facts are from *USA Today,* August 24, 1988.

walk out of a window or something. And I could sleep in a way that the slightest sound woke me.

"I worked for Elvis into the 1960s, and we always stayed close. It's strange, all these books written about Elvis, about his growing up, what he did (*we* did). . ." Gene paused thoughtfully. "Those people who wrote about Elvis' growing up didn't even know him then. I *know* what went on because I was there! I loved Aunt Gladys like a mother. Someday I think I should write a book. . ."

From the moment I finally met Gene – while on location in the Los Angeles area, helping prepare the Home Media Elvis documentary* in June – I appreciated his warmth and "realness" (which were also obvious over the phone in April). Gene has the blue eyes with the Presley "twinkle" – and a tremendous sense of humor. But to return to our conversation. . .

"I saw Elvis a few weeks before August 16," said Gene. "He told me, 'Gene, I envy you. You can go anywhere. If you want to stop someplace for a beer, you can. I'm living the most miserable son-of-a-bitchin' life anyone could live!' Elvis also told me," he continued, "shortly before the sixteenth, that he would be going away for a while, but that he would contact me later." Then, when Gene heard Elvis had died, he said he couldn't believe it, felt something was wrong – and then *knew* something was wrong when he went to the viewing.

"The first thing I saw when I went to the coffin," Gene related, "was the hands. They weren't Elvis'. You see, Elvis' hands were big and beat up – calluses on the knuckles, scars, a crooked finger – all this from karate, breaking boards, smashing bricks. The hands in the coffin were small and as smooth as a woman's, smooth as a baby's behind. They were definitely not Elvis'. Plus, the sideburns were glued on; one was sticking straight out at the side. When I noticed this, some man came over and patted it back down, like he was sticking it back on. The nose was all wrong – pugged. Elvis had a straight nose. The eyebrows were wrong, the forehead wrong, hairline wrong. I could even see where the hair had been glued on around the forehead – you could see the glue."†

---

*The *Elvis Files* documentary, about an hour in length, will be available in coming months in video stores; a television presentation, incorporating perhaps an hour more of footage, will be announced late this fall.

† A fan from Cleveland, Tennessee, wrote me stating that there were "two doctors living here who were working the E.R. the day 'Elvis' was brought in. They were there when he was pronounced dead. Recently, there was a story in the local paper about this, and they both said that they didn't know it was Elvis until they were told. They never would have recognized him."

"Could it have been a wax dummy?" I asked Gene.

"Could have been," Gene responded. "*I* thought it was."

"Many who viewed the body in the coffin noted what they termed as 'beads of sweat,'" I told him.

"That's true," Gene answered. "I saw it, too."

Laughingly, I reminded Gene that dead bodies don't sweat. He said, "I know. Plus," he added, "if it was a wax dummy, then there had to have been an air conditioner in the coffin. I think there might have been. I was one of the ten pallbearers, and that coffin was so heavy I fell to my knees. The coffin was *too* heavy to have had just a body in it."

"One of Elvis' friends," I added, "said the same thing, that he knew it was not Elvis in the coffin, and asked Vernon Presley what was going on, where Elvis *was*. Vernon told him that Elvis was *upstairs . . .*"

Gene then told me that that could have been true, relating to me a story about the special powers Elvis had. "Elvis was psychic, he could do strange things," said Gene. "One time, he called us out to a porch – it was summer and there was no breeze, nothing, just still, quiet air. Elvis said, 'Gene, be quiet and watch this.' Elvis then put out his hands toward some shrubs and concentrated, moving his hands slowly back and forth. Suddenly, that part of the bushes began to move, like a breeze moving them – but just the part Elvis was aiming at, nothing else. I saw it.

"The reason I'm telling you this now is that when we were carrying the coffin out the front door, this large tree branch suddenly slammed to the ground! The tree it came from was still green and alive, and so was the branch. There was no reason it should crash down near us. It was like someone was 'upstairs,' mentally making it happen. Like with the bushes. Maybe this doesn't make sense, but if you knew Elvis, saw what he could do sometimes, then it does make sense."

As we talked further, I got the distinct impression that the family – excluding Priscilla, Lisa, and Vernon – were not in on a "death hoax" (assuming this was what was being enacted). (All this was underlined in an October 1988 conversation I had with a man identifying himself as Elvis [see File Case No. 16].) Asked about how Vernon, Lisa, and Priscilla behaved at the viewing and funeral, Gene said that that, too, was strange. "Our family cries and carries on when someone dies. But they didn't do that. Vernon acted a little upset, but not like a father who had lost a son, just kind of disturbed. And Lisa was running in and out, riding her golf cart – not like someone whose daddy was lying inside in a coffin."

In my initial conversation with Gene, over the telephone, I

asked him if he ever received any calls from Elvis or from someone sounding like Elvis, since August 16, 1977. He told me he had.
In my later California conversations, when I repeated that question, he tilted his head to the side and, with that Presley humor
sparkling in his blue eyes, replied, "Did I say that. . .?" I smiled and
said, "Yes." "Well," he went on, "I'm not saying I have. And I'm not
saying I haven't. . ."

Assuming that there is much that the family cannot divulge,
and respecting the reasons why, I drew back. Yet something inside
me also said that if Gene Smith talked to Elvis, knowing Gene's
loyalty I was sure that whatever Gene was now coming public to
say on the documentary was "permissible."

Yet I had to ask: "Is it possible Elvis is alive?"

Gene held contact with my eyes. "Yes," he spoke slowly. "It's
highly possible."

FILE CASE
No. 16

Surprises, and Grand Finale— Or Is It?

The great end of my life is not knowledge but action.
—THOMAS HENRY HUXLEY

Question: The controversy surrounding Elvis' "death" continues to be a focus of the mass media – such as *Life* magazine's 1990 story of his supposed "suicide." Is there anything left, still, to surprise us?
Answer: Absolutely. Although no satisfactory explanations of the curious events of August 16, 1977, have been given by the family, experts have recently uncovered some amazing facts, a close friend of Elvis' has tripped up on television, and Elvis' family doctor has changed his opinion.

O n August 16, 1977, came the "cry heard 'round the world." Perhaps this worldwide lament was in part due to the fact that there was, to most observers, no warning. After all, an Elvis concert tour was to begin that day; Elvis' fans would be there to greet him. Little did they know that this sixteenth day of August would be recorded in history as Elvis' grand finale.* "We

*The number sixteen, as we have seen throughout this book, is significant to Elvis in other ways than as the date of his death (the sixteen Cadillacs in the funeral procession, etc.).

243

never had the chance to say goodbye," was oft repeated by the millions shocked by Elvis' sudden "death."

Elvis' leaving fast became the tragedy of tragedies, one that led me to create a novel, *Orion,* that focused upon a man who did not want to be a god anymore. In it, although I did not want to write a biography of *Elvis,* I did want to capture the essence of his soul. Whether subconsciously I suspected – *then* – a possible death hoax on the part of Elvis is debatable; consciously, however, I knew Orion would fake his death. Thus, I used a combination of religion, mythology, and my own reading of *The Passover Plot* to form the story of *Orion,* little knowing that much of what I wrote as fiction in 1977 would prove to have substance in 1990! (For instance, I read *The Passover Plot* years before August 1977, never knowing that it was one of Elvis' favorite books until after the fact; i.e., the "death." That I was the recipient of a dog-eared, "marked-up copy" over a decade later is but one of the many mysteries in this human puzzle. Somewhere along the way, after writing *Orion,* I was told that Elvis did indeed consider *The Passover Plot* a favorite, as is outlined in File Case No. 5.)

I find it hard to use the term "death" when writing about Elvis, preferring, as do many, to use the words "left" or "gone." Songwriter Carole Halupke, Georgia's Songwriter of the Year 1985, had captured that thought in the following lyrics to the song "Orion," written for the novel:

You came from out of nowhere with your haunting melody.
We laughed and cried and screamed and tried to touch our fantasy.
You danced and sang your way into the hearts that cry for you.
'Cause, now we cry, Orion, what did we do to you?

Orion, we chased after you while following a dream
But now the dream is echoed in the songs you loved to sing,
To those who listen close a note of sadness whispers through,
Orion, what did we do to you?

You opened up your soul to let us see your love light shine
And we were glad to take your gift but gave no peace of mind.
We never got the chance to say goodbye, God be with you,
And now you're gone, Orion, what did we do to you?

The conjunction of *Orion* with Elvis' "death" has made me the hub of a many-spoked wheel. Beyond the thousands of letters with information, I have also been the recipient of hundreds of letters, thoughts, and poems written *to* Elvis and/or *about* Elvis.

Because they are written from the hearts of those who love him, I am compiling them, combining them with art and having them set to music – a collection by which the fans can give back to Elvis what he gave to them. Music for the collection, *Roses to Elvis,** will be produced by Larry McBride, founder of the music group Alabama, who in 1983 was named Producer of the Year for the song "It Feels So Right." The songs on *Roses* are sung by Sue Ellen.

A sample of one of the poems I'm talking about is the following, "Elvis, Is That You?", by Paul E. Phipps, of Muncie, Indiana:

Elvis, is that really you,
Beneath that bronze and clay?
Or is it just a replica
Of one who is gone away?

Are you on some distant shore
Basking in the sun?
That's something you could never do,
You always had to run.

Your fans come here from everywhere
To see your lovely place.
They come to see the *Lisa Marie*,
"The Hound Dog II" and the Music Gates.

From everywhere in the world they come
To pass through Graceland's gates,
The King is gone, but his legend lives on,
So the tributes still are paid.

As I recall and recollect,
The early days of youth –
The whole world was rocking to
The sound of "Blue Suede Shoes."

Is that great voice we grew up on
Forever to be stilled?
Or did the numbers all line up just right,
Was some prophecy fulfilled?

Should we believe the rumors
That say you're living still?
Or are they all lies and you really died
In your mansion on the hill?

---

*The net profits of the collection will be directed to organizations for the prevention of child abuse.

The questions are so many,
The answers are so few,
And I just can't help from asking myself,
"ELVIS, is that you?"

A big surprise on the horizon is singer Trent Carlini (opposite page)* of Italy – new superstar of the '90s – who sings the theme song, "Maybe Tomorrow," in conjunction with the *Elvis Files* video/TV documentary produced this year. "Maybe Tomorrow" is also written by Carole Halupke. It, like the other *Orion* song, was originally written for the novel (soon to become a major motion picture). The song is produced by Larry McBride:

Living just ain't living
When you're doing it alone,
And everywhere I go I find
My mind takes you along.
And at night I sleep on your side
With the dream you left behind.
Maybe tomorrow
I'll find peace of mind.

Maybe tomorrow
The sun will rise a different way,
Maybe tomorrow
I'll find what I've been looking for today.
Like an old-time melody renews a faded memory
Maybe tomorrow
Your love will set me free.

I still go down to the place in town
Where we had so much fun.
But a crowded room
Is a lonely tomb
When you're dying for someone.
If I thought it'd help
I'd take myself
Far away and try to hide.
Maybe tomorrow
I'll find my love has died.

ORIGINALLY, FILE CASE NO. 16 WAS TO DEAL PRIMARILY WITH THE telephone call I received in the early hours of October 1988 from a man identifying himself as Elvis Presley. (I taped the call. When

*From the album "Welcome to the Human Race." To order: Call 1-900-Country, or write P.O. Box 1, Nashville, TN 37202.

I was in California recently, I played the tape for Gene Smith, Elvis' first cousin. ("Without a doubt," he said, "that is Elvis' voice, no doubt about it.") However, before I walk you through that call, I need to spotlight a most mind-boggling recent development.

Also, I thought I had completed *The Elvis Files,* when I received a confidential telephone call asking me to compare the handwriting on Elvis' death certificate with Elvis' handwritten 1970 letter to President Nixon. "You will find the handwriting is one and the same," I was told. I contacted Mr. Paul Weast, a forensic document examiner and Master Certified Graphoanalyst, court-qualified as an expert. His report was as follows:

Paul R. Weast

Master Certified Graphoanalyst

Certified Document Examiner

April 17,1990

Gail Brewer-Georgio
1416 Lakeshore Circle
Gainesville, Ga. 30501   File No. Q-41390-E

     Re: Medical Examiner's Report on Elvis A. Presley

Dear Ms. Georgio;

Pursuant to your request received April 13, 1990 I have examined
the following:

QUESTIONED

Exhibit Q-1

A photo copy of a report entitled Office Of The County Medical
Examiner, 858 Madison Ave.,Memphis, Tennessee 38103.

     REPORT OF INVESTIGATION BY COUNTY MEDICAL EXAMINER

This is purported to be a copy of the Medical Examiner's report
on the death of Elvis Aron Presley on August 16,1977. All
information is handwritten and purported to have been written
by the Memphis Medical Examiner, Dr. A. Nichopolous.   The
signature at the bottom of page one is not readable.

EXEMPLARS

KNOWN HANDWRITING FOR COMPARISON

Exhibit E-1

A photo copy of a handwritten letter on American Airlines
inflight stationery.   It is addressed to President Nixon and
consists of six pages. It is not dated.   On page five it is
signed Elvis Presley. Page six lists several telephone numbers
and is also signed Elvis Presley.

page two
File No. Q-41390-E
Gail Brewer-Georgio

Exhibit E-2

A photo copy of a handwritten letter dated 1/17/63. It is
addressed Donna and is signed Elvis Presley.

Exhibit E-3

A photo copy of a Bill of Sale of Southern Motors,Inc. No.
2042. Bears handwritten notation and is signed Elvis Presley.

Exhibit E-4

A photo copy of a restaurant guest check signed Elvis Presley
and the notation " Tip $3.00"

Exhibit E-5

A photo copy of a thank you note, postmarked Memphis, Tenn.
Nov. 16,1973. It is signed Elvis Presley.

Exhibit E-6

A photo copy of hand printed Christmas Gift list for 1965.
At the top it is imprinted Elvis Presley.

Exhibit E-7

Photo copies of the face of two checks bearing a corner card
reading E.A. Presley 3764 Elvis Presley Blvd.,Memphis, Tenn
38116. They are drawn on National Bank of Commerce. Check
number 168 is dated May 14, 1977 and is signed E.A. Presley.
Check number 200 is dated Jan. 14, 1972 and is signed E.A.
Presley.

Exhibit E-8

A photo copy of a page from Vida's Autograph Analysis Collection.
It bears reproductions of Elvis Presley autographs. One at

age 24 in 1959. Next is dated 1956, next 1967 and the last is 1977 and labeled " only five months prior to his death."

Exhibit "C"

A photo copy of the first page of the Medical Report greatly enlarged. It has a signature clipped from the Nixon letter and pasted under the name Elvis Presley Blvd. to illustrate the close similarity.

I understand that each of these Exemplar documents can be authenticated as genuine samples of Elvis Presley's handwriting and signatures.

METHOF OF EXAMINATION

The signatures reading Elvis Presley or E.A. Presley and the handwriting and handprinting attributed to Elvis Presley have each been carefully examined by stereo-microscope and by viewing with transmitted light on a light table. Each has been measured for the degree of slant, size, spacing, alignment and proportion. Individual letter forms have been examined and compared. Transparent photo copies were produced and viewed in a greatly enlarged state with an overhead projector. Transparent photo copies were overlaid over each other for comparisons.

RESULTS OF EXAMINATION

The degree of slant, letter size, spacing, alignment and proport- ion matches on all documents . The numbers and words reading 3764 Elvis Presley Blvd on the Medical Examiner's report match numbers and signatures on the President Nixon letter. The name Elvis Presley in the address match several signatures of Elvis Presley. The word Entertainer on the ME report matches very closely the same word written by Elvis Presley in the Nixon

page four
File No.Q-41390-E
Gail Brewer-Georgio

letter. Several of the small letters f match very closely as do two of
the capital letters F .Capital letters B also match.

OPINION

It is my professional opinion as California Courts qualified
examiner of questioned documents that the handwriting on the
questioned   Exhibit Q-1, "Report of Investigation By County
Medical Examiner " was probably produced by the same person
who produced the handwriting on Exemplar Exhibits E-1 through
E-8 and the signatures that read Elvis Presley or E.A. Presley.

Photo copies of all listed documents are attached to this
report an incorporated herein.   Documents supplied to me for
examination are hereby returned to Gail Brewer-Georgio.

Thank you for the opportunity to be of service in this matter.
If I can be of any further service please call on me.

Respectfully submitted,

Paul R. Weast, MGA,CDE
Master Graphoanalyst
Certified Document Examiner

PRW/ bl

Encl: As cited

The reader will have seen Elvis' letter to President Nixon, earlier in the book. It was, of course, one of Elvis' handwriting samples examined by Weast. I now include some of the other writing Weast looked at: the Medical Examiner's Report (or death certificate); some signatures, including some on checks; a signed restaurant receipt; and a 1963 handwritten and signed letter:

PERSONAL HISTORY: Suicide attempts ☐   Suicide threats ☐   Hobbies, aptitude and skill with firearms, chemicals ☐   Domestic, premarital or marital conflicts ☐   Financial or business reverses ☐   Social or religious conflicts ☐   Legal difficulties ☐   Criminal record ☐   Unemployment ☐   Fear of disease ☐   Other (specify) _____

CONDUCT BEFORE DEATH: Efforts to prevent help ☐   Efforts to obtain help ☐   Suicide attempt: Admitted ☐   Denied ☐   Refusal to talk ☐   Written declaration of intended suicide ☐   Accusations against others ☐   Other (specify) _____

	LAST SEEN ALIVE	INJURY OR ILLNESS	DEATH	DISCOVERY	MEDICAL EXAMINER NOTIFIED	VIEW OF BODY	POLICE NOTIFIED
DATE	8-16/77		8-16-77	8-16-77	8-16-77	8-16-77	8-16-77
TIME	08:00±		Pronounced 1534	1400±	1600	1730	1530

	LOCATION	CITY OR COUNTY	TYPE OF PREMISES (HOSPITAL, HOTEL, HIGHWAY, ETC.)
INJURY OR ONSET OF ILLNESS	Home		
DEATH	DOA Bm H — Resc. attempted		
VIEWING OF BODY BY MEDICAL EXAMINER	Bm H		

MEDICAL ATTENTION AND HOSPITAL OR INSTITUTIONAL CARE

NAME OF PHYSICIAN OR INSTITUTION	ADDRESS	DIAGNOSIS	DATE
A Nichopoulos	medic	HCVD / Cor. Pulm.	

CIRCUMSTANCES OF DEATH

	NAME	ADDRESS
FOUND DEAD BY	Ginger Alden	Same
LAST SEEN ALIVE BY	"	
WITNESS TO INJURY OR ILLNESS AND DEATH	None	

NARRATIVE SUMMARY OF CIRCUMSTANCES SURROUNDING DEATH:

Found on floor of dressing room by above⊙ who had
been sleeping in adjoining room. No indication of foul play.
Had been ok in early am. Had ? playing basketball
in early am. Found coroner signed for autopsy.
To be performed at Bm. H.

Q-1

Below is part of the original certificate, showing the weight
170 pounds written in:

If Motor Vehicle Accident Check One: Driver ☐   Passenger ☐   Pedestrian ☐   Unknown ☐
Notification by ___ City Homicide ___   Address ___ City ___
Investigating Agency ___ SCME + MPD ___

DESCRIPTION OF BODY: Clothed ☐   Unclothed ☑   Partly Clothed ☐   Circumcised Yes ☐   No ☑
Eyes Bl ; Hair Bl ; Mustache O ; Beard O
Weight 170 Pounds   Length ___ Inches   Body Temp ___ Fahrenheit   Date and Time ___
Rigor: Yes ☑   No ☐   Lysed ☐   Livor Color O ; Fixed ☑   Non-Fixed ☐

Vida's AUTOGRAPH
ANALYSIS COLLECTIONS.

ELVIS
JAN 8, 1935
AUG 16, 1977

1959 Age 24
height of career

1956 Spiralling movie success

1967 Elvis marries Priscilla

5 months prior to death

box 2267, Toluca Lake, Cal.,91602

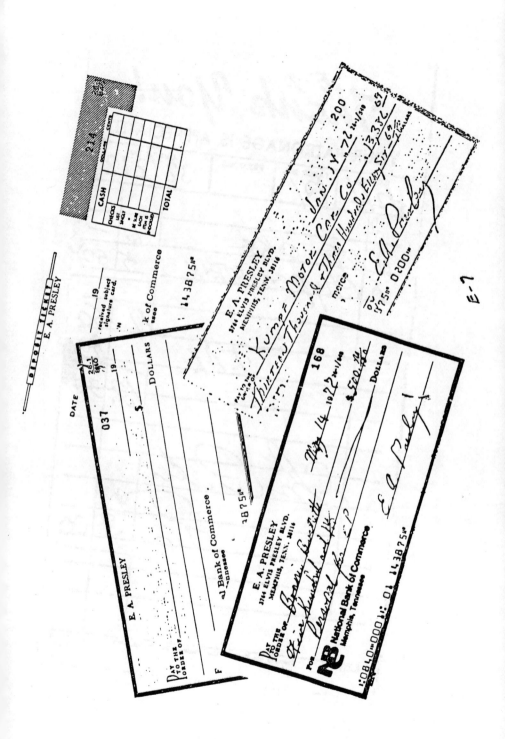

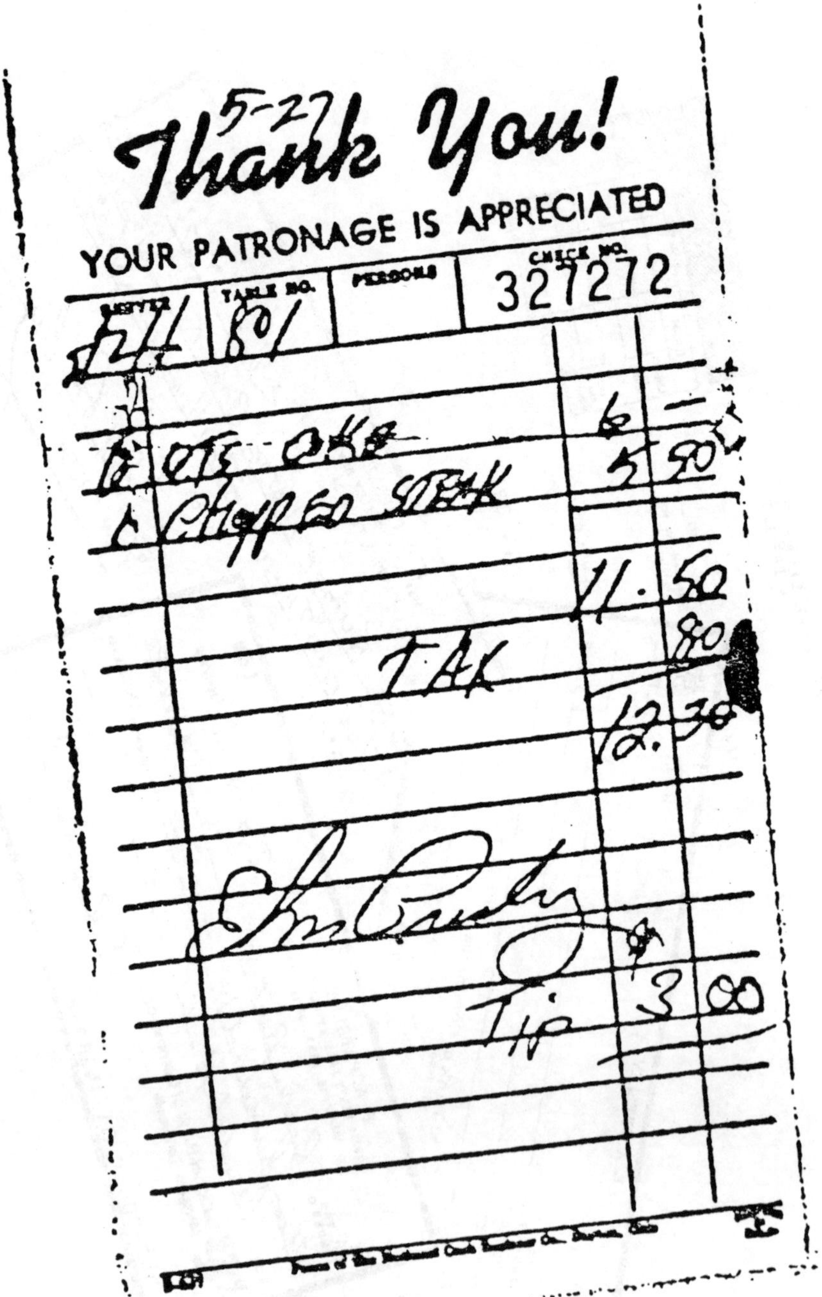

Dear ~~Vienna~~

My how time does fly, its seems that only a few days ago that the New Year of 1963 had just come in. Now the year 1963 has passed and we find that we are entering into a new year, 1964. I sincerely hope that you had a wonderful year in 1963 and that 1964 will be a much better one for you and yours.

May I extend to you my deepest gratitude and sincere thanks for your wonderful and loyal support in the years passed. It is my wish to please you with my entertaining and I do appreciate the wonderful cards and letters that I received from you. I sincerely hope that you will find the time to continue to write.

I had a very nice Christmas and Birthday at home with my folks, and I do hope that you had a nice one, also.

I will be returning to the West Coast in the next few days to start working on a new picture. My latest picture which I recently finished will be released sometime in the summer. I hope you liked the recent release which is titled "Fun In Acapulco", if you have seen it.

I will be in Nashville one day before my return to the West Coast to record more songs.

I will close for now. I hope to hear from you again soon.

Sincerely,
Your friend as always
Elvis Presley

1/17/63

It appears that my caller was correct. Weast's conclusions indicate that ELVIS FILLED OUT HIS OWN DEATH CERTIFICATE! And, perhaps *because* he did, this explains the 170 pounds weight written in on what was probably the original. Elvis is like the rest of us! At 250 pounds, he was overweight and perhaps thought, "Aw, what the heck, I'll get back down to 170!"

Obviously, courts of law are filled with opposing "experts," each challenging the other. Mr. Weast could meet with such opposition. However, while I was in California helping to film the *Elvis Files* documentary, I showed the death certificate and Elvis writing samples to Monte Nicholson, who as an investigator with the Los Angeles Sheriff's Department is also rather expert at handwriting comparisons. Nicholson concurred with Weast's findings.

"I feel very sure that I will be challenged by other document examiners who will be out to prove me wrong just for their own publicity," Paul Weast wrote me, further stating: "The handwritten 'Elvis Presley Blvd.' on the ME report is most convincing. The chances that an ME would write 'Elvis Presley' so nearly like Elvis himself writes it are pretty high odds. One letter [another writing sample] does not match exactly, but no one writes exactly the same every time. The slant and size match. That alone is not all that is common."

This book is not a court of law. But just as I originally had the tape with *Is Elvis Alive?* examined by a qualified voice expert, thus I had the same done with the death certificate.

A further piece of handwriting (opposite page) has come to my attention recently. It is part of a brief documentation from the FBI Files on Elvis Presley. Note that it bears a date of December 14, 1977—a date four months after the month in which he is said to have died. Note the circled printing, "NAM Frederic Peter Pro." Compare the word "NAM" with the word "NAME" on a segment of the last page of Elvis' 1970 letter to President Nixon (included, opposite bottom, though not in File Case No. 1). Compare, too, the "F" in "FREDERIC" with the "F" in "CONFIDENTIAL." Preliminary handwriting reports show that it is Elvis' notation (circled) on the December 14, 1977, FBI report. It appears that Elvis is making a correction to the report's typewritten "FREDERIC N. PRO." Since, according to FBI files, Elvis was being victimized by Pro, Elvis appears to have written the correct name of his antagonist.*

*Again, reader, you must be the judge. Not all of you will agree. If you have doubts, write the government for copies and have these same documents examined by experts of your own.

ROUTINE

CLEAR   32/34/77   b7C

FM DIRECTOR (87-343603)

TO MIAMI (196-68) ROUTINE

NEW YORK (196-66) ROUTINE

MEMPHIS (196-23) ROUTINE   NAM FREDERICK PETER (N)

BT

CLEAR

FREDERICK M. PRO: ET AL: ELVIS A. PRESLEY (DECEASED) - VICTIM:

ITSP: FBW: MF: CONSPIRACY: OO: MEMPHIS.

REBUTELCAL TO MIAMI, DECEMBER 14, 1977.

THIS IS TO CONFIRM REBUTELCAL IN WHICH AUTHORITY WAS   b7C

GRANTED FOR SA ████████████ TO TRAVEL FROM NEW YORK TO

MIAMI TO CONDUCT INTERVIEW OF ████████████   b7D

BT

WASHINGTON HOTEL) PHONE ME 85900
Rm 505-506.
UNDER THE NAME
OF JON BURROWS

PRIVATE
AND CONFIDENTIAL

atten, President Nixon

via Sen George Murphy

from

Elvis Presley

DURING THE LAST PART OF MAY, THIS YEAR, ALBERT GOLDMAN, AUTHOR
of the 1981 book *Elvis,* together with Elvis' stepbrother David
Stanley, appeared on national television stating that Elvis Presley
had committed suicide. This claim was followed up by a front-
cover feature in the June 1990 issue of *Life* magazine, which
headlined it: "THIRTEEN YEARS AFTER THE DEATH OF ELVIS PRESLEY
NEW EVIDENCE POINTS TO AN INESCAPABLE CONCLUSION: SUICIDE."

Goldman's book *Elvis* had, earlier, been a negative portrait of
an obese, drug-ridden Elvis – a book that many of his fans felt was
one-sided, holding little compassion or sympathy for the total
man. The *Life* article penned by Goldman told that he was doing
a revision of his Elvis biography and that he was wrong about
Elvis' taking an accidental drug overdose, as stated in the book.
He should have read the signs more closely, he said; he now was
convinced that Elvis committed suicide. Part of Goldman's new
conclusion stems from David Stanley's statement that Elvis had
said goodbye to his stepbrother a few days prior to August 16,
informing David that he wasn't going to be seeing him anymore.
David is now convinced that Elvis *knew,* in fact, that his demise
was imminent – that, indeed, he was *planning* it.

David Stanley, along with his mother, Dee, and brothers Rick
and Billy, in 1979 had written *Elvis, We Love You Tender* (telling the
entertainer's story to Martin Torgoff). Besides Elvis' saying goodbye to David, the Stanleys reported in their book that, during Elvis'
final tour in June 1977 – moments before he was to be televised –
Elvis turned to stepbrother Rick and said, "Know what, Rick? I
may not look too good for my television special tonight, but I'll
look good in my coffin!" It is not difficult to see why David concluded that Elvis was planning his death.

In my opinion Elvis was, yes, planning a death – but not a
suicide.

Elvis' deep religious nature would have been appalled by the
idea of suicide. In fact, David Stanley wrote at length about his
feelings about it in *Elvis, We Love You Tender.* He recalled a time
when he and Elvis were watching television and the news of Freddie Prinze's (NBC-TV's *Chico and the Man*) suicide was broadcast.
David reported that Elvis turned away from the TV in disgust and
said, "That's really the chicken-shit way out!" David further
elaborated by saying he did not believe Elvis would ever kill
himself on purpose, stating, moreover, that Elvis held a strong
religious resistance to suicide. "The Lord's way would never be to
kill yourself," David reported Elvis as saying. "Elvis' sense of
manhood and dignity would never allow him to take the 'easy' way

out," David underscored Elvis' remark. David also wrote, about Elvis' last few years, how he had "laid back" and taken it easy.

Now, all of a sudden, a decade later, David Stanley changes his mind?

But let's take a look at other events that occurred on that "final" night and early morning of August 15–16, 1977.

Elvis' nine-year-old daughter, Lisa Marie, had been at Graceland on an extended vacation away from her mother, who now lived in California. Surely if Elvis planned to do away with himself it would not be during one of his precious daughter's visits! What's more, Lisa's bedroom was the only other bedroom upstairs at Graceland, and she had access to her daddy's bedroom. Can you imagine Elvis chancing his suicided body's being discovered by his little girl? Surely, if suicide was on Elvis' mind, he would have sent Lisa back to California to Priscilla. Instead, Elvis had kept Lisa with him despite his upcoming tour. It was, in fact, as if he *had* to keep Lisa there – for another reason. Was it because his "death" would soon be reported and he took care to see that Lisa *was with him,* that *she knew he was not dead* – despite world news reports?

And what about Elvis' father, Vernon? Remember, the most important people in Elvis' life in 1977 were his daughter and his father. The fact that Vernon had suffered several severe heart attacks was a constant worry to Elvis. Certainly he would not have committed an obvious suicide and chance his father's finding the body, bringing on Vernon's death? This is not the Elvis we've read about.

However, if Elvis were to "fake" his death, then in order to protect Lisa and Vernon they would have to be in on it; and despite a certain nerve-wrenching few hours, they would not be exposed to the trauma of a suicide.

Plus, everyone at the time told that Elvis had been in good humor and spirits, especially with Lisa there. They had spent the past two weeks "playing," especially in Memphis' Libertyland Amusement Park, where they frolicked like kids. "They had a ball," Paul Lichter writes in his 1989 Elvis book *All My Best.* There were movies to see, golf carts to ride...

That last night and morning saw Elvis in good spirits, too. In fact, at around 10:30 P.M., August 15, Elvis headed out to visit his dentist, Dr. Lester Hoffman, for some emergency dental work. Hoffman agreeing to see Elvis at that unusual hour, Elvis, his fiancée, Ginger Alden, friend Charlie Hodge, and cousin Billy Smith piled into Elvis' Stutz Blackhawk – and off they went. At the dentist's, Elvis asked that his teeth be cleaned. New fillings were put into Elvis' upper-right bicuspid and upper-left molar, Dr. Hoffman marveling at how well-cared-for were the singer's teeth.

Does all this sound like a man who was planning a suicide a few hours later? Have you heard of anyone calling his dentist late at night for a hygienic dental appointment when a plan of suicide loomed in the near horizon? Nonsense.

Still full of cheer, Elvis and his small group returned to Graceland, talked, and he played the piano and sang. Shortly before dawn, Elvis decided to play racquetball, a game including Ginger Alden and Billy and Jo Smith, Billy's wife. According to all accounts, Elvis was cutting up and laughing while on the court.

After racquetball, Elvis and Ginger retired to his bedroom to watch TV and read; it was now around 6:00 A.M. Ginger fell asleep some time after; Elvis got up and went into the bath-room—a large bathroom/lounge, with its own back entrance.

Around 9:00 A.M. was the time estimated at which Elvis' "rigor mortis" was said to have begun to set in. This would indicate that Elvis had to have died soon after leaving his bedroom for the bathroom.

Except that...

It appears that while Ginger slept, Elvis did not stay in the bathroom, but probably used the back entrance to go downstairs. How do we know this?

Paul Lichter, president of the Elvis Unique Record Club, an organization licensed by Elvis Presley Enterprises, had sent a registered letter to Elvis. It arrived at Graceland on the morning of August 16, 1977, and was signed for by Elvis. Here is the receipt:

Lichter told me that upon checking with the post office, the letter was signed for at 9:30 A.M., which not only blows holes on the 9:00 A.M. rigor-mortising claim, but points out that Elvis did not seem to be in a "suicidal" mood. It also illustrates that David and Rick Stanley did not know what Elvis was really up to that last morning: where he was, even what he was wearing, what he was reading.

The Goldman book and the Stanley book contradict even themselves with other small details, such as how on one page Elvis was found wearing "blue pajamas" and a few pages later "yellow-and-blue" – and on and on. Goldman states publicly that he was wrong in his first report on the circumstances of Elvis' death, and so does David Stanley. If they were wrong first time around, they could be wrong – and doubtless were – the second time around, late this spring. Out of all of this confusion the blaring truth remains: Elvis' death is highly questionable.

Confusion and contradictions concern who found the body, the most popular story being that it was Ginger, who called Elvis' friend Al Strada (sitting downstairs in the kitchen), and then that Al called Joe Esposito, whose location has varied. Paramedics were eventually called; they stated in newspaper interviews that they did not recognize the body as that of Elvis Presley. Even the Stanleys' book reports that the body in the coffin looked "frighteningly unfamiliar."

It certainly is not this book's purpose to debate Albert Goldman and David Stanley, item by item. And the many contradictions have already been related in File Case No. 13, and even to a larger extent in my earlier book, *Is Elvis Alive?* It won't hurt, however, to repeat what was told me by Gene Smith, Elvis' first cousin, outlined in File Case No. 15: that the hands in the coffin "weren't Elvis'."

I am sure that Albert Goldman is sincere in wanting to update his book, and probably believes the suicide theory. But how can David Stanley believe it, when he elaborated in his book about how set against suicide Elvis was? What's more, all of the Stanleys have written and spoken of Elvis' great love and protection for Lisa. How any of them could even for a moment fathom Elvis', or any loving father's, committing suicide in his daughter's presence is outrageous. Even more than Elvis' going to the dentist hours earlier suggesting he had no suicidal plans, his daughter's presence at Graceland makes the theory totally unacceptable. (Actually, the fact that Elvis insisted on going to the dentist is *indeed* favorable to Elvis' being *alive*. Did Elvis have his teeth cleaned and fillings replaced because he knew he was going away and might not have immediate access to dental care until another identity was established?)

Because the FBI files run 663 pages and are too complex to dissect totally at this writing, I suggest that those who flatly deny the possibility of Elvis' being alive should find and read them all (some are in File Case No. 1). Pay particular attention to 1977 and the years following. You will discover that both Elvis and Vernon had been involved in a dangerous situation, with Elvis listed as "victim" by some pretty tough folks – many of them now behind bars – this due, in part, to Elvis' input. That Elvis and his father were testifying against these men and the multi-million-dollar criminal activities they headed put both Elvis' and Vernon's lives at risk. The fact that Vernon had a serious heart condition distressed Elvis, particularly because the entertainer knew the stress Vernon had to live under because of the FBI connection. Although I, personally, believe that other factors played a part, too, in the probability of Elvis' hoaxing his death, the trouble he and his father had gotten into as Mob victims was the catalyst.

The FBI Files on Elvis Presley before and after his "death" should be read with care and instruction. Certain confidential lines are blacked out. Still, there is enough to illustrate that some pretty rough events were occurring – and that the "only way out" was death. One cannot "kill" the already dead, can one?

AS THE READER KNOWS BY NOW, JOE ESPOSITO WAS/IS ONE OF ELVIS' closest friends. I have been on two TV shows with Joe: *Larry King Live* (CNN) and *Geraldo* (CBS). Both times Joe slipped up: He talked of Elvis in the present tense; admitted to the "beads of sweat on the body in the coffin" (despite the truth that dead bodies do not sweat); and verified that Priscilla was already at Graceland at the time of Elvis' "death."

Joe's biggest slip to date occurred on June 18, 1990, on Geraldo Rivera's "Did Elvis Really Commit Suicide" show. Joe refuted David Stanley's claim that Elvis took his own life, talking about Elvis' personality, how he never would have killed himself in his bathroom, etc. Joe was also angry at David for linking up with Albert Goldman, who, Joe said, "crawled out from under a rock." Very angry over Stanley's association with Goldman, Esposito stated the following on the air: "We're here to say Elvis Presley did not commit suicide, and it's only out there because somebody wants to make a dollar. Albert Goldman lives off of people that are dead. He assassinates people after they die. This man's a little worm. I wish he was here. [Goldman was not on the show.] He should know how I feel about him, because I'm talking about him and he's not here to defend himself, and that's how *Elvis feels* about this situation."

Joe added later: "Everything [Elvis] did in life was overdone, and that's why he did not commit suicide, because if he was going to commit suicide, he would have overdone that. Believe me, he would have done something extravagant, wrote a letter or something. He would not end up killing himself and committing suicide in his bathroom."

At another time, in reply to Geraldo's insistence that "Goldman is not here to defend himself," Esposito countered: "Just like Elvis isn't here to defend himself either."

But: "...and that's how Elvis feels about this situation"!

This slip of Joe's* has brought me (and doubtless Geraldo Rivera) an onslaught of letters! And just think: Goldman wrote his book *Elvis* in 1981, four years after Elvis' "death." Therefore, Elvis, if dead, could feel nothing about this "situation." Plus, present tense!!! Joe, Joe, Joe!

A sampling from a letter to me follows, and part of a letter to Geraldo himself for allowing this slip to go over his head. Linda H. S., of Maiden, North Carolina, emphasized her agreement with Joe Esposito that Albert Goldman "assassinates dead people." And she was in ecstasy that Joe used the present tense when speaking of Elvis:

> Wow! wow! wow! I have this on tape. . . . At the end of the show, Joe said, "In the first place, how can he commit suicide. He's living in Kalamazoo, Michigan. He's alive. (Or "He's dead" – I can't remember the exact wording here.) Of course, Joe said this last part as a cute joke.
>
> I know you have heard, by now, about Colonel Parker on the talk show recently in California† saying that Elvis told him he wanted out. That the pressure was too much. That he felt he had disappointed his fans and himself. The interviewer asked if Elvis

---

*In the Introduction to Joe Esposito's book *A Legendary Performance* (Buena Park, CA: West Coast Publishing, 1990), he states: "I consider myself the luckiest person in the world to have shared Elvis' finest hour and his final hour." ("I thought Elvis died alone!" wrote Mary K., of Tylertown, Mississippi, after reading Esposito's statement.)

† Although several people wrote or called about Colonel Parker's response to the suicide question, I have no information about when or where Elvis' manager made the statement.

committed suicide, and the Colonel replied, "No, sir, he did not!
I told him a way out and he took it." Another big Wow!

D'Lores A. Gossen, of Ogilvie, Minnesota, wrote to Geraldo
himself:

> I was very surprised, as others are, that during one of Joe's state-
> ments. . .you didn't pursue it further. It just went right on by you.
>   After Joe said, ". . . and that's how Elvis feels about this situation,"
> there was a pause – plenty of time for you to ask him to explain that
> statement!. . . Joe slipped up, and you completely missed it! He
> spoke of Elvis in the present tense, and you cannot deny that, nor
> can Joe take it back. Obviously, Elvis has an opinion on Albert
> Goldman. More than likely, Joe's descriptions of Goldman are in
> reality Elvis' feelings. . . .
>   Geraldo, I think you were asleep at the wheel during that obvious
> revelation of Joe's. I'm surprised that members of the audience did
> not comment on any of it! (Coached again?) How are you going to
> feel when the news comes out, after you've been fighting it all along,
> afraid it will be another "Capone's vault"!. . .You absolutely refuse
> to even consider the likelihood that Elvis is alive. You could be
> having a hand in on one of the biggest stories of our lifetime, but
> you are so stubborn!. . .
>   It has also occurred to me that you know *exactly* what's going on,
> and that Elvis is alive.

D'Lores also mentioned the Colonel Tom Parker interview in
which he denied the idea that Elvis might have committed suicide.
"Colonel Parker's word was golden [to Elvis]. I challenge you to
have Colonel Tom on your show," she told Rivera. "That could
prove to be a dynamite show. . . . The man *is* eighty-one years old,
but I'm sure he's still fully capable of keeping the best of men on
their toes – and that includes you, Geraldo!"

FURTHER EVIDENCE THAT ELVIS IS ALIVE – ALTHOUGH NOT IN
Kalamazoo, as Joe Esposito jested – came, syndicated in newspapers across the nation on June 5, 1990, in an article headlined (generally): "ELVIS LIVES, AT LEAST ON CENSUS FORM."
"Even the Census Bureau says it has evidence that Elvis lives –
the King returned a 1990 census questionnaire," the article read.
"The bureau office, in Huntsville, Ala., got back a completed form
indicating Elvis is residing in northern Alabama. It's not all tedium
for census workers screening forms for completeness; they get to
howl over some of the answers mailed in," the article concluded.
  Last Christmas, a Birmingham-based veteran photographer,

Carol Sheehan, had just completed reading my book *Is Elvis Alive?* Shortly afterward, a friend told her that she believed Elvis was living on a farm just outside Birmingham. Sheehan and her husband, Michael, drove out to the farm. "I parked about a mile away," she wrote me, "walked back, and hid in the bushes with my camera while Michael sat in the car with a two-way walkie-talkie and served as my lookout. As the day wore on, I was able to get several photographs of Elvis. . .a slimmed-down, relaxed Elvis playing with his horses and taking solitary walks across the 150-acre farm."

The photographs, in my opinion, do not reveal enough of the man's face to confirm that it is Elvis, but Carol Sheehan found a crumpled piece of paper in the bushes and said she would have it checked out by Paul Weast to see whether it was in Elvis' handwriting: a list of musicians' names and salaries. In any event, Carol says that "Blount County (where the farm is located) came apart at the seams and the farm was sold," after she sold her story and photos to the *National Examiner*, which used one of them on its front cover, August 15, this year – together with a multi-page story done by *NE* reporter Bob Boyd!

Obviously, if he is alive, Elvis Presley is wealthy enough to have several residences. Northern Alabama may or may not have been one of them.

JULY 11, 1990, AS *THE ELVIS FILES* WAS GOING TO PRESS, NEWS FLASHED across national television stating: "Elvis' doctor says Elvis was murdered. Watch ABC's *Entertainment Tonight*. . ."

Good grief, I thought. Last month it was suicide! How can one man have died so many different ways: heart attack, drug overdose, cancer, brain tumor, suffocation in a carpet, suicide, and now murder? And all of these allegations come from those who were "close" to Elvis! Is it any wonder that, thirteen years later, many of the fans – as well as this author – ask questions? Recall that it was this same Dr. George Nichopoulos, Elvis' personal physician, along with Dr. Jerry Francisco, Shelby County Medical Examiner, who in 1977 officially listed "death" as "cardiac arrythmia" (or heart attack) as cause. Now, all of a sudden, "Dr. Nick" remembers it was *murder?*

I immediately tuned in to the program.

It announced that Elvis died from a fatal karate blow to the neck, according to Dr. Nick, via co-writer Murray Silver. Dr. Nick was quoted as stating he should have insisted that X-rays be taken (to show broken neckbone?). The camera then switched to Dr. Francisco, who was dealing his own death blow to Dr. Nick's story:

X-rays were taken . . . no broken bones whatsoever.

O.K., so who's lying this time around? Every time these folks speak, they insist they are ready to tell the "real, real, real truth" – which says they lied first time around, correct?

Obviously, since there exists no medical evidence of murder, Dr. Nick's story bears a large enough hole to drive "sixteen coaches" through. But just for logic's sake, let's consider the murder theory, for motive:

- *Financial gain?* Who would be beneficiary of such gain? Nine-year-old Lisa Marie Presley. Would a small child have the power and motivation to land a fatal karate blow on a 250-pound father who had an eighth-degree black-belt karate rank? Hardly. And since it was known that Elvis had changed his will in March 1977, who else would gain? Surely, heart-attack victim Vernon (Elvis' father) possessed no such strength or motivation.
- *Robbery?* Someone stole into much-secured Graceland, past gate guard(s) in bright daylight, past Al Strada and Joe Esposito, past Ginger Alden and into Elvis' bathroom (the bandito knowing Elvis would be there around 9:30)? Of course, this robber would also have had to be a karate champion, to boot. After no resistance from Elvis, the bandito gave the final blow? What did he take away? Elvis' bible, book of numbers, pictures of Gladys? Hardly. Robbery can be safely ruled out.
- *Murder by contract?* A kingpin hires a hit man to take out Elvis? This is the most feasible of all murder theories (since we know by FBI files that Elvis' life *had* been threatened) . . . except that: Wouldn't a kingpin be smarter than counting on the karate expertise of a hit man against a black-belt champion, and want to use methods less chancy? And, what's more, do the job in broad daylight, with grounds guard(s) and potential witnesses? And against a Federal Agent who may have been guarded? I would think murder by gun or car explosives more in line. After all, Elvis was a karate expert, and I imagine he'd be a little curious if some stranger suddenly appeared in his bathroom in full karate stance.
- *Inside job by friends/family?* Is Dr. Nick accusing someone who was present or in the near vicinity – such as Al Strada, Joe Esposito, the Stanleys, Elvis' father, Priscilla, cousins, Grandma? Even if any of these folks had desire or motive (which they didn't), were any of them equipped to be karate partner to Elvis Presley? Poison by drugs would be far safer

and healthier on the part of the attacker. Plus, if Dr. Nick lied about the heart-attack story and knew a crime had been committed, why did he wait so long to try to get the guilty culprit? Did he think so little of Elvis that he willingly covered up the murder of a man who had been so kind to him?

. . . And how can charges of suicide, murder, etc., explain away the documented evidence given in this book?

Does this author – myself, I mean – have the "real, real, real, real story"? No. But I have more of it than has been told, to date.

Poor Elvis! I fear his final epitaph may read: *Died sometime toward the end of the twentieth century of convulsive laughter from reading his yearly obituaries!*

AND NOW, A WORD OR TWO FROM TWO CELEBRITIES. JERRY GLANVILLE, former coach of the Houston Oilers football team and new coach of the Atlanta Falcons, a firm believer in Elvis' being alive, has written an autobiography, *Elvis Don't Like Football,* together with *Sport* magazine editor J. David Miller. An extract from the book, due out in August this year from Macmillan Publishing Company, appeared in *Sport* in July. The article ends, affably, with Glanville's comment: "I'll always wonder, though, how Elvis could walk away from the Houston Oilers. Maybe he was embarrassed about dropping that pass. Maybe he just decided he don't like football. Singers and football players are a lot alike – you wear tight pants and jump around a lot. But then again, nobody ever blindsided a singer. I still say Elvis should've coached in the AFC Central against guys like Chuck Noll and Sam Wyche. Now that's a reason to fake your own death."

The reader will remember my mentioning, earlier in the chapter, an October 1988 telephone call I received from someone special. . . .

At around 2:30 A.M., the phone rang; my husband answered it. A gentleman was asking to speak to me. My husband reminded him of the time and asked that he call back in the morning. The man apologized, but said it would be one of the most important calls I would ever receive.

I took it.

"My brother works for Elvis," the man said, indicating that, at times, he did too. He told me I was correct about Elvis' governmental involvement, indicating that he could not say more than that. "When it [Elvis 'death'] first happened, Elvis became depressed. Finally, though, he pulled out of it and began traveling around the world. . ." He paused. "Elvis walked in the room when you were on the Oprah show and shook his head sadly, saying, 'I don't know why she puts herself through this.' "

Finally, I said I would have to talk to Elvis.

"That's why I am calling," he admitted. "Elvis will call you in ten to fifteen minutes. If he changes his mind – which he does a lot – I'll call you back, so you won't be waiting." He then added: "I trust you're a lady and won't tape the call?"

"I'm not in bed with a recorder," I replied.

"But you *do have* a recorder, don't you. . .?"

It almost sounded as if I was *supposed* to record! that he was reminding me to do so!

My problem was that my husband and I were still at our old house in Marietta, Georgia, although most of our furnishings had been moved to our new home in Gainesville – including my good new AT&T equipment! I ran downstairs, after hanging up the phone, recalling a box of things out in the garage that held an old bulky tape recorder, the kind with a suction cup.

The suction cup was so worn, I found, that it wouldn't stick to the phone, and the only tape I could find was a used one that I had to record over. Thus, the first half of the tape came out very low and was at times inaudible. The second half was clearer, for two reasons: I held the suction cup down, and Elvis' (?) voice had "opened up" – he said he had been asleep just before calling me.

Realizing, of course, that the voice could be that of an impersonator, I asked him about a friend we share in common (information that an impersonator could not know). He answered correctly.

Our conversation is part of the tape included with this book, *The Elvis Files*. Because of places on it that are difficult to hear, below I pull out the major points that my phone caller made:

- He was in a state of shock over Lisa Marie's wedding.
- He was at the wedding, as was Priscilla.
- I was not supposed to ask him about people in particular, because he did not want to get other people involved.
- He said he was going to be in Washington, D.C., for the next month or so.
- When I asked him if the Stanley boys knew he was alive, he said they didn't. I mentioned Rick, in particular, and he answered, "Ricky does not know." I asked him if Rick was as religious as he appeared, and he said, "Ricky's very religious, wouldn't question that at all. He's had his hard times, his prob-

lems. He's married, has a family. . ." He said that he and Rick used to pray together – countless times. There was great affection in "Elvis'" voice for his stepbrother.

- When we talked about Lisa, I asked how the world would accept Elvis' being a grandfather. "It's how *I'll* accept it," he said.
- He then stated that he hoped he would be "out" before the baby was born, that the dust would settle by then.*
- I kiddingly told my caller that when I am asked how I knew it was a wax dummy in the coffin, I say, "Because of the wick on the top of the head." This tickled him, causing him to reply, "Well, thank goodness nobody lit it. It would have been a nuclear meltdown, the biggest meltdown of the century!"
- When I asked about his health, he said he had lots of problems – little nagging problems, nothing that was life-threatening. As for his weight: "I lost some weight, but put some back on." Then he said something about not liking a vegetable diet.
- When I told him I had defended the "drug stories," he said, "If I was on as many drugs as people say, I wouldn't even be talking now."
- He complimented me, said I was a good writer, a good fielder of questions, but that just as I was sitting there *thinking* I knew the truth, he was there and *knew* the truth, knew what was going to happen. He said that things would be happening soon. When I asked if he was going to come back, he replied: "I pray to God so. . .I don't want to be disappointed again."
- Our conversation was very easy, very natural. He even kidded that he *was* dead but would be alive again in a couple of hours. He also said that he had called people who had hung up on him. He told me that I was doing a good job, that he would try to call me again and send me ammunition (*The Passover Plot?*), told me I could not contact him but that he would have to contact me. "Maybe I can help you with the press," I said, and he amusedly retorted: "I have enough of that!"
- "I hope people treat you kindly," he said in a low voice – his voice sounding so very much Elvis. The emotion I felt is hard to describe. "When I was a kid," he went on, "people treated me cruelly. But they were nicer back then, compared to today. I know you're going to have a nice life. God will take care of us all. Whatever card He deals us, we'll have to play. God bless you. . ."

---

*The news of Lisa's pregnancy had not been made public; this call came six days after her marriage. Thus, how would an Elvis impersonator have known this?

And God bless you, Elvis.

Whatever be the truth – whether Elvis is alive, whether all the "evidence" is but a series of giant coincidences – Elvis Presley was/is a giant star in the universe, a beloved son, father, husband, friend, American patriot – and a "Light" to whoever has paused to bask in its warmth. Elvis, you did indeed open up the window of your soul!

This is *not* the end.

A Selected Elvis Bibliography/Sources for Books and Other Materials

Benson, Richard. *The Minstrel.* Memphis: Minstrel Publishing, 1976.

Cogen, Arlene, and Charles Goodman. *Elvis, This One's for You.* Secaucus, NJ: Castle Books, 1985.

Columbus, Maria. *Elvis in Print* (forthcoming, 1990). P.O. Box 1457, Pacifica, CA 94044.

Cotten, Lee. *The Elvis Catalog.* New York: Dolphin/Doubleday, 1987.

De Barbin, Lucy, and Dary Matera. *Are You Lonesome Tonight?* New York: Villard Books, 1987.

Dundy, Elaine. *Elvis and Gladys.* New York: Dell, 1985.

Edwards, Michael. *Priscilla, Elvis and Me.* New York: St. Martin's Press, 1988.

Farren, Mick, and Pearce Marchbank. *Elvis in His Own Words.* New York: Omnibus Press, 1977.

Fitzgerald, Jim, and Al Kilgore. *Elvis: The Paperdoll Book.* New York: St. Martin's Press, 1982.

Geller, Larry. *If I Can Dream: Elvis' Own Story.* New York: Simon & Schuster, 1989.

Gibson, J. Robert, and Sid Shaw. *Elvis.* New York: McGraw-Hill, 1985.

Goldman, Albert. *Elvis.* New York: McGraw-Hill, 1981.

Gregory, James. *The Elvis Presley Story.* New York: Hillman Books, 1960.

Grove, Martin. *Elvis: The Legend Lives.* New York: Manor Books, 1978.

Haining, Peter. *Elvis in Private.* New York: St. Martin's Press, 1987.

Hammontree, Patsy Guy. *Elvis Presley: A Bio-Bibliography.* Westport, CT: Greenwood Press, 1985.

Hanna, David. *Elvis: Lonely Star at the Top.* New York: Leisure Books, 1977.

Harbinson, W. A. *The Illustrated Elvis.* New York: Grosset & Dunlap, 1976.

Harmon, Sandra, and Priscilla Beaulieu Presley. *Elvis and Me.* New York: G. P. Putnam, 1985.

Hebler, Dave; Red West; and Sonny West (as told to Steve Dunleavy). *Elvis: What Happened?* New York: Ballantine Books, 1977.

Hill, Ed (Stamps; as told to Don Hill). *Where Is Elvis?* Atlanta: Crossroads Publishers, 1979.

Hodge, Charlie, and Charles Goodman. *Me n' Elvis.* Memphis: Castle Books, 1985.

Holzer, Hans. *Elvis Presley Speaks.* New York: Manor Books, 1978.

Hopkins, Jerry. *Elvis: A Biography.* New York: Simon & Schuster, 1971.

———. *Elvis: The Final Years.* New York: St. Martin's Press, 1980.

Jenkins, Mary, and Beth Pease. *Elvis: The Way I Knew Him.* Memphis: Riverpark Publishers.

Lacker, Marty, and Patsy and Leslie Smith. *Elvis: Portrait of a Friend.* New York: Bantam, 1979.

Lichter, Paul. *Elvis, All My Best.* P.O. Box 339, Huntingdon Valley, PA: Jesse Books, 1989.

Mann, May. *Elvis, Why Don't They Leave You Alone?* New York: Signet Books, 1982.

Mann, Richard. *Elvis.* Van Nuys, CA: Bible Voice, Inc., 1977.

Marsh, Dave. *Elvis.* New York: Warner Books, 1982.

Nicholson, Monte. *The Presley Arrangement.* P.O. Box 7406, Oxnard, CA 93031-7406, 1987.

Parker, Ed. *Inside Elvis.* Orange, CA: Rampart House, Ltd., 1978.

Peters, Richard. *Elvis: The Golden Anniversary Tribute.* London: Pop Universal/Souvenir Press, 1984.

Presley, Dee, and Billy, Rick, and David Stanley (as told to Martin Targoff). *Elvis, We Love You Tender.* New York: Dell, 1979.

Quinn, William G., and Kathy Westmoreland. *Elvis and Kathy.* Glendale, CA: Glendale House Publishers, 1987.

Reggero, John. *Elvis in Concert.* New York: Dell Books, 1979.

Stanley, Billy. *Elvis, My Brother.* New York: St. Martin's Press, 1989.

Stern, Jane and Michael. *Elvis World.* New York: Alfred A. Knopf, 1987.

Tamerius, Steve, and Fred Worth. *Elvis: His Life from A to Z.* Chicago & New York: Contemporary Books, 1988.

Tharpe, Jac L. *Elvis: Images and Fancies.* University of Mississippi, 1981.

Vellenga, Dirk. *Elvis and the Colonel.* New York: Delacorte, 1988.

Wiegert, Sue. *Elvis for the Good Times.* Los Angeles: Blue Hawaiians for Elvis, 1978.

Wootton, Richard. *Elvis.* New York: Random House, 1985.

Those interested in ordering the novel *Orion*; the book *Is Elvis Alive?*; soon-to-be published poems and thoughts of love to Elvis, entitled *Roses to Elvis*; the *Breakthrough* video; the *Elvis Files* documentary; recording information on the Sivle Nora album; the record "Wherever You May Be" (Paul Richey); the 1977 Poolhouse Picture; or other data should send a self-addressed, stamped envelope to: The Arctic Corporation, 1416 Lakeshore Circle, Gainesville, GA 30501.

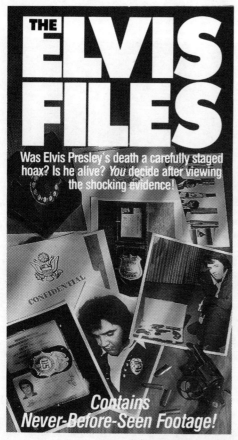

THE ELVIS FILES

Was Elvis Presley's death a carefully staged hoax? Is he alive? *You* decide after viewing the shocking evidence!

Contains Never-Before-Seen Footage!

YOU'VE READ THE BOOK. NOW WATCH THE INCREDIBLE VIDEO!

The startling, provocative story revealed in author Gail Brewer-Giorgio's compelling book is now available on videocassette from Media Home Entertainment!

• Exclusive release — first time on video!
• Includes never-before-seen footage!
• Astounding facts and evidence on the "death" of the King of Rock 'n' Roll!

Only $19.98
Suggested Retail Price

"The Elvis Files" is available wherever videocassettes are sold or rented.

To Order Direct: Call 1-800-733-9800*